Three Bags Full

*"Everybody has his own delusion
assigned to him: but we do not see that part
of the bag which hangs on our back."*
—CATULLUS, *Odes*, XXII

HBJ

Three Bags Full

ESSAYS IN AMERICAN FICTION

Philip Young

HARCOURT BRACE JOVANOVICH, INC.
NEW YORK

ISBN 0-15-190174-0
Library of Congress Catalog Card Number: 73-174517
Printed in the United States of America
B C D E

Some of these essays, in somewhat different form, originally appeared in
*The Atlantic Monthly, JGE: The Journal of General Education, The
Kenyon Review,* and *The New York Times.*

Quotations from "The Bridge" are from *The Complete Poems and
Selected Letters and Prose of Hart Crane,* copyright 1933, 1958, 1966
by Liveright Publishing Corp., reprinted by permission of the publisher.
Quotations from T. S. Eliot's "Sweeney Agonistes," "The Dry Salvages,"
and "Landscapes" are from *Collected Poems 1909–1962* by T. S. Eliot,
copyright 1936 by Harcourt Brace Jovanovich, Inc., copyright © 1963,
1964 by T. S. Eliot, reprinted by permission of the publisher. The lines
from "New Hampshire" are from *The Poetry of Robert Frost,* edited by
Edward Connery Lathem, copyright 1923, © 1969 by Holt, Rinehart and
Winston, Inc., copyright 1951 by Robert Frost, reprinted by permission
of Holt, Rinehart and Winston, Inc. Lines from "Our Mother Pocahontas"
by Vachel Lindsay are reprinted with permission of The Macmillan
Company from *Collected Poems* by Vachel Lindsay, copyright 1917 by
The Macmillan Company, renewed 1945 by Elizabeth C. Lindsay. Lines
from "Cool Tombs" are from *Cornhuskers* by Carl Sandburg, copyright
1918 by Holt, Rinehart and Winston, Inc., copyright 1946 by Carl
Sandburg, reprinted by permission of Holt, Rinehart and Winston, Inc.

This book is for Katherine

CONTENTS

PREFACE

Part of the rite of admission to graduate school, thirty years ago at a large Midwestern university, was an interview with its dean. A Famous Name of whom I had not heard, he was settling into senility, but had uncovered the secret of success in the profession. Find yourself a single writer, he told me—not too big a one nor yet too small—and fix on him till you know practically everything there is. Then write about him. Keep turning it out. You absolutely can't miss. Exactly, I remember thinking, but precisely, the wrong idea. The right one was to know as much as possible about as many things, which is what I set up to attempt. Now, three decades later, who sits here remembering? Our Hemingway Man.

That wasn't the way it started. The writing, that is, goes back to another day years afterward when, having picked up an "interdisciplinary" degree, I was an instructor at a large Eastern university. My chairman took me aside and told me straight: if I wanted to be an assistant professor I had really better get Published. Soon. (Yes, sir! Yes, sir!) But how? At someone else's instigation my doctor's thesis, which was on Hemingway, was dying out there at some provincial university press and, busy with my teaching overload, I had never even thought about posing as a scholar or critic. (I knew that certain professors "published," but I thought they did it out of some profound irritability, or because they couldn't make it in class.)

As it happened, however, I was at the time reading Poe pretty hard, him with all those beautiful dead or dying ladies, and I'd been wondering what could be the matter with a man that he should write like that. So I went to the New York Public Library to look it up. Survey the field and report the findings, that was the way. And before too long I did have a towering stack of notes on sick-Poe theory. Lest it collapse, I divided it in two piles, labeling one Conceivable, the other Idiotic. Then I shoved all the former into a waste basket. (For all I knew, Princess Marie Bonaparte's *Edgar Poe: étude psychoanalytique,* a Conceivable example, was itself demented, whatever Freud really thought about it; easier to handle was a real American book that explained how all Poe's troubles resulted from a lopsided forehead.) So I surveyed *half* the field, wrote it up and mailed it off, and got a prompt acceptance, plus promise of early publication. One for my master! I immediately passed him the news, and two weeks later had his formal letter to the general effect that I was canned.

I never did get to be an assistant professor—nor an abominable Poe man either. But with this breakthrough in pathological scholarship (*American Literature,* XXII [January, 1951] 4, 442–54), along with involuntary removal from the classroom, I had made a discovery. Which was that whereas the Rewards of Teaching are real, they are often exaggerated or sentimentalized, while the pleasures of getting into print go oft unmentioned and are tangible. Getting ready for a class, moreover, not to mention reading exams, somehow does less for a man than the realization that there's something in the typewriter: even if, so far, it's practically illiterate, it

underpins everything else you have to do that day. It's harder
to write than teach, at least in this case. But in this case it
has also been more fun. And so here we have another book.
(One for my dame!) To be sure it may seem presumptuous,
this coming on like three men in a tub. Three Bags Empty,
or Full of What? But there is precedent. All gall is divided
into three parts.

How I came to be a Hemingway man, after certain vicissitudes, is related in the first essay of this book. The doctor's
thesis mentioned earlier did get published eventually, and
one thing led to another for so long that you can't really
knock the people who figure I never read anyone else but him.
My admirers, on the other hand, have long implored me to
vacate that platform, where the act began to wear on both
of them some time ago. Very well, I'm about to take their advice; it's too late to check back with the dean. But first a
backward glance o'er travel'd roads. (Heav'ly.)

The story of my struggle with Hemingway, and his with
me, was written when after a good ten years I tired of an-
swering the same questions. (Did you know him? Why did he
try to stop your book? What did he say after he read it? Et
cetera.) It really was a bit of an epic, and I put the whole
thing openly on paper. This was the true start of things; might
as well lead off with it.

The second piece in this first section is very different—a
near-deranged return to the note-piling of the Poe epoch,
prompted by an outburst of books on Hemingway that appeared in the early Sixties. In a manic moment I had promised to go through them all; the problem was how to make
readable an account of so much that wasn't. At least it was a
gutsy try, and I was pleased to learn years later of a university where a couple of graduate students, their professor's

book having been an exhibit in the display, kept supplying Periodicals with fresh copies of the Autumn 1964 *Kenyon Review* as he repeatedly removed them from circulation.

Now of course the *Kenyon* is gone, and those books keep right on coming. Let them come for all I care; the baa-baa role wasn't all that fetching anyway. But in 1966 A. E. Hotchner's *Papa Hemingway: A Personal Memoir,* which became as expected a very best seller, seemed exceptional, and once again I did cut it with my hatchet. This renewed violence was prompted by accounts in the papers of how Hemingway's widow was trying to stop the book, which I saw at the same time I was reading the book itself in a magazine and getting the sneaky feeling that there was a lot more wrong with it than she probably knew. It was rumored that Mrs. Hemingway was *not* one of my admirers, but I got in touch with her anyway, and visited her in New York, and she was completely cordial. More, she told me how to reach most of the far-flung people who appear in the book, and these in turn advised me that the parts of it involving them were unfounded or distorted. All this confirmed my hunch that one who never knew Hemingway personally might with sufficient ingenuity have faked Mr. Hotchner's *Personal Memoir* for him. (Subsequent disclosures reconfirmed it.)

This malign critique had repercussions more audible than are common. *Atlantic Monthly* got a lot of mail, most of it agreeable, and the man who played the title role in a broadcast called "Mike Wallace At Large" called to ask if I would confront Hotchner on his show. I said that I would but Hotchner wouldn't. And he wouldn't. Wallace and I, however, recorded an interview, and Hotchner appeared a couple of days after I left town to hear what I had said and refute it. This he attempted by trying to discredit the witnesses. (That Hemingway called this one "Youngerdunger" at least once I have no trouble believing, but it is certainly not true that he sued me, nor was it so that I was hired to finger Hotch by Mrs. Hemingway and her lawyers.) Some people thought I was a fool to give a wicked journalist a crack at me on the air like that, with no chance to respond; the same ones figured I would get sued when later I called the book a fake on the "Today" show. But I wasn't, and as a disinterested observer I felt I'd discredited the thing as intended. Which was the end of that.

Or would have been, but for the fact that, in the face of a mutual antagonist, Mary Hemingway and I had become friendly. Otherwise I would never have found myself, a couple of years later, secured in her bank, or the library of her apartment, groping in the great stacks of manuscript her husband had left behind, for the purpose of ordering and identifying things. From doghouse to penthouse in fifteen years, it was good to be back in New York—employed. I tell about that in the last part of Part One. I could never be happier working than I was in that vault if I lived to be a hundred.

My second bag is made of different stuff—older fiction, worn somewhat thin long ago by the repeated handling of the critics. The problem is therefore different: how do you take in all that's been said already and still respond to a book in such a way that it still seems, as it is, alive? Sometimes, as in the first specimen here, and also in that compendium Hemingway review, there is a further problem: how do you keep it alive when you're dealing not with the books but with other critics of them? Tempt not a desperate man. I once wrote a piece called "Scott Fitzgerald's Eliot: *The Waste Land* and Other Poems" which showed how, inadvertently or otherwise, *The Great Gatsby* contains quite a few lines that appear to come directly out of T.S.E. And that is probably how, already fond of literary reverberations, I advertently fell into Fitzgerald's practice. The occasion for review was a collection of

Hawthorne essays that weren't, to be truthful, urgently needed—also a new edition of Hawthorne's *Works,* which the literary world was not pleading for either. My idea was to keep the reader awake by spasmodically ringing bells in his ears. Thus thirty-one poetical quotations, twenty of them from *The Waste Land,* were stuck in the text like plums in the pudding. How many, O gentle Reader (Wordsworth), can you pluck?*

Next we consider three Classic American Nineteenth-Century Novels. When faced with the like of these what gets tested, at least in the beginning, is not so much your ingenuity, taste, or judgment, as your nerve. What typically happens is that on the basis of previous arrogance you get asked to write, say, an introduction to a new edition of some book that's been written about a hundred or so times before. It's not worth doing if you've nothing new to say, and at the moment you don't. But it's an honorable challenge and you pick it up, though with a secret suspicion that nothing is *going* to occur to you. That is what, as those who don't play it don't realize, makes this a game for men. (As opposed to women, who are reputed to say no when they are thinking yes; for men the situation is reversed.) And then they have to bring it off.

Each encounter of this sort is of course different, though there may be a pattern to it. In rereading *Typee* the thought occurred that it might be possible to establish hardy new roots for an old cliché: that the exotic island in that book was "Melville's Eden"—from which he is cast out with a vengeance. In going through *The House of the Seven Gables* again I thought I saw how an even older cliché—the "moral"

---

* The publisher will issue a citation of merit to anyone who mails in a list correctly identifying all quotations, together with a jacket from this book. Address all entries to Ticknor and Fields, 24 Tremont St., Boston, Mass.

of the book, which is Hawthorne's, he claims—might have its roots cleanly clipped, one after another, so that other "morals" might grow. And with *The Adventures of Huckleberry Finn* I probed about down there underground in search of dark meanings that seemed real enough to me, but had never seen light of day. (I had an additional motive here; the essay is a chapter in my *Hemingway,* but it was meant to stand on its own anyway, and is just about the only section of that book that's never had to—by being reprinted, that is, entire and by itself. We'll see.)

The last piece of Part Two, which deals with the discrepancy between America as we know it and as we find it in modern fiction, is different again, and on several counts— most particularly in that it was originally a lecture, and is somewhat dated. It would not have been difficult to change the style, and update it. (Indeed if I were to bring it more nearly to the present, and were to pass by J. D. Salinger, all the rage at the time, for say John Barth, and the appalling blackness of *Giles Goat-Boy,* the argument would be strengthened.) But the itch to revise has succumbed to the temptation to preserve at least a hint of the occasion on which the talk was delivered: this was the first literary lecture given—in July of 1962, at Penn State—to the first flight of trainees for the Peace Corps. The summer air was alive with hope that night, John Kennedy was in the White House, and not *all* was wrong with the world.

The third section of all this is a last different matter, two specimens of work-in-progress called Studies in Classic American Myth. Once there was supposed to be a volume of such essays, and one day there may be. But I started the project twenty years ago, and so far have published only these two pieces of it—which I wanted to have in this book in case I never get around to finishing the other one. (A primary problem has been that this time my notes for every single study pile high enough to feed a whole tome, and no one can justify writing seven books that he would not care to read himself.) About the whole project, however, or these samples of it, only a few things need saying here.

One of them would be that what's meant by "American myth" is myth-by-analogy: narratives tha have had great popular currency in this country over a long period of time, that have functioned in our culture, and still do, much as myths work in civilizations old enough to have real ones, and which are open to the same sorts of interpretation. In the traditional tales of Pocahontas and Rip Van Winkle I heard at the start faint gongs announcing no one knew what, subliminal murmurs in an unintelligible tongue. Never explained either was the enormous attraction these mythic characters have had for American artists and audiences. Nor had anyone dug long and hard enough to show how widespread, deep, and ancient are the precedents for them. And so to dig, account for, articulate, and interpret was the plan. What's in my first bag is more widely known. But I suspect that it's in this last one that the best wool is gathered. The topics are out of childhood, but the studies of them are as adult as I can make. Nothing, then, for any little kid who lives down the street.

PART I *Our Hemingway Man*

HEMINGWAY AND ME:
A RATHER LONG STORY

2 July 1961 it was, late of a hot bright Sunday morning, when dark amid a blaze of noon the phone rang with the news of Hemingway's sudden departure from the living. All the instruments agreed: the day of his death was a hot bright day, and the shock of it ran the whole world round. His scorn for the "cowardice" of self-destruction, especially as he had planted it in the thoughts of the protagonist of *For Whom the Bell Tolls*, seemed to rule it out for him—on the entirely foolish assumption that a man who had expressed his bitter distaste for suicide could not in another country, condition, and era commit it.

We were conditioned to expect that Hemingway's death would come with a bang when it came; following the airplane crashes in Uganda in 1954 there had already been obituaries. Most important, I had recently learned through an unusually direct and accurate operation of the literary grapevine that the author was a great deal sicker than the press, on his two hospitalizations, had announced or been in a position to know. But the news hurt anyway.

After great pain, claims the poet, a formal feeling comes. What came instead were more phone calls—later a couple of telegrams, later still letters—all excited and to the same effect:

You called it, Young! These messages belong to a rare species of the genus Congratulation, but the recipient was not gratified. Nor was the remark particularly accurate, as anyone who reads my book will see, unless by extrapolation from it. But there is more to this than first appears, and it is fortunate that an objective statement of the problem already exists.

In a preface to the new edition of his *Art of Ernest Hemingway* the British critic John Atkins provides a sort of "Coming Attraction" for my tome:

. . . shortly after my own book appeared there came an extremely interesting study by Philip Young. I understand that Hemingway tried to prevent the publication of this book. Its treatment was very intimate . . . and if its diagnosis was accurate it was a brilliant piece of work. If, on the other hand, the diagnosis was specious and only apparently consistent, it was a piece of impudence. According to Hemingway, it was a collection of mistaken conclusions based upon partial information. . . .

Fair enough, as a statement of a difference of opinion; and understandable enough the "irritation of Hemingway and his widow" toward Young that Atkins mentions later on. But then, with reference to Hemingway's first protagonist, Nick Adams, comes the trouble:

Many of us had been puzzled by our own reaction to those early stories. . . . We felt they contained some deep significance. It is to Young's credit, I think, that he revealed this significance by showing the subject-matter to be the aftermath of fear. . . . All his life he had exposed himself (overexposed himself, claims Young) to things he feared. It may be a distasteful thing to discover, but I cannot help feeling that Young virtually foretold self-destruction.

"Distasteful" is not entirely adequate. But the question is, if the diagnosis were specious and mistaken, how could Young have "virtually foretold" suicide on the basis of it?

It is important first to get the picture hung straight. Move number one is to repeat that Young did not predict suicide. He described a situation, a pattern, a process in Hemingway's life and work in which the act of suicide would not be altogether inconsistent. Second move is to state that nobody I know of recognized such a prediction, nor was I ever aware of it, except by hindsight. But I think—I feel?—that there is a deeper problem only a very few have been tactless enough to raise.

Suppose, as is the case, the author had in advance warned his literary analyst of the enormous damage a psychological working over could do him. Suppose, further, he had mentioned a very long letter, almost certainly to the same effect, that he had composed but, since it could only, he said, give the critic worry, he was not going to mail. (To tell a writer he has a neurosis, Hemingway did write me, is as bad as telling him he has cancer: you can put a writer permanently out of business this way.) Suppose, then, that critic, critic's critic, editor, and publisher all believed that Hemingway was needlessly and irrationally alarmed about the matter and so went ahead and produced a book which contains, among other things, a description of a syndrome the critic thought he had found in the author's work, which he believed the author's experience had caused him to delineate carefully there, and from which an after-the-fact prediction of death by his own hand could be, and was, imaginatively inferred. Could a head-on collision with such material conceivably have anything at all to do with the destructive way in which the syndrome worked itself out? If a diagnosis implies a prognosis can the diagnosis operate so as to induce the prognosis? Or help prevent it? Or have no effect at all?

Before questions of such complexity the critic is understandably mute. He does not know enough about the places and how the weather was to make even an impudent guess. Among the countless events that crowd a man's life, and this was a very crowded one, it is utterly beyond him to measure the effect of any single event. All he can know certainly is that for a year or two the "threat" of his book had an unmistakable effect on Hemingway and that in subsequent recorded interviews, right down to the last one, Hemingway was mindful of it.

But worry the critic has had—letter mailed or no. However his full discomfort, like his alleged prediction, came only after the fact. At the time of his struggle with the author, which developed into a struggle with himself as well, he simply could not get it into his head that a totally obscure $3,100-per-year instructor at the Washington Square College of New York University could actually hurt the most confident (apparently) American novelist of his age—and, next only to Faulkner, the best one. Neither could any of the others involved. Save only Hemingway.

In short, the critic is not as sure as he once was (once he felt quite sufficiently sure) that in his eventual "victory" a greater degree of right triumphed over a lesser degree. This is no matter of *mea culpa*, which would constitute an act of impudence to pass all men's believing. (Anyway, much of the tale is less morality play than farce.) And the critic will still defend the thinking according to which he and others, not knowing their own infernal strength, if Hemingway was right, built the case for publishing the book. Nor would he hesitate to make the case for bringing it out again. But it helps to admit at the start that like the ancient subterranean brook which is flowing still under Washington Square something is running under his reasoning, silently tugging at the foundations of it.

I had liked this writer for a long time, and had even ported a *Portable Hemingway*, along with a very few other books, halfway across Europe during World War II. But the story really starts later, with some well-remembered moments of a postwar afternoon in one of Iowa City's most wretched apartments for young marrieds when the pieces of my fragmentary reading of him began to fall into place—and, simultaneously, to align themselves with a recent and then-heterodox rereading of *Huckleberry Finn*. What I knew I had, if it would flesh out, was the argument for the subject of the doctoral dissertation I had to write. Flesh out it did, as things went along, in all kinds of ways.

The story consists more of endings than starts, however, and the first one came in 1948 when I finished the job—the first book-length study of Hemingway, I believe—and lurched off with the degree. There are two arguments among several to be found in that strenuous effort, as in this book, which are necessary to an understanding of subsequent events. First: the notion that the so-called "Hemingway hero" as I defined him was pretty close to being Hemingway himself. Second: that one fact about this recurrent protagonist, as about the man who created him, is necessary to any real understanding of either figure, and that is the fact of the "wound," a severe injury suffered in World War I which left permanent scars, visible and otherwise. I should also put it down for later relevance that in the beginning I answered a frequent question—What does *he* say about all this?—by explaining that since I knew roughly how he felt about critics and academics I was pretty certain he would not reply and hadn't asked him. When the question became oppressive I did write to ask if he wanted to comment and I was correct in the first place; he didn't answer. (At least I can take satisfaction in knowing that I did not start the procession of "these damn students" who "call me up in the middle of the night to get something to hang on me so they can get a Ph.D.") (Or, as he metaphorically looked at it, did I?)

The first of an impressive number of celebrations attended

this ending; as for my work, it was supposed to pass and be forgotten with the rest. And, except for doing a nice little piece of business on the interlibrary loan circuit, it had begun that process even as my wife and I made our way to New York. But that first finish was undone when I was conned by some generous and well-intentioned people into a tedious interchange with a couple of university presses. And that misadventure ended when after eight months one unmentionable editor (he had once shot an antelope or something and was a great fan of *Green Hills of Africa*) returned the volume with the explanation that he was going to publish instead a work which would pretty much upset it. (Just how I was not to learn, since if that book appeared the secret never leaked.) Meanwhile, however, a good friend and colleague at N.Y.U., William M. Gibson, had read a copy and had sent it to a trade publisher with a college department, Rinehart and Company, where was employed a friend of his named Thomas A. Bledsoe.

Mr. Bledsoe was soon to figure largely in this story. He in turn became a friend and also established himself as the best all-around editor I ever encountered. He compounded at least one spectacular mistake of mine; he was forever on the road when we should have been in action back at 232 Madison Avenue; when he was there he was badly overburdened with all sorts of other books. But he worked with energy, intelligence, taste, and understanding from start of this to finish and I am still in his debt—especially for a couple of organizational and strategic ideas that worked.

The first smart thing Tom did was make a prompt offer, which was that if I would clean the thing up so as to get the Ph.D. out of it (largely because the subject resisted the same there was less of that than is normal), and if I would arrange things so that Hemingway shared less of the stage with Huck Finn, then Rinehart would publish it. Astonished with delight with a new dimension to things, I attended my first of those let's-get-together-soon-I-mean-it New York luncheons, and became quite looped in a happy, expansive sort of way.

Thus for several months, exercising in the still night when only the moon raged, and the lovers lay abed, I remorselessly did the job over, chapter by chapter, adding one and junking another, until it was finally finished. But we only thought it was done, because right then, as if out of nowhere, came the announcement of Hemingway's first book in exactly a decade. This novel appeared initially in some improbable magazine; once each month I minutely observed the current idiosyncrasies of Col. Richard Cantwell, protagonist of *Across the River and Into the Trees*. Of all living readers only John O'Hara and Carlos Baker, I believe, have refused to call this near-parody of Hemingway a bad book. But I wonder when a critic-errant ever had a more astonishing adventure with a new work; it was precisely as if the author had got hold of my manuscript, incomprehensibly had determined to prove its notions to the hilt, and had brilliantly succeeded. For without pretending otherwise, the Colonel was about as close to his author as it is possible to get and still be called fictional, and now it was *Hemingway* who was demonstrating how his life had centered on that violent World War I misfortune. Here was staggering evidence for my argument, and nothing to do but put it in. Put it in I did. And finished again.

Even at this time I knew that when critic and editor have done all they can for a manuscript a common practice is to send it out to an Independent Expert. So I said if you're going to do this, how about Malcolm Cowley? He had been a friend of Hemingway's for many years, had himself written well and substantially on the subject, and was rumored to be available for such assignments. I had never met him at this point, but Tom knew him and thought he was a good if obvious choice. So the critic's critic was employed.

Cowley was to become the unintentional agent of a great deal of trouble, but at first he certainly earned his money. In April of 1951 he sent me directly a detailed interim report, which was a thoughtful thing to do, as I could begin considering changes at once. He related as well a good deal of factual information which I couldn't put in the book but which was reassuring anyway. In particular he brought up places where I had given impressions I hadn't intended and places where I had made bad guesses, and he objected to several things that I felt I wanted to leave the way they were. A month later he submitted his formal report, and I profited once more. He was gratifyingly enthusiastic about the first two and last two chapters, less so about the three in between, which I had already tediously reworked. But he had some solid objections, and I did a few things yet once more, finally in late May winding it up again.

The subsequent celebration took a nasty turn and became a wake. After reading the study Cowley had sent an informal account of it to Hemingway, commending much of it to him, and Hemingway had unaccountably got a very odd impression of what I had done. He proposed at once to stop it; and when Cowley had the letter to this effect, he reported it, with his hair on end, to Bledsoe, who had said nothing to me while I was still at work on this book of criticism. The letter was from Ernest to Malcolm and dated 22 May 1951.*

---

* Not even that date is a quotation (Hemingway didn't write dates in that fashion), and it may be necessary to make clear why it is not. In May of 1958 Hemingway wrote out an edict, with his wife as witness of it, to the effect that his letters, or even parts of them, were never to be published. One comes to understand his reasons. His letters are typically open and free-wheeling (and often very funny); he took few pains with the composition of them; he wanted to be remembered for his work, not his biography. But no one knows what "never" to be published, in this case, means. One thing it almost surely does not mean is "never." It certainly, however, does not mean

What Cowley reported in horror I read in shock. About this book of Young's, Hemingway wrote. He was absolutely determined that no biography of him was going to appear while he was alive to stop it. All he had to do was refuse to grant permission for quotation from his work, and then if the project went ahead all he had to do was turn it over to the lawyers. He was sorry, but every single time he had tried to be polite or helpful or frank to someone who was trying to make money out of his life it had gone badly. Thus if Mr. Young planned to publish his life while he was still in it, he would block him. He had no desire to be rude to Mr. Young or Mr. Bledsoe, but this was his considered stand and he did not intend to budge.

Perhaps this looks easy. I had most assuredly not written his biography—nor have ever wished to—and as for making money no one was more surprised than I, except the publisher, when the book did turn a profit. But to me it looked more than a little ominous. The book was criticism. But maybe you could call it "biographical criticism"; it did unfashionably contain enough biography to demonstrate that the experience of the hero was typically a refraction or projection of the author's. A sense of foreboding I couldn't account for distracted me even as words for a message of clarification began to form in my mind. But it was instantly decided that Rinehart would do the straightening out, and I acquiesced. Thus began what I still think of as The Year (it was really longer than that) of the Great Mess.

The struggle that followed was in large part real enough, but some of it was unreal and some of it was ridiculous. The real questions were, first: what are the rights of living authors,

---

"now." In savage retaliation to this policy I hereby refuse myself permission to quote from my own letters, or from Cowley's or Bledsoe's either.

and what the rights of critics? Second: at what point can criticism become an invasion of an author's privacy? And how much privacy can a writer expect when he has allowed himself to become an internationally public figure, or even, according to some, had worked very hard at promoting the image? Lastly, and this was much the toughest of the lot: given a respect for the author, which grew as the struggle progressed, how far is the critic willing to venture, even in defense of the author against many other critics, in violation of the author's deepest wishes that certain theories about him not be published? (As I said, much of the debate was then as now as much with myself as with Hemingway.)

As for the false part: in addition to being no biography written to cash in on his life the book was in no way, as he warily seemed to feel, an attack on him. Quite the contrary. And as for invading privacy, I had from the start been careful to include absolutely nothing of a factual nature that I had not already seen in print, although I knew a great many other things. Only my organization of the facts, which was really a perception of how I thought and think *he* had, not far beneath the surface, organized them, was new. And as frustrating as anything was that the single impediment to publishing the book when it was ready was the pre-announced refusal to grant permission to quote from his work and, if I quoted anyway, to take legal action. The joker in this pack was that nobody but Hemingway thought he would have a case. Despite his confident belief, which without any appreciable effect first Cowley, then Bledsoe, patiently explained to him to be almost certainly unsound, the considered opinion of the literary-legal experts like Morris Ernst was that if a case came to court in which a critic had without permission quoted for legitimate purposes and was not trying to sell the author's work as his own, the court would almost certainly find for the critic. (This was, however, a useless opinion in this instance, and Hemingway simply ignored it, probably figuring as I did that it didn't matter, since no reputable publisher at that time was likely to go to press without having satisfied the convention.)

In the light of the reality of central problems, however, it is remarkable how much of what happened was farcical. In the first place nobody, but nobody, except Hemingway answered his mail promptly. (When this eventually dawned on him he cut it out.) Indeed Bledsoe, who was in the naval reserve, went off at one critical point on an extended sea venture, having stowed away in his gear a letter that he thought he'd left behind for his immediate superior, Ranny Hobbs, to deal with. There was nothing to be done; I didn't even find out which ocean he was on.

Second is the fact that at this time Hemingway was living in San Francisco de Paula, which is a hamlet near Havana, Cuba. Now the mail clerk at Rinehart, whom I once or twice encountered on the elevator, appeared to be a nice enough girl. But I don't believe she ever did really master what I came to think of as the Cuba Concept. This had nothing whatever to do with politics, Castro not having yet been heard of. It was made up of the notion that Cuba lies outside the territorial limits of the United States. Thus mail journeying there by plane required three cents, I think it was, in extra postage to make the trip successfully, clear customs, and get unpacked. As a result of the clerk's failure to comprehend this, our letters, already long overdue, would typically wing south only to float back as it seemed on the trade winds, covered with blurred purple lettering which when deciphered and translated always turned out to signify Returned for Insufficient Postage, and had to wing it again. (The misconception must have been contagious; toward the end even Hemingway, in reverse, picked it up.) Then a fit of petty jealousy brought in the United States Post Office; two of our most winning bits of diplomacy touched base first at San Francisco, California, only later to take off, somewhat dispirited, in a proper direction.

And, Lord help us, there were the lawyers. Hypersensitive to Hemingway's pithy references to law and lawsuits, Official Rinehart (but never Bledsoe) ran scared all the way. I may not have all of it exactly straight, because much of this specialized activity, or inactivity, was not deemed suitable for my observation. But if the reports I got were accurate *three* firms had the manuscript to check out for libel—of which of course there wasn't any. One lawyer broke his hip, became intensely irritable, and refused to do any work during a lengthy stay at the hospital. After another long delay another lawyer announced, under some pressure, an Imminent Opinion ("by Monday"), whereupon he expired over the weekend. Then I heard that Stanley Rinehart and Charles Scribner appeared to have the thing about patched up on the front-office level when Mr. Scribner died. And all that time—it was nearly a year— until Hemingway wrote to ask why in hell he never heard from the *author* of the damned book, my hands were tied (and sweating).

Obviously things moved very slowly in this adventure-by-mail, which needs only a little cleaning up for family consumption and a little care in correcting the spelling (else one would be quoting).* We had not even got started with the

---

* Hemingway had, to use his wife's phrase for it, "this crazy thing about spelling," which was chiefly that he usually inserted an "e" in words that do not conventionally retain it—e.g., liveing, writeing; the extra vowel in his *Moveable Feast* exists in honor of the practice. It is possible that he had some subtle purpose in mind here, but that would not account for the various ways in which the word "psycho-analytic" was later to appear; nor does it make his position impregnable when in the *Feast* he kids Fitzgerald for having known him "two years before he could spell my name" (which usually came out "Hemmingway"). (But truth to tell it is doubtful that Fitzgerald could have survived the first cut in a fourth-grade spelling bee, while Hemingway, if he put his mind to it, could.)

correspondence when, six full months after Cowley's original shocker, he wrote Tom again. By this time the situation had become so miserable for him he wished he'd never heard of the wretched book. Word of it had apparently reached Hemingway from some additional source; anyway, we learned that by now the author was so disturbed that he had written his own publisher a whole *series* of letters on the subject. Since Cowley had commended the project to him in large part, he now seemed to Hemingway vaguely aligned with the enemy. Understandably, the critic's critic wanted to take his leave of the affair at this point—which only made Hemingway all the angrier at the man he referred to in one letter as an old, close friend (the same man who had done a good, honest job on the manuscript, and whose offer to return his check for it Bledsoe naturally refused). It is not pleasant to recall the time many years later when Cowley told me that following this mix-up he never once heard from Hemingway again. But I also know that Hemingway subsequently praised one of Cowley's books, and I remind myself that he has a compensatory privilege in being one of the very, very few who are going through all the manuscript Hemingway left behind.

Up to this point neither Tom nor I had written Hemingway, nor had we heard directly from him. On 3 December 1951, however, Tom did write, as Cowley had done and as we should have done six months before, in an attempt to bring the whole matter into focus. Some time later (due to insufficient postage our letter had only just arrived) the author replied at great length. And an open, rambling, and friendly letter it was. But it boiled down to his insistence that too much had already been written about his life. First there had recently been Cowley's own long biographical study in *Life* which, well-meaning as it was, had the effect of moving attention from his work to himself. Then there was the notorious *New Yorker* "profile" by Lillian Ross, another good friend.

Despite her complacence, this had horrified him when he read it in proof, but he had done nothing to interfere with it. The result of all this (and much more), he felt, was that his writing was being judged from the standpoint of these widely read biographical impressions and not on its own merits. He had not discouraged any of these people (they had all needed the money) but by now he had had bloody well enough. Although he had been a very long time hearing from us and wondered why and intended to be firm, he did not wish to seem rude or intractable, he said. He predicted that pretty soon there would be no writers, only critics, who would go off to Hollywood and be wrecked by the movies. What did we want to bet that Arthur Mizener wouldn't soon be on TV? All we had to do was get him another Scott Fitzgerald. I have nothing against Professor Mizener, but it was a most ingratiating letter, which ended wishing us a good holiday.

The holiday was Christmas, and better than a month was to elapse before Hemingway was to get a response to his most friendly overture. But it should not be assumed that Bledsoe and I were idle all that time. Indeed not; we were busy making things infinitely more difficult. Christmas time, for all healthy-minded college and university English teachers, is also Modern Language Association time, when we stage our own peculiar version of a convention. The proceedings that winter were in Detroit and I had been invited to read a short paper on Hemingway. I did, it was a mistake, and when Bledsoe finally answered Hemingway's letter (he'd been extensively on the road again), he reinforced the error, proudly describing the reception of the talk, which he had attended.

Tom's letter, again returned for more stamping, arrived on the evening of 16 January. The next morning Hemingway replied to it and by now his patience was tiring. He pointed out that in a frank and friendly way he had spelled out his position, only to wait a month for a response to it. If Mr.

Bledsoe was too busy, why didn't he hear from Mr. Young? Was it true that Mr. Young was corresponding with a critic in the Sudan?* He couldn't understand why, if Mr. Young had time to be traveling about giving papers on his work, he couldn't find time to write the author about it. *And* send along a copy of the talk. He closed, but on 31 January added a postscript explaining that he had put the letter aside for two weeks so that he would not be the only person involved who answered his mail. He also stressed his eagerness to read my paper: he felt it might help him in his present efforts.

The trouble was that, as assigned, my effort (restricted to something like twelve minutes) was a critique of three Hemingway papers that preceded it. Two of those papers were by chance psychoanalytic in approach—John Aldridge's "Jungian," and Frederick Hoffman's "Freudian." To establish the widest possible area of agreement among us I followed the lead, voted for Freud, and, carrying the tendency of Hoffman's remarks to what seemed a logical conclusion, ended with what I still take to be the appropriate psychoanalytic terminology. Hemingway's sense of indignation at this vocabulary did not surprise anyone. My position is what needs explaining.

There were two lines of defense at this dreadful juncture. One is that I stumbled on the psychoanalytic theory and its terminology *after* I had completed my own analysis of the wounding process and its results, which I felt Hemingway had delineated carefully only to have the whole matter ignored by his swarming critics. I remember this clearly. As part of my General Education, back in Iowa, I was reading *Beyond the Pleasure Principle* when it suddenly broke over me that Freud was writing about precisely the kind of thing I had con-

---

* Probably a reference to Atkins who was, I believe, in the Foreign Service.

structed out of Hemingway's scattered descriptions of it. Told that Freud had undergone a lot of modification, I got hold of Fenichel, recommended to me as the most authoritative of the post-Freudian Freudians, and there I found a more detailed account of the same business. What I had called, in a very special sense, "primitivism," Fenichel called "primitivation"; I had written "shell shock," he called it "traumatic neurosis." All I had done in the paper was to supply these and other terms, and to remark how skillfully Hemingway had illustrated them in fiction.

The second point is that for the MLA there was no need to waste even thirty seconds acknowledging the obvious fact that the critic was no trained analyst. I have a recent anthology called *Psychoanalysis and American Fiction,* which has fifteen contributors; all of them, including myself (but not on Hemingway), are English professors or literary critics or both, and not one of them felt the need to point out that he has no medical license to practice. It might have been unreasonable to have expected Hemingway to know this, but in our branch of service, as the saying goes, it goes without saying.

Rinehart clearly was betting no money at all on my diplomatic talents; before my first letter to Hemingway had passed a board of review Bledsoe had written again, and on 12 February received an eloquent reply. First noting that for once sufficient postage had been supplied, only to have the letter go to California (he enclosed the envelope), Hemingway gritted his teeth and remarked once more how much he looked forward to hearing from me in person and reading my paper. But he said he had a real objection to people who won't leave writers alone to do their work (precisely why, except for my reluctant, unanswered letter of years before, he had not been aware of my existence until hearing from Cowley). And people don't wish writers luck. They annoy them and worry them instead of simply hoping they will be healthy, live a long time escape financial and female difficulties, and most of all go on writing. Writing is very tough work, he said, yet it requires mechanisms as delicate as the most delicate mechanisms imaginable. If someone comes along, not himself an expert, and takes the machine apart for his own benefit, it's all very well to say that he has a right to take any old machine apart, but Hemingway did not feel the right existed while the mechanisms were still in good running order. And that was what he meant when he said some criticism constitutes an invasion of privacy.

A man who cannot, first shot, put down two English sentences in a row that are nowhere barbarous did not need telling that writing is an extremely difficult way to pass the time. But the important fact to me was that on 6 February I had the first chance to present the case myself—which, despite the cogency of Bledsoe's and Cowley's letters, I probably should not have relinquished in the first place. I explained my previous silence, pointed out that the connection between himself and his recurrent protagonist was not in my mind the central idea of the study, and tried to salvage what I could from the Detroit debacle. I expressed my admiration for his work, noted that my own book had come to mean quite a bit to me, too, and closed.

At this point Hemingway went on a fishing trip, and it was one month to the day of my first effort when he sent the most memorable reply I ever got from anyone. It began with a simple offer: if I would give him my word that my book was not a biography disguised as criticism, further that I was not psychoanalyzing him alive, then he had no objection to my publishing it. He was not going to go over the whole business again, he said. But then he wondered if I really understood how damaging it could be to a practicing writer to tell him he has a neurosis. It damages him with all his readers and could so injure the writer himself that he could no longer write. He

said he had found my Detroit paper, which I had so kindly
sent him, very interesting; but he was shocked by my use of
serious medical language. He repeated it: The paper he
thought interesting, and likewise the conclusions of it, but he
was shocked by the terminology when there were no medical
qualifications for employing it.

What followed, as he tried to explain the amount of trouble
I had caused him over the past ten months, shocked me. It
surely seemed to him, he said, that there were enough dead
writers to work on to allow the living to work in peace. So
far I had caused him serious worry, hence a serious interruption in his work. First there was Cowley, who had disturbed
him with that first report, and next, leaving a mystery, had
washed his hands of the thing. Then there was all the rest.
The disturbance caused by me, he said, had been very bad
for a man who was trying to keep his mind peaceful during a
year which had already seen the death of his first grandson,
the serious illness (cancer) of his father-in-law, the death of
his mother, the death of a former wife (mother of two of his
three children), the suicide of the maidservant of his house
on the heels of a previous attempt, the death of his last old
friend in Africa, and then the death of his very dear friend
and publisher, Charles Scribner. On top of everything were
piled the menace of my book and then the neurosis or neu-
roses charges made in Detroit. Out of all this he said he sin-
cerely hoped my luck had been good; his assuredly had not.
(Many of his letters had been composed on an obviously de-
crepit typewriter but this one was handwritten, three pages of
it, and he explained that the lines were askew because of the
hot day, which made his forearm sweat on the paper.)

The effect of seeing myself in the company of such events
was nearly catatonic, so that, although I thought of little else,
two weeks elapsed before I was able to respond and to clear
the response again with the board. I had begun to think my

initial sense of doom was profoundly justified. There did not seem much point in explaining that I had studied a good many writers, most of them dead, without coming up with a set of ideas that would support the like of my doctor's thesis and the consequent book. What I said instead was that the easy way would be to give the word he asked for. I could satisfy the letter of his conditions. But I˙was less sure about the spirit of them. He had been so decent throughout this business that I couldn't tell him less than the truth. The biography part was simple, but not the psychoanalytic; perhaps I should have offered simply to remove what little I had got from the analysts. I was glad to read, eventually, Mark Schorer's judgment that this material was handled with "great sensitivity," but a couple of other reviewers were to remark that my case would stand without it, and as already noted there had been a time when it had not been around to cut. But the shoe I handed readers to put on if they wished seemed to fit so well I could not resist offering it, and I tried instead to explain. There were only a few hundred words of offensive matter; it dealt with *nothing* but the wound; *I* had not done the psychoanalyzing—had, rather, quoted from two analysts and called their theories plausible and incomplete. One thing I was trying to show, I wrote him, was the remarkable resemblance between a psychiatrist's description of how a man acts who has been badly hit and his own account of, say, Nick Adams fishing the Big Two-Hearted River (which he had complained no one had ever understood). I also told him that however much things had gone astray I had surely never intended to injure him in any fashion. If a critic could hurt a writer with his readers, then it must follow that he could help; I hadn't wasted the better part of the last few years trying to knock anybody down. I said I felt badly about having caused him so much trouble, and that I did, very much, wish him well.

It was not surprising when at this point Hemingway lapsed into a complete silence. As the weeks went by, it became clear that we were on dead center. Ranny Hobbs sent a cable asking for a favorable decision on my letter; a few days passed; then he received a cable from Hemingway saying that he was thinking my letter over as I had done his. He would write soon. But he did not, for a long time. The situation had ceased to be bad and had become desperate; conceivably the whole project should have been dumped at this point. But that did not really seem an option to me, because of a scarcely less serious situation that had developed simultaneously with these events.

Following the postwar G.I. bulge of students, enrollments at N.Y.U. dropped precipitously, and as an untenured instructor in 1951 who had not published anything breathtaking, I was perishing fast. Although no one had told Hemingway this, I was, by the time now reached in the story, unemployed for a whole year. Except for the mercies of the American Council of Learned Societies, which paid a small wage to keep me from leaving the profession (as I had come near doing in Detroit), and for the fact that Carolyn, my wife, had a part-time job as hostess in a tea-roomy sort of restaurant, I don't know what we would have been eating. Further, I had no job for the next year, and when I eventually landed one it was strictly a temporary appointment, so that I faced unemployment again for the following year. Lastly, since the book had long ago been announced all over the place I was receiving a certain amount of static from the wrong quarters about not being able to deliver.

Thus I felt that if I was unable to get Hemingway's go-ahead for what I thought the right reasons I had very little choice but to try to get it for the wrong, and so on 23 May 1952 I wrote again, explaining very briefly my predicament. I also said that, although it was none of my business, it was hard for me to understand why, because she needed the money, he had assented to Miss Ross's "murderous" *New Yorker* profile but would not permit a book which made the strongest case it could for his importance. Anyway, I felt now there was only one thing I could do. If he would not grant the conventional permission then I was quite prepared to re-write the book paraphrasing all the quotations. I was positive he would prefer his own language to mine, but it was up to him how it went. Bledsoe wrote to confirm it: Rinehart would publish the book that way. Five days later I had a cable from Hemingway telling me to inform his editor that permission to quote was granted. He said he hoped I was happy.

Over the years I had accumulated a good deal of circum-stantial evidence of Hemingway's generosity. He liked very much to be generous; perhaps for some reason he needed to be. I thought then that however much he deplored what he thought I was doing to him, he seemed now to want to be generous with me, and I wrote to thank him. I remarked that I could scarcely be happy when it was so clear he was not, but that I was grateful and accepted his kindness not only because I needed it but because I thought—as Cowley thought—that he would be pleased with much, not all, of the book.

The insufficient postage problem originated with Heming-way this time, so that two weeks later I got a letter that had been written before the cable was sent. It was a warm letter. He said that as a matter of principle he would maintain his stand with Mr. Bledsoe forever, but that however mistaken he thought my book, he felt badly at its being held up and my chances for making a living impaired. Since he was granting the permission, it would only worry me to have a very long letter he had written me, so he was not mailing it. Then it was as if all his skies cleared and the sun poured down. He would tell Scribner's, he said, to pay to me instead of him his share of my permission costs (this was done), and if I had practiced economy in quotation to hold down expenses, he would be pleased if I would quote more extensively. (I hadn't realized the quotes were to be paid for, so there was no need of this.) Lastly he wrote that he was real sorry, buddy, if I was in crummy shape financially. He could let me have a couple of hundred and I could still feel free to call him a bastard if I wanted. If I was broke I couldn't be sued.

I did call on the Scribner editor, Wallace Meyer, who gave every appearance of having expected a man with at least two heads. Settling down, we went over the principal quotations I was going to make; I seemed again to have passed some sort of examination; then I wrote Hemingway at once (no board of review any more) accepting his generosity with the permissions fees and declining with thanks the two hundred dollars. I listed each and every quotation, including bits from things not published by Scribner's, and assured him that there had never been a moment when I felt like calling him a bastard.

There followed a rapid exchange of entirely cooperative and cheerful letters. After discovering precisely and down to the tiniest detail what words of his I was using, and commenting on several passages of them, he approved them without protest, exception, or change. Habitually he would extend the friendliest of best wishes, remark the heat, and include some little diversion such as an anecdote. I did what I could to reply in kind.

Negotiations had been going on for over a year now but the end was once more in sight; the manuscript, all tattered and torn, was once again at Rinehart ready to go. And then publication of *The Old Man and the Sea* was announced. I had known "a new book" was in the works. Hemingway had written that he hoped I would like it—that although he had gone through it over two hundred times it still did something

to him. Mr. Meyer had predicted I would like it: there was
not, he said, a single four-letter word anywhere in it. (Not
even, I thought, "this" or "that" or "fish"?) But I had not
known publication was imminent. So back from the printer
came all my pages. I read an advance copy on its arrival, and
did at that time like it, and wrote a new rousing climax to the
chapter on the novels which (hopefully) had already climaxed twice. Then a few months later my book, officially
dated 1952, unbelievably did appear—on the twenty-sixth
day of February in the year of our Lord nineteen hundred
and fifty-three.

I remember little of that celebration except driving back
late from Tom's house on Long Island, with a knowing but
now silent and vicariously exhausted Carolyn beside me, and
finding myself irrevocably committed to the George Washington Bridge, hence to New Jersey—which would not have been
absolutely unacceptable but for the fact that we were then
living in the Bronx. I remember, too, the morning after, when
of all books published that day the *Times* reviewed mine, and
Charles Poore offered me a medal for composing the atrocity
of the year. (February was pretty early in the year for that,
but then it turned out he was editing a Hemingway omnibus
for Scribner's.) I stifled an immediate response to the gist of
his attack: he must be crazy to say that I had said Hemingway was crazy, thereby proving that I was crazy. And that
was the last bad review I saw.

Partly because I had not realized in how many out-of-the
way places book reviews are made, I was astonished by the
number that appeared. (For instance, there was the *Public
Spirit* of Hatboro, Pennsylvania—"highly recommended"—
which metropolis I had never heard of.) The book came out
shortly afterward in England, where reviews were equally
generous, and then, translated, in Germany, where sales were

excellent. It was published as well in Spanish, and has long been postponed to appear with Hemingway's *Collected Works* in Italian. A substantial piece of it was in a French journal, and bits of it came out in such unlikely tongues as Telugu, Bengali, and Marathi. Best of all, it was pirated in the Argentine, and when Rinehart went to collect it was discovered that the publisher, a Peronista, was both bankrupt and in jail, which is the start of a saga the reader is to be spared.

From feature stories in the papers to solemn academic exercises, several writers paid the honor of plagiarism. (If imitation is the sincerest flattery, then what's plagiarism?) (Almost as good as piracy.) There were television plays, at least two movies, and one live play (which happily closed before it ever got to Broadway) that revealed a bungling study of the book. So much of this went on that I finally decided to crib myself, and by invitation wrote another *Ernest Hemingway*, the first pamphlet in the flourishing Minnesota series on American writers. This has now appeared in three English versions, three Japanese, two Spanish, and one each in Italian, Portuguese, Arabic, Korean, and Pushtu (which, according to my *Britannica*, is the language of the Afghans, 90% of whom are, it says, illiterate). The book itself, reverting to type, went out of print the very week it was voted into the new White House Library, and it took nearly three months of real effort to locate a fresh copy for Washington.

Mindful of this run, the original question left unanswered becomes central: what did Hemingway say? Several reviewers had wondered about this; the *Times Literary Supplement* had asked it, and more, with a vengeance: "Though simple and at first sight devastating, the argument is solidly based on a thorough analysis. . . . What will happen to Hemingway when he has read this book?" Curious to find out about this myself, I mailed him the first advance copy I got hands on, and in view of his great alarm, followed by the enthusiasm, I was surprised at the speed with which he returned it—the wrapping reversed, my name and address carefully lettered in. Very well, I thought, it can't hurt him a whole lot if he doesn't read it. That returned parcel was the last contact.

Before long, however, I began hearing from people who knew him, and it became clear he had read the book all right. Then, when he took the Nobel Prize, *Time* ran a cover story on him, and the anonymous interviewer who went to Cuba asked him what he thought of it. "How would you like it," he asked, "if someone said that everything you've done in your life was because of some trauma?" Also, with reference to the amazing list of his physical injuries I had compiled, he objected that he didn't "want to go down as the Legs Diamond of Letters."

Many years later, in August of 1965, *Atlantic Monthly* ran some free verse of doubtful quality by the author and along with it an interview by Robert Manning, which seemed to have been conducted in the same period as *Time*'s and remarkably resembled it. On this occasion Hemingway is reported as saying of the book: "If you haven't read it, don't bother. How would you like it if someone said that everything you've done in your life was done because of some trauma? Young had a theory that was like—you know—the Procrustean bed, and he had to cut me to fit into it." (The mystery of the similarities is cleared up by our man in Havana, who submits intelligence to the effect that there was only one interview—and some correspondence: the *Time* reporter was Robert Manning, too.)*

---

* Mr. Manning had added a little to the record by noting in a letter the great care with which Hemingway had obviously read the book and the good-humored way in which he rejected it, so that his remarks, Manning says, look more hostile in print than they sounded in conversation. In a subsequent and only mildly obscene letter to his interviewer Hemingway rewrote my list of his wounds so as to make

An indecisive but somewhat different exchange took place later in *Paris Review*. Editor Plimpton:

Philip Young in his book on you suggests that the traumatic shock of your severe 1918 mortar wound had a great influence on you as a writer. I remember in Madrid you talked briefly about his thesis, finding little in it, and going on to say that you thought the artist's equipment was not an acquired characteristic, but inherited, in the Mendelian sense.

Ernest Hemingway:

Evidently in Madrid that year my mind could not be called very sound. The only thing to recommend it would be that I spoke only briefly about Mr. Young's book and his trauma theory of literature. Perhaps the two concussions and a skull fracture of that year made me irresponsible. . . . I do remember telling you that I believed imagination could be the result of inherited racial experience. It sounds all right in good jolly postconcussion talk, but I think that is more or less where it belongs. . . . On the question you raised, the effects of wounds vary greatly. . . . Wounds that do extensive bone and nerve damage are not good for writers, nor anybody else.

To which one can only say that the gulf between these remarks and Mr. Young's trauma theory (which is of course by no means original with him) could not be bridged in a sentence—and wouldn't require a chapter either.

The only other reports received on the subject of the author's reaction to the critic's book have come from old acquaintances unforgot, and the last one reliably described came not long before Hemingway's death. Professors Leslie Fiedler and Seymour Betsky, both then of Montana, had called on the author in his Sun Valley home. A short time later Fiedler was in my house, where he briefed me on the

---

it hilarious. He also added to the reference to Legs Diamond his disinclination to enter literary history as a clay pigeon.

shocking, unpublicized condition of the writer's physical and mental health—which is why I was not as startled as many by the news of his explosive end, while at the same time being perhaps more moved by it. Fiedler was unable to recall what had been said about the book, but Betsky did remember and wrote me that to the best of his recollection Hemingway's exact words were: "Mr. Young is a good man and he is certainly entitled to his opinion of my work. But I think in his book he was riding a thesis and I think the thesis distorts the work somewhat."

I wish I had expressed that last myself. All theses distort the work in some degree. In trying to get at the figure in the carpet (to give a tired metaphor just a little more exercise) the man who thinks he has found the essential pattern ignores, at least for the time it takes him to demonstrate it, the whole of the rug for the figure in it. But when he is done, he hopes that the pattern will sink back into the carpet, and the carpet none the worse for wear. Even, maybe, if the revelation was truly new and sufficiently convincing, all the more to be valued.

1966

THE END OF
COMPENDIUM REVIEWING

Nothing like starting with a confession: this was to have been a whole lot grander. I had dreamed up a poor academic slob who, as the consequence of having placed one paragraph in *The Explicator,* had got in a position where he understood himself forced to read his way through a whole crush of books published since 1960 and having to do with Hemingway. I had an assortment of gimmicks whereby the character, though feeling rather square about the project, actually fought his way through the books, taking notes on 4 x 6 cards (often illegibly, while drunk). I planned to chronicle his contemporaneous and most unreasonable domestic difficulties, and even thought to appear myself, in the role of a Greenwich Village barfly disguised somewhat as José Ferrer playing Toulouse-Lautrec. Further, I had pretended to invent two of his department's impecunious but very real graduate students who, sworn to secrecy, were to read the French and German entries for as little cash as possible, since—can you believe it?—my protagonist's Ph.D. Reading Knowledge of these tongues, largely spurious in the first place, had long since deserted him in the second. (This device I have cleverly chosen to retain—along with, for the sake of brevity, my still-born hero's 4 x 6, Greggorian-Choctaw style.) And finally

there was to be a real O. Henry finish which would have produced a rich harvest of pity and fear. But since the fantasy
was too implausible even as fantasy for me, at least, to bring
off, I have had to fall back on the simple truth. The slob, *c'est
moi.*

The thing of it is, for a long time I have been sick of reading about Hemingway. I could still occasionally read him, but
not about him. So I quit. But I discovered something. Once
you're pegged it's not all that easy to get off the peg. One
trouble is, you get tired of saying that, whatever it may be,
you haven't read it. (*What do you read?*) And so, in a period
of mental alienation, I announced buoyantly that I was going
to get Caught Up, and read Every Damn Thing that could
be called a Hemingway-Centered Book or Pamphlet, hard or
soft, that had come out since 1960. (A nice round number,
and somewhere about the time I quit.) If being our Hemingway Man was inevitable, why not relax and enjoy it? (Relax!
Enjoy! Is to laugh.)

For a while everything was fine. It took many weeks to
accumulate the books; so long as they were coming in I felt
no need to read them yet; I continually congratulated myself,
and with reason, that I had at least been sane enough not to
propose reading the torrent of essays and articles. But all of
a sudden it dawned on me: maybe the flow, bookwise, was
not going to stop. If not, it was the old story: in postponing
my fate I was aggravating its severity. Therefore on 4 July
1964 *I* stopped. This even though I might easily have put off
the evil day by awaiting two announced but as of then unpublished books on Hemingway; one by Nelson Algren, which
might be interesting; the other by Sheridan Baker, which
might even be good. Or, for that matter, I might have postponed the misery by continuing the search for two published
but hard-to-get-hold-of efforts: Kurt Singer's *Hemingway's
Badge of Courage,* date, place, and publisher undetermined,

and Jerry R. Krzyzanowski's *Ernest Hemingway,* Warsaw: Wiedza Powszechna, 1963. (I had a reader lined up for *this,* and finally learned why I couldn't get it: the demand in Poland is such that the book went out of print practically on publication, and the paper shortage is such that they don't reprint you unless your name is Marx, or Lenin.) But since my project's other virtues were doubtful or worse, I was concerned to present my effort, even without these four tomes, as An Immoveable Feat.

And so that night, despite a painful burn from a sparkler, I counted the shaky pile: thirty-two items to hand. (It looked like more.) I measured it: twenty-two and one half inches. (Very disappointing.) I carried it to the bathroom and weighed it: only eighteen pounds. (Too many paperbacks.) But there were still thirty-two full titles: that's a lot. What to do next with this mess? I spread it out all over the floor of my "study," then spent half the night on hands and knees arranging and rearranging the books in smaller piles, according to various notions of genus and species, and kicking over three beer cans in the process. Toward morning I had one pile on one side of a wet rug, eight piles on the other, and went to bed feeling slightly better. On the Sabbath I faced up to them, started reading and (since I have almost no memory) making notes.

I. *Primary Sources*

A. POETRY

1) Ernest Hemingway: *Collected Poems.* Pirated Edition. San Francisco: no publisher, 1960. First collection of all his known, published verse. Six pieces from magazines of early Twenties, ten from *Three Stories and Ten Poems* (1923). Mostly imitative; or adolescent if not childish. Something

wrong some place: impossible to reconcile man we see in *Wild Years* (*infra*), let alone *Moveable Feast,* with man who wrote, did not throw away, even published the lyrical "Soul of Spain" (*e.g.,* Part IV entire: "After a while there were no bullfights. What the hell no bullfights? No you really can't mean it no bullfights. But there were no bullfights."). Only poem much worth reading: "The Age Demanded." (Scholars please note: Title is from, poem is answer to, part of Pound's "Ode pour l'Élection de Son Sepulchre.")

Am told Hemingway left behind another book of "poems," written over later years. Malcolm Cowley has read it. Tells me they're "Kiplingesque," won't do anything for or to his reputation. So they'd better be better than these.

B. JOURNALISM

1) Ernest Hemingway: *The Wild Years.* Edited with Introduction by Gene Z. Hanrahan. New York: Dell, 1962. Is paperback collection of seventy-three features written for one-half cent/word for *Toronto Star Weekly* and *Toronto Daily Star,* 1920–23. Inauspicious-looking: ridiculous title, irrelevant introduction, cover photo of Hemingway with great curvy-horned African animals shot maybe fifteen years later. Also, features meant to be read at distinct intervals, not in couple of sittings. But all's not lost. Engaging picture of makings of what could have been World's All-Time Foreign Correspondent. Enterprising, independent. No faking. (Any young American in Paris knew he should really go for those *apéritifs;* he describes same [correctly] as having "basic taste like a brass door-knob.") Hardheaded, hard to fool, amused. Serious, witty, determined, mighty smart. Two sharp, very early interviews with Mussolini; trip with wife to Pamplona bullfights when they're only Americans in town. Much else: Toronto, Chicago, Paris, Germany, Switzerland, Italy.

Editor expresses pious hope (gulp) Hemingway "would have been pleased" with this book. Hemingway on subject of even *listing* his journalism (in published letter to first bibliographer, late L. H. Cohn): "It is a hell of a trick on a man. . . . No one has any right to dig this stuff up and use it against the stuff you have written to write the best you can." (Naturally he assumes critics would be stupid enough to use it against him. False assumption. Book should've been published, okay. But in hardback, edited by competent responsible person.)

II. *Secondary Sources*

A. SIBLING BIOGRAPHY

1) Leicester Hemingway: *My Brother, Ernest Hemingway.* Cleveland: World, 1962. Begins saying much printed about brother "heinously and hilariously inaccurate." *E.g.,* "He never ran away from home," as "freely reported by biographers" (me too): "Ernest always sent postcards." (Oh.) But *chief* trouble is: Ernest sixteen when Leicester born; by first page Chapter Two Ernest ready to go to war; early years, important years, mostly missing. Then, when close contact (mainly during Key West period), simply anecdotal: hunting, drinking, endless fishing. These were *Esquire* years, Leicester's is *Esquire*-type portrait (though now it's *Playboy*, and *Playboy* did serialize it).

Two interesting sections, however. First on background for famous heroine of *Farewell to Arms.* In life Catherine Barkley was Agnes H. von Kurowsky, Bellevue-trained daughter of German-American father. (Leicester found nice picture of her, prints it.) She somewhat older, but Hemingway obviously had affair with. Also, much of hospital stuff in novel —head nurse finding empty bottles in Lt. Henry's room, etc.—

happened. Hemingway intended to bring Agnes back from Italy and marry. *Now:* have long been two literary versions of end of this. In *Arms,* of course, she dies in childbirth; in "A Very Short Story" unnamed protagonist comes home alone, expecting Luz to follow, but gets Dear John letter instead: she going to marry Italian major. Doesn't marry him either, and John contracts gonorrhea in Chicago taxicab. No sign Leicester ever heard of story, but aside from venereal element, not substantiated here, now apparent "A Very Short Story" tells how it actually was, novel how it might have been.

Leicester pretty clear on brother's break with parents after war. Mostly because of their almost unbelievable Victorianism. Also they insisted he go to work, which writing wasn't. Rather grim tale. Ernest "formally drummed out of the home" on twenty-first birthday. Break somewhat patched up, but when *Sun Also Rises* appeared parents bug-eyed in horror; when writer and first wife Hadley divorced, Leicester heard father say, "It's the disgrace. I'd rather see him in his grave." This, too, was partly smoothed, but estrangement such that when mother died 1951 Ernest sent sister "a note and money, asking that she take everyone to dinner in his name. . . ."

Incidental Intelligence: Model for apparently immortal restaurant in "Killers" was "Kitsos," Near North Side Chicago. Model for Harry Morgan, protagonist of *To Have and Have Not,* was Josey Russell, who ran rum from Cuba to Florida Keys. After father's suicide Ernest told Leicester "Pray as hard as you can, to help get his soul out of purgatory"; what other people don't understand is "things go right on from here." (Leicester says all during marriage to number two, Pauline Pfeiffer, Ernest was "as strong a Catholic as she was"; he broke with it when he broke with her.)

Here, too, is best account yet of Hemingway's final illness: twenty-five shock treatments for depression, weight down to 155, long list of physical ailments. Also manages to get across brother's "zest," extraordinary desire to learn, very wide interests. But for writer, and brother of famous one, he seems either awfully dead-pan or out of touch; dealing with World War II years, *e.g.*, mentions "Jerome Salinger, who was a good CIC man with the division." Period. Finally, though, one excellent passage sums up book, also much of Hemingway:

Ernest was never very content with life unless he had a spiritual kid brother nearby . . . someone he could show off to as well as teach. He needed uncritical admiration. . . . A little worshipful awe was a distinct aid. . . . I made a good kid brother when I was around.

In connection with this biography, see also widely ignored novel:

2) Leicester Hemingway: *The Sound of the Trumpet*. New York: Holt, 1953. Was partly warm-up for biography. Poor novel, roughly as John to William Faulkner; same superficial resemblances to big brother. But all of sudden book comes to life when Ernest appears, under name of Rando Granham; gives kid brother second-best table. All most literal, covering much of ground biography covers, with nothing changed but names. Line between fiction and biography getting hard to draw. Of which more later.

3) Marcelline Hemingway Sanford: *At the Hemingways: A Family Portrait*. Boston: Little, Brown, 1962. Unpretentious job; good pictures again. But she has one thing on Leicester. Was close enough to Ernest in age (less than two years older) to have been with him through high school. Items of literary interest: his great reading as kid, Horatio Alger to "every word of the King James version"; how he heard tales from Indians and others up in Michigan and used same; that his style was becoming individual, as present writer argues, in high school—*i.e.*, *before* Kansas City *Star* days. Small shocks of recognition: *e.g.*, mention of picture (apparently one

printed in book) Ernest sent home from Italy, after his wounding, of "nice-looking bearded older man . . . Conte Greppie": Count Greffi of *Arms,* no? (Doubt she heard of him.) Some legends contradicted: Hemingway never kept out of school to study cello, as he claimed; did not ruin eye boxing. Some bolstered: he did rescue Italian soldier *after* had been nearly killed himself (this once dismissed as impossible). But nothing here, except his wider experience, to show why he not she became writer.

Without him, no book, but as per title emphasis on family, not Ernest. Looks this way: In portraying parents, first as Dr. and Mrs. Adams, then under different name in *For Whom the Bell Tolls,* Hemingway greatly underplayed them. In many ways remarkable, admirable people. Family life happy, extremely active; had lots of cash, spent it well. Father quite a fellow, nearly professional naturalist, pioneering M.D. Mother's been made out foolish, religious culture-vulture; was equally talented; was Gave Up Singing Career for Marriage type, but actually Did. Turned down offer of contract from the Met; in 1895 gave concert in old Madison Square Garden: one thousand smackers. After marriage was making same sum per month—plenty money, those days—as voice teacher (this while novice doctor-husband making fifty dollars). After death of husband and loss of singing voice became painter; sold pictures for good prices, lectured "all over the country." And though Marcelline wouldn't like it, reader can largely credit parents' radical Victorianism for son's generation-leading rebellion vs. all that.

More on this break with family. Ernest said Oak Park people didn't "live all the way" like Italians. Relationship with family pretty much as in story "Soldier's Home" (though neither she nor Leicester seems ever to have read *it*). Young writer's early works snapped it. Marcelline bought *Three Stories and Ten Poems,* nearly passed out. Especially over

"Up in Michigan": Ernest had put names of old family friends into "this vulgar sordid tale." Says *in our time* did it for parents. She's got wrong title; no matter. Father "wrote to Ernest and told him that no gentleman spoke of venereal disease outside a doctor's office." This, too, patched up, but finally permanent disaffiliation: "In her late seventies Mother mentioned her desire to sometime have a reply to her annual birthday letters to Ernest." On same note, see Acknowledgments at end. Names thirty-seven people who helped with book, many of them relatives, but not Leicester, who was friendly with Ernest. In his novel Leicester has Rando (Ernest) speak to brother Danforth (Leicester) of "our unmentionable sister." Had several sisters, but little doubt that late Marcelline, whom Ernest was raised insofar as possible with as twin, is one they had in mind. Sad.

B. VULTURE BIOGRAPHY

1) Kurt Singer: *Hemingway: Life and Death of a Giant*. Los Angeles: Holloway House, 1961. This, or maybe next below (forget), was first of obscene paperbacks appearing mysteriously from nowhere before corpse even cool. Author credited with forty books, has doctorate Political Science, U. of Indiana. No more promising: Dedication to "James A. Michener . . . who inherited the Hemingway crown"; or Foreword, explaining book finished in great haste because we simply couldn't wait.

As for text, some of it interesting, fresh—indeed original. Lots of sex. Items: was *friend* who got gonorrhea in Chicago cab. (Singer joins rest in never having heard of story.) Hemingway "had his first woman when he was thirteen." Enter mysterious "Mrs. X" in Chicago he spent many afternoons with, listening to stories of her lovers, "their techniques," and learning from her "art of love-making." Then in Paris detailed account of event with one Heloise, described as "frail wisp of a woman" (but apparently pretty fat in the middle): "Taking his hand, she helped him explore her breasts, the curve of her waists and thighs." In Chicago another affair with Maria, Italian slum girl, action and conversation both recorded. In Spain, a starving twelve-year-old Rosita; she lifted him up (all 200 lbs., no doubt) and carried him to bed when he sick. Lastly, in Key West, add boy, José, he fished with—until boy made pass at him while he slept.

On second thought, not hard to be fresh, original, if you make it up. Some novel theories, too. Example: Lady Brett Ashley, forty years known to have been based on Lady Duff Twysden, "was a composite of the women he had known, Hadley, the Parisian coquette, Heloise, and the many name-less faceless wenches who had hung on his arm or bit his ear." Has vision as well. Example: On Ezra Pound in St. Elizabeth's Hospital: "Eventually [1958], the aging poet was set free. He died a few years thereafter."

Book (scrapbook) ends in plunge through chaos. Last example: To put criticism in proper place, in own small book on Hemingway, cited Marianne Moore's well-known concession about poetry: "I, too, dislike it: there are things that are important beyond all this fiddle." Cf. *this* paragraph:

Mostly [Hemingway] shrugged off his critics saying, "There are things that are important beyond all this fiddle."

(Footnote: Letter from "Singer Features, In the Heart of Disneyland," and dictated by Mr. Singer, reveals that his hard-to-come-by *Hemingway's Badge of Courage*, mentioned above, was "anthology and contained no new material." Damn.)

2) Alfred G. Aronowitz and Peter Hamill: *Ernest Hemingway: The Life and Death of a Man*. New York: Lancer, 1961. This one has Bibliography yet—even Acknowledgments; best is of debt to "Professor Arthur A. Fiedler of Montana State

University." (Come Back to the Pops Again, Les, Honey!) Some fresh stuff here, too, but more reliable. Got first wife, Hadley, speculating after his death about possibility her husband and Brett, or Lady Duff Twysden, "had an affair." ("I think it's perfectly possible . . . but I think they didn't actually. . . . That isn't the kind of a thing a husband talks to his wife about too much, don't you agree?") Also have remarks of first son, John; among other things he contradicts my notion woman in "Snows of Kilimanjaro" is based on Pauline Pfeiffer. (Authors suggest, most implausibly, Zelda Fitzgerald; probably everybody wrong.) Book anecdotal and partly paste-up with some pretty big unpaid-for chunks from other books. But as rush-to-press journalism could be worse. Next is (is worse):

3) Milt Machlin: *The Private Hell of Hemingway*. New York: Paperback Library, 1962. Private, *hell;* now is public. Discovery in a barber shop; author Managing Editor something called *Argosy*. Says he knew Hemingway for over decade; handicap doesn't show. What shows: "mountain of books and clippings and magazine articles I poured through."

But more memorable side of Machlin is hellish creative. Most impressive achievement is to take nice, shifting distinction between young Hemingway and young Nick Adams and clobber it. Thus by simply substituting "Ernest" for "Nick" substantial contributions made to knowledge of Hemingway's youth. Example of method: takes story called "Battler," carefully not acknowledging existence of same, removes "Nick," inserts "Ernest," comes out with section of heretofore unknown biography. Makes other characters in story (Ad Francis and Bugs) actual personages with those names, lifts their conversation from story intact, inserts it. Thus the "still trusting Hemingway," not Nick, got knocked off train by brakeman; same kid, Ernest, narrowly escaped pasting only when Bugs sapped Ad. Etc., etc. Method has extraordinary possibilities; any number can play. But snags, too: when novelist kills off

hero—Col. Cantwell, say—what to do with Hemingway alive?
(Easy, as Machlin shows: say Cantwell is *not* Hemingway, is
one Col. Charles T. Lanham.)

Biographer occasionally reveals humbler side. *Asks* (un-
expectedly): Was "lusty Gypsy woman Pilar" of *Bell* named
after Hemingway's boat, Pilar, "or both named after some
unknown woman in his past?" (Answer, according to
Leicester: Both named for Spanish shrine.) But has little
patience for questions, and real contribution many critics
might envy: makes separation of writer from written impossible. So long, Bouffon! (The style is the man.) So long, Mark
Schorer! (The style is the meaning.) Hello, Milt Machlin!
(The man is the fiction.)

C. MISCELLANEOUSLY BIOGRAPHICAL

1) Lillian Ross: *Portrait of Hemingway*. New York: Simon
and Schuster, 1961. This is reprinting of famous 1950 *New
Yorker* "profile," but now appears as book, with preface on
Furor it Caused at the Time. Chiefly among people who read
it as devastating attack, making subject out an ass, a nut, and
"an ignorant bastard," who "thought of establishing a scholarship and sending myself to Harvard." *She* calls piece "sympathetic," points out that before publication she sent proofs to
Hemingway and he said he liked. Further, when he heard
about uproar he wrote again she shouldn't worry.

All very well. Or is it? Piece is colorful, funny, often ingratiating, though lots of curious Indian-talk in it (hmm . . .)
and no sense subject was of great stature she claims he had.
No doubt whatever about those letters; his generosity bound-
less. But I was also hearing from him in those days. Understand you get jail for quoting unpublished letters of his, but
can reveal to waiting world he wrote me he didn't think he
talked half-breed Choctaw (hey, watch it!) and didn't think

she gave much impression of a writer who worked as hard as he. But what the hell. No harm intended though much received. (This submitted gratis for the record. Machlin, *supra*, quotes Hemingway saying Ross profile "had done more to destroy his faith in his fellow newsman [sic] than anything in his life.")

2) Leo Lania: *Hemingway: A Pictorial Biography*. New York: Viking, 1961. Bad, very bad. Pictures mostly overfamiliar, except for fourteen of Ava Gardner, Burt Lancaster, Gregory Peck, *et al.* (They appeared in movies with Hemingway titles.) Further index to quality: "Short, Happy Life of Francis Macomber" is called "The Macomber Affair" (movie name).

Text is worse. Hunks picked up and dished out from unnamed, but easily identified, books. Is work of outsider. Way outside. Writes of "Hemingway's temptation to return [from Chicago!] to the flesh-pots of Oak Park," his hometown (which, as Leicester noted, "was proudly described by its residents as 'the place where the saloons stop and the churches begin'"). Only real interest is trying to figure out book's source. New York publication, but amount of Nobel Prize money given in kroner and pounds, not dollars. "Leo Lania" elsewhere identified as pseudonym for "Lazar Herrman." Who he? Appears publisher tried to make book look as if had been translated into German; almost certainly was translated out of it.

3) Carlos Baker: *Hemingway: The Writer as Artist*. Third edition. Princeton: Princeton University Press, 1963. Relevance of this that, since Hemingway didn't publish anything important between second edition and this one, added matter would have to be biographical—as such might provide advance notice of what Authorized Biography Baker is doing will be like. Right on both counts. New chapter called "The Death of the Lion"; forecast is for mixture of cloudy and fair.

Biographical treatment is tasteful, reserved, dignified, accurate. (And for first known time Baker here, right on p. 335,

slips and gets title to *Green Hills of Africa* right. Attaboy,
Carlos.) But biographer still at sort of respectful (bardol-
atrous?) distance. Account of last years not "immediate," not
even frank. Doesn't take life out of subject, but avoids or
plays down the wild or unpleasant. No more than hint of
latter-day forbidden drinking. (Friends said, recorded elsewhere, "What's he trying to do? Kill himself?") No mention
of fact he was twice in mental hospital for depression; this
mildly significant: accounts more than any other single thing
for suicide at which chapter title points. Somebody doesn't
watch out, we going to get, in name of Good Taste, a freshly
washed, shaved, combed Hemingway. Best biographies never
known for politeness, never written to please publisher, widow
of author. Cf.:

4) Carlos Baker: *The Land of Rumbelow*. New York:
Scribner's, 1963. Novel (and better one than reviewers let
on). Relevant because (on one level) is book about Baker
writing book about Hemingway, despite routine dodges and
disclaimers. Novelist named Nicholas Kemp—combo, perhaps,
of names of two Hemingway protagonists, Nick Adams and
Harold Krebs (of "Soldier's Home," who was at Belleau
Wood, where Kemp lost arm in same war). Kemp ran away
from home, is big-game hunter, wrote autobiographical stories
about boyhood, etc., etc. Baker's Dan Sherwood, English professor with Jersey plates on car, manuscript on Keats in tow
(for which read Shelley), is Baker. He's writing book on
Kemp out in Arizona, where Baker wrote his *Hemingway*.
Just as he finishes book Kemp brings out first novella, described to fit *Old Man and Sea*: exactly what happened just
as Baker's *Hemingway* appeared. Many other parallels.

But gets complex. Hemingway had middle name (Miller)
he didn't use. So has Kemp but (Baker and Miller being a
little too close?) the middle name is Young. Well now: Prof.
Sherwood went to Amherst, is short, was boxer. (Prof. Baker

went to Dartmouth, is tall, athletic prowess not known.) Who went to Amherst, is short, and (for brief but anyway deplorable period) was wrestler (not boxer)? Damned if *Young* didn't (isn't, didn't).

Plot (*i.e.*, on *à clef* level) thickens. Enter another, younger critic from Minnesota (where younger Young once taught, where his pamphlet on Hemingway [*infra*] was published). This dope is *also* writing on Kemp. Kemp in turn has been put in position, he feels, where he will greatly damage young man's career if he, Kemp, stops publication of critic's stuff; this Kemp would like to do, since he resents application of Freud: precisely, but exactly, Young's predicament for many painful months, 1951–52. Kemp's letters to Sherwood sound as if Baker had been reading and copying Young's mail from Cuba (Rum-below?). But he hadn't (didn't, hasn't).

Enough, enough. Sherwood decides he will put Kemp's biography in his book; would hurt too many people (Hemingway's stock objection to biography while he lived). Professor ends convinced should *be* no biography; not while Kemp lives, anyway. Here cf. introduction to first edition of Baker's *Hemingway*, where points out he not writing biography then, though subject's life would be "a proper story, and in some respects a heroic one. But the time to tell that one has not yet come. It can wait." (Foreboding, that.) Well, he waited. Some ten years. Now time has come. But if book is what it ought to be, somebody still going to have to get a little hurt.

D. CRITICISM (In English)

1) John Killinger: *Hemingway and the Dead Gods: A Study in Existentialism.* Lexington: University of Kentucky Press, 1960. Absolutely inevitable somebody'd get around to

this. But Killinger got there just too soon: Hemingway alive when he wrote; demise might have been crucial. (Am thinking of Camus, to effect there's only "one truly serious philosophical problem and that is suicide.") Be that as may; critic uncovers some striking parallels between notions Hemingway expressed and those of big-game existentialists. Thus thesis has limited plausibility. But same thing will work on whole flock of nonexistentialist writers, so in end have feeling of nice try, better luck next time out.

2) Stewart Sanderson: *Ernest Hemingway.* New York: Grove, 1961. First published in Scotland. Neither good nor really bad; doesn't seem to have *tried.* (But has special interest for present reader. If imitation's sincerest form of flattery, what's shoplifting? Surprisingly unpleasant, especially when they print as gospel what you gingerly guessed. However, one gets out from under on page 96ff., when magically transformed into "Philip Green.")

Critic understands what he's read, writes decently, plays minor variations on other people's themes. Then, after 118 pages, simply stops. (Had to answer phone, go to john or something; forgot to come back.) Flaccid, tired, disengaged; reminiscent of only other British book, John Atkins' *Art of Ernest Hemingway,* 1952. Maybe British just not up to playing tough games anymore.

3) Joseph Defalco: *The Hero in Hemingway's Short Stories.* Pittsburgh: University of Pittsburgh Press, 1963. Book was apparently University Florida Ph.D. dissertation. Very favorably reviewed by Baker. Own arrogant opinion: they should take back degree. By page 6 following titles mentioned: *The Waste Land, Moby-Dick, Adventures of Huckleberry Finn;* never gets one quite right. Which is nothing. In seven pages, during incredible discussion of "Killers," misspells Ole Andreson's name twenty-one times. Trivial. But for level of edification consider introductory this:

Much is lost to the reader in viewing *The Adventures of Huckle-berry Finn* simply as a story of a boy on a raft floating down a river. . . . It would be equally inconsequential to designate [sic] *Moby Dick* as a story solely about whaling, or *The Scarlet Letter* as a description of life in early Puritan Boston. These novels are considerably more.

Thank *you*, Paul Revere. Many other ingenuities—like man who "commits suicide by cutting his own throat." (Not somebody else's throat.) Repeated references to conflict of child with parents as "triadic." (Proves author can count to three; glad to see it.) Worst of all, such as this (p. 1, chapt. I): "Moreover, due regard to the coequality of the two [form and theme] as fictive processes leads to a more coherent understanding of the whole as an artistic totality." Come again? No! —don't bother!

However, book at times illuminating. This because critic had secret connection to author's intentions and consciousness. Thus can reveal that when Hemingway called first hero "Nick Adams" he "intentionally used a symbolic name as a conscious device to illustrate what the character himself would reveal. . . ."(Nick equals Satan, Adams equals Adam; thus a "tension," Q.E.D. But—heck!—it doesn't stick; Nick later becomes Grail hero, Lazarus, and some other guys.)

If I crucify this jerk, would that make him Christ symbol? Back to "Killers." Ole Andreson "exhibits the qualities of the traditional wounded hero-king. . . ." As for Cook, "we again see [him] functioning as the wooing mother-surrogate." (Jesus, don't we ever!) That a snake "is symbolic of the emasculated or ineffectual father" is called "fact." Defalco, poor melancholiac, can't see a sunrise without spotting a foreshadowing of "the coming of night again." (O You Andrew Marvell!) Are at least half-dozen crazy readings; one leads to fancy theories about guilt of incest in "The Battler." ("Of course," as Hemingway has Bugs point out in story, "they wasn't brother and sister no more than a rabbit.")

Things Taken Out of Context? Cross my heart: in context is worse. Assume no one at Press read this, partial absolution granted. But appears Prof. Harry Warfel "directed" project; *he* should have read it.

4) Earl Rovit: *Ernest Hemingway*. New York: Twayne, 1963. This is pretty fair book. Man did plenty homework, assimilated same, then strikes out for self on solid ground. Good on Hemingway's two "heroes," "Hemingway hero" and "code hero," and renames them "tyro" and "tutor." Okay, or better, by me. *Not* okay by me: Discovery story called "Fifty-Grand" is "supremely comical"; present writer gets Holy Hell for missing joke, still can't see it.

Principal troubles: Critic gets in very deep with psycho-analytic stuff, then is shipwrecked on question of identity of Hemingway's "artistic ancestors." Tutor as father, "Hemingway heroine" as mother, pretty unconvincing; so is explanation of novelist's "return to the world," Lt. Henry to Robert Jordan, on psychoanalytic grounds. Worse is unrelenting rocky thesis that writer's literary affiliations are not with Twain, Crane, and the rest but (Marie, Marie, hold on tight!): Emerson and Whitman. Insists on making "persuasive case" for "placing Hemingway firmly within the Transcendental aesthetic tradition." Recurrent shock of unrecognition is numbing; little transcended but reason. And to allow argument, is forced to dismiss author's writing off (in *Green Hills*) of what Rovit calls his "Transcendental grand uncles" as "just another indication of Hemingway's incompetence in the handling of abstractions foreign to his immediate experience." Well, now. True that Hemingway not much of a hand with abstractions; true further that Rovit handles same pretty well. But that won't fly. However, in addition to handling abstractions pretty well, Rovit even better defending writer against his detractors. And, though couple of his theses abortive, competition is such that this is best full-length Hemingway book since Fenton's, decade back; possibly better than that.

5) Philip Young: "Ernest Hemingway." In *Seven Modern American Novelists: An Introduction,* William Van O'Connor, ed. Minneapolis: University of Minnesota Press; London: Oxford University Press; Tokyo: Donald Moore Books, 1964. This is revised, updated, hot off press version of Minnesota Pamphlets on American Writers, No. 1. After editions in Spanish (two), Italian, Arabic (which end is up?), Portuguese ("copyright 1960 by Leon Edel," man who gets around), and with Korea and Japan (in *third* version) soon to be heard from—nice to see this back in English. But professional ethics prohibit doing justice to succinct, eloquent little masterpiece.

E. CRITICISM (Continental)

1) John Brown: *Hemingway.* Paris: Gallimard, 1961. Bit of an oddity: book on American novelist by American critic composing in French. Author a Foreign Service officer, cultural attaché, etc. (Present writer somewhat embarrassed by Brown's friends, while living in Rome, at not having read. Now have.) Also odd sort of book: seven parts made up of quotes about Hemingway as man and writer; chronology of life; summaries of, excerpts from, novels, etc. And photographs. Only section really critic's is Part III. Here, comparisons and contrasts with Faulkner, discussion of style (sources and influence), discussion of "hero." Chief point in last is, far from being callous, hero is so sensitive he's forced to become "un homme anesthésié"—this accomplished by plunging into alcohol, physical activity, writing. Book aimed at French audience, for which good introduction. See also:

2) *Ibid.* Milano: Feltrinelli, 1964. "Traduzione dal francese e reduzione italiana di Livia Livi." Pretty much same book, with changes directed at Italian audience.

3) G[eorges].-A[lbert]. Astré: *Hemingway par lui-même.* Paris: Éditions du Seuil, 1961. This number 46 in series called "Écrivains de toujours." Doesn't acknowledge fact, but chiefly exploits, with skill, last few pages of earlier, American, book arguing essential Hemingway story makes "myth" relating "greatest of all American stories . . . the meeting of innocence and experience . . . the Fall of Man, the loss of Paradise" and Eden (quote from Young's *Hemingway,* 1952). Astré also sees this meeting, or conflict, as "un problème remarquablement américain," and makes of Nick Adams, and young Hemingway, an Achilles figure, confident of immortality, who confronts Europe (again representing mature experience, Paradise Lost, death). "L'initiation d'Ernie [*sic*] [est] comme celle des fabuleux héros d'autrefois. . . ." This is tendency of critic's mind. Also works out notion again that whole conflict "entre l'illusion d'immortalité et expérience précoce du mal et de la mort" is foreshadowed in *In Our Time.* Sees *Sun* and *Arms* as revealing total failure of the "rêve américain." Finishes it off by seeing *Bell* as transforming death into victory, and *Sea* as "un mythe odysséen," in which Hemingway through old man is reconciled to fate, with no more need of feeling immortal or even of having to win. This brings "Les Bonheurs D'Ulysse." Okay.

4) *Ibid. Ernest Hemingway in Selbstzeugnissen und Bilddokumenten.* Hamburg: Rowohlt, 1961. ("By his own testament and in pictures"—but title, in French or German, is misleading.) This is das selbe Buch auf Deutsch, ich glaube, ich hoffe.

5) Quentin Ritzen: *Ernest Hemingway.* Paris: Éditions Universitaires, 1962. Author is young Parisian M.D., moonlighting critic as well, with books also on Simenon and Chek-

hov. Copy at hand inscribed to present writer, who preferred to discuss interesting symptoms, at Paris cocktail party, Dec., 1962. But nice man, nice book. Thesis is that Hemingway was artist, not thinker: "Il croyait en ce qu'il avait vu, senti, touché . . . " etc., etc., which is what Hemingway said about Goya. Book conducts running battle with one Maurice E. Coindreau's *Aperçus de la littérature américaine*, which apparently presents cliché objections: Hemingway never grew up, had limited view of life, was defective in feeling. Last of these *aperçus*, anyway, as Ritzen shows (and so have Brown and others), is itself defective in feeling. All trouble comes from approaching as if Hemingway were philosopher; was poet, says Ritzen (who as M.D., incidentally, accounts for suicide as result of "long melancholy"). All very French, very intelligent—except on *Death in PM:* "One could prefer, in Hemingway, this work to all the others; as in Melville one prefers *Moby-Dick*." *This* one couldn't.

6) Hermann Stresau: *Ernest Hemingway*. Berlin: Colloquium Verlag, 1958. (Zounds!—note date: didn't *have* to and *did*. Donnerwetter noch einmal!)

Ah well. Book is introductory; plenty biography and description of novels. But as for much of rest: Germanic tough going. Not for all of, though. *E.g.*, on Hemingway's "style of narration"; "Sie ist scheinbar realistisch, in Wirklichkeit symbolisch; sie ist scheinbar primitiv, in Wirklichkeit einfach und ausserordentlich kunstvol." ("It is apparently realistic, in reality symbolic; it is apparently primitive, in reality simple and extraordinarily artful": not bad, what?) Not so tough, either, when critic leans on only secondary source mentioned, 1954 German translation of Young's book: "Gewiss ist Hemingway ein washechter Amerikaner" (a washable—*i.e.*, died-in-the-wool—American). His "epischer Kosmos" imaginable only in America, and "Von allen, die ihn je beeinflusst haben, ist

Mark Twain derjenige . . . und zwar dessen Buch *Huckleberry Finn.* . . ." But look:

Es ist einfach [Ha!], weil zuweilen ein überlegener Geist eine Form findet, welche jene Fragen nicht einzeln, sondern alle gleichzeitig beantwortet in einer Art der Aussage, die das Problem aus den zeitlichen Voraussetzungen löst und ins allgemein und zeitlos Bedeutende hebt.

(Never *mind* context. You couldn't hack that either.)

F. COLLECTIONS OF ESSAYS

1) *Hemingway and His Critics: An International Anthology,* Carlos Baker, ed. New York: Hill and Wang, 1961. Has good introduction plus as good a check list of Hemingway criticism as exists. Collection includes *Paris Review* interview by George Plimpton, most standard American critics: Trilling, Wilson, Beach, Levin. But emphasis on foreign criticism: Mario Praz (Italy), late Arturo Barea (Spain), Ivan Kashkeen (Hemingway's best Russian critic and one of best anywhere), H. E. Bates (England), André Maurois (France), etc. Hemingway, as per introduction, "citizen of the world." (Vatican and Kremlin issued statements on occasion of his passing, along with White House, as if he world statesman.) So collection's angle quite proper.

2) *Hemingway: A Collection of Critical Essays,* Robert P. Weeks, ed. Englewood Cliffs, N.J.: Prentice-Hall, 1962. Good collection, good introduction, in good series ("Twentieth Century Views"). Table Contents is roster of Classics in Field: Cowley's pioneering (1945) introduction to Viking *Portable Hemingway,* even earlier Brooks and Warren analysis of "Killers"; then Halliday on the "symbolism," Levin on the style, Ross on the personality (the *Portrait, supra,* complete). Also

coherent sections from principal critical books. Lastly some *recherché* items: D. H. Lawrence typically perceptive on Hemingway's first real book; exhumed debate, on justice of award of Nobel Prize, between Leon Edel (con) and Young (pro). (Young wins in a breeze; promises never to write on Henry James.)

3) *Ernest Hemingway: Critiques of Four Major Novels,* Carlos Baker, ed. New York: Scribner's, 1962. Another damn Casebook (sorry: "Scribner's Research Anthology"). Suggested Topics for Controlled or Library Research: also (lest anyone miss sales pitch) long list of Available Scribner Hemingway titles in back. But is decent collection of criticism of *Sun, Arms, Bell, Sea.* Baker courageously places own symbolic reading of *Arms* against Halliday's widely reprinted objections. (This is significant debate; see refinement and reassessment by Bern Oldsey, *Wisconsin Studies in Contemporary Literature,* IV [Spring-Summer, 1963], esp. pp. 195–98.) But most interesting contribution is by Hemingway: first publication of what's called "original conclusion" of *Arms.* Since Hemingway said he rewrote ending any *number* of times (it varied), for "original" read "earlier"? Anyway, is very different ending from one we know; also very inferior.

G. BIBLIOGRAPHY

1) Hans W. Bentz: *Ernest Hemingway in Übersetzungen.* Frankfort am Main: Hans W. Bentz Verlag, 1963. Terrific labor of love for small market, but not without browsing interest, viz.: are five German editions of *Über den Fluss und in die Wälder; Arms* is translated into Gujarati, Lettic/Latvian, Macedonian, Marathi, etc.; other books into Grusian, Azerbaijan, Oriya, Turkmenian as well as Turkish, Slovenian as well as Slovak. If you had all Japanese editions, would have 52 books; if all German, 69. International indeed. Included is

piece of curious information: something called "The Animals of Farmer Johns" was translated into Swedish, 1954. Well now.

H. COMIC BOOKS (But No Pictures)

1) Anon.: *A Critical Commentary: The Sun Also Rises.* New York: R.D.M. Corp., 1963. First (?) of four such pamphlets. Sleuthing discloses R.D.M. is Research, Development, Management. Sure have researched, developed, managed the hell out of this. Now even students of Hemingway have ponies. Progress. Item has Biographical section, Analysis Plot and Characterization, Criticism, Summary of Characters, Study Topics, Bibliography. Even has sense of humor: "Remember, though, nothing can supplant the pleasure and excitement of reading the great books themselves."

2) Anon.: *A Critical Commentary: A Farewell to Arms. Ibid.*, with much of equipment, including errors, lifted from pamphlet above (or vice versa). But Commentary more challenging. Hits peak in discussing affair of Catherine Barkley and Frederic Henry—especially latter: "There are no indications of any potential dual activities for the two lovers. As a matter of fact, we are not clearly informed about Henry's hobbies or pastimes." Pity. (And anyway, as matter of fact, we are.)

3) Thomas R. Goethals: *A Critical Commentary: For Whom the Bell Tolls. Ibid.* Author identified as "Ph.D. Columbia," where also apparently teaches. Biggest joke here: job is well done. Excellent background on Spanish War, very good critique of novel, especially weaknesses of.

4) Anon.: *A Farewell to Arms: Notes.* Lincoln, Nebraska: Cliff's Notes, 1964. Smart fellow, that Anon. On sources: Henry-Barkley love story "obviously" invented; later "probably" invented (quit too soon: keep going to "possibly" invented and through possibly not and probably not to not

invented and he'd have it). On novelist's lack of spontaneity: "Writing did not flow out of Hemingway like it apparently did from Thomas Wolfe." Nor does it flow so elegant out of Anon. like it apparently did from practically anybody. *E.g.,* on the Romantic love affair, again: "Henry is interested in Miss Barkley"; later "Henry is on the make"; later still "Henry is on the prowl"; lastly "he is simply on the make." Analysis of story: "The plot goes: boy meets girl, boy loses girl, boy gets girl back. . . . Hemingway leaves out the last chapter, so to speak."

Most helpful section is of "Notes." Examples, chiefly oenological: "*Strega:* An Italian liqueur." "*Grappa:* A type of Italian brandy. Strega is a liqueur." "*Vermouth:* A spiced wine. It is the other ingredient in a Martini, the first being gin or vodka." "*Provisional visa:* A visa is a stamp on one's passport. . . . A provisional visa is just what Henry explains it is." "*Porcelain stove:* It is exactly that, a large affair of porcelain. . . ." "*Mineral water:* Soda, like in 'Scotch and Soda.'" (*Sic.*)

Sic, sic, sic. Most pregnant line goes: "Tragedy is always hovering nearby." Most surprising Note explains: "*Fiasco:* Chianti, an Italian red wine."

1964

I DISMEMBER PAPA

After a splendid dinner at the *finca* outside Havana in the winter of 1954, Ernest and I were lingering over a crackling cold Sancerre. He was more subdued than usual, and suddenly he said, "Listen, Phil. Any man's death diminishes me. Because, dammit, I'm involved in mankind. So don't ask, kid, for whom the bell tolls—it tolls for you."

The trouble with this memorable "conversation" is that it didn't take place. (I never laid eyes on Hemingway.) The setting is pretty much lifted from A. E. Hotchner's high-flying *Papa Hemingway*. To get the quote, I pulled down *Bartlett's Familiar Quotations* and roughed it up a little. The fact that Hemingway was in Africa at the time is no matter.

It is conceded that in the course of their fourteen-year palship "Hotch," as he is called, did see Mr. Hemingway—on more than one occasion. There is a possibility that they did, as alleged, print a card announcing their incorporation: "Hemhotch, Ltd." But, witness this book, the partnership was more limited than Hemingway could have imagined. Its junior member ran off with the treasury: a betrayal of confidence way the hell and gone beyond free-lance cynicism. Further, and every bit as bad in a different way, the hunch is that a really ingenious and knowledgeable fake (who had never met him either) could have rifled Papa's countless letters—also many books, magazines, published interviews, and newspapers—and come up with a best-selling hotch-potch that would not differ radically from this one.

The reasons for suspecting this book of a certain amount of bluffing are four. First, both partners in Hemhotch are tellers of really tall tales. Then there is A. E.'s bemusing ignorance of some fundamental facts about Hemingway's life and work. Third, the book transparently contradicts itself in several places, and in such a fashion that the author simply cannot have it both ways. Last, and most important, there is a basis for speculating that some of the conversations that make up the better part of Hotchner's Loot Song never occurred.

Several reviewers have expressed deep misgivings about the taste and propriety of this book ("disgraceful," "shameless," "contemptible"). But no one seems to have called any substantial part of it into question, though little more than common sense is required to question Hotchner rather early in the game, and to doubt as well that Papa was much concerned to tell him the truth. Almost at the start Hemingway appears to have discovered that his fawn would relish almost anything. And so he fed it tidbits in generous variety as long as he was having fun. Thus it is that we learn Hemingway could talk so eloquently to bears and a gorilla as to practically unhinge them; that Legs Diamond's gorgeous mistress gave him $300 for servicing her twice at "21" (once in the kitchen, again on the stair landing); that he lost his virility with his second wife and magically regained it with a prayer, promptly converting to Catholicism; and so forth. After deducing that his subject's account of a bout with Mata Hari would have had to take place after her execution, Hotchner says, "I was always on the lookout" for this sort of fiction. But if he was, he never let Papa know it, or the reader in on it.

Hotchner lets Hemingway tell him a real funny story involving the shyness of Max Perkins, which led that editor to put down on his calendar a four-letter word from *A Farewell to Arms* that he didn't want to speak but which had to be deleted from the manuscript. If Hotchner knew as much about that novel as any careful reader, he'd know as well that this graybeard of an anecdote cannot possibly be attached to that book for the simple reason that its manuscript contained *several* words that had in those days to be cut, including a much tougher and more offensive one. Similarly, if our portrait artist were even reasonably informed on his subject, he would not have provided us with a learned footnote to the effect that the unfavorable reception of *Across the River and Into the Trees* constituted "the first setback Ernest had received since the publication of his first book." And if he knew as much about Hemingway's life as can be found in the crudest of paperback biographies, he would not have presented Ernest pounding a punching bag in a music room added on to his ancestral home in Oak Park—a room which is supposed to have been built on an inheritance from a father who did not die until a decade after these workouts are supposed to have occurred.

Somewhat less trivial are the palpable contradictions within Hotchner's own covers. Sometimes it is Hemingway who, according to the story, is allowed to contradict himself. Thus, for instance, Papa tells him that all his books started as short stories; "I never sat down to write a novel." This is simply untrue, and not many pages later A. E. has Ernest describing how he very deliberately and "finally got around to doing my war novel," only to bring him back a few chapters later with "I've never yet set out to write a novel—it's always a short story that moves into being a novel." The discrepancy is not particularly important, but the silence of the biographer at such moments is worth thinking about.

———

Not long ago an English novelist got into a bad storm flying here from London, while the only draft of a new book huddled against the weather in his luggage. It occurred to him that if the plane crashed he would be dead, and his wife and children abandoned to an expensive world, but all he could *worry* about was his bloody manuscript. This is a common affliction, and it is well known that Hemingway had a bad case. "Ernest always treated the pages of a manuscript-in-progress as Crown Jewels," writes Hotchner, and once he has him go to a Havana bank to get one out of the vault. Yet it does not bother Hotch to present a vivid account of Papa in his fishing boat, the *Pilar,* trotting out the manuscript of *Across the River and Into the Trees* for A. E.'s inspection— and this on a day so stormy they had to give up and go ashore. Or stop him from two far more incredible stories about the same manuscript, "hand-written and Ernest's only copies." One of these recounts how Hotchner most unaccountably managed to leave the last three chapters of the same book on the Simplon-Orient Express. Then he tells how when he got to the rail yards in search of his loss he found the right car, and how, although it had already been cleaned, everyone had overlooked a "nine-by-twelve manila envelope" in plain view on the wall of his compartment, "lodged in the frame" of one of those tourist scenes that decorate such accommodations. Consider if nothing else the dimensions, including the thickness, of such an envelope stuck in such a crack, and it seems clear why "I never told Ernest. Or anyone else."

On one page an incompetent driver and Hotchner are en route by car to Milan, with Hemingway as a truly expert "full-time navigator" (with an "excellent sense of direction, and infinite patience . . . a post that he always relished"). On the next page they are all utterly lost—circling Milan "for an hour and a half" ("there was nothing to do but circle and hope for the best"). But as a rule, that is *not* Hotchner's method. Late in the book he attacks a magazine that had "wormed its way into the [Mayo Clinic's] confidential records and had smeared its pages with the contents of the file on Ernest. . . . Where the facts were missing," they "filled the gaps with conjecture."

What fill most of the gaps in Hotchner's record are the materials out of which he has fashioned the conversations which may indeed make the book, as Mrs. Hemingway argued in court, more "by" than "about" her husband. They are said to be the product of notes Hotch secretly kept "during all the time I knew him," and of the tapes on which he recorded the boss. But as one of the participants in this drama has pointed out, "He couldn't possibly have been taking notes. Not even he could have, and gotten everything so wrong." As for the tapes, one need only listen to a widely marketed recording of some of them, called *Ernest Hemingway Reading,* to hear what *that* device (a toy, good for laughs) was worth as a biographical source.

In other words, it is awfully difficult to believe that Mr. Hotchner has accurately described the matter out of which his book was made, and just as hard to resist the notion that this *Personal Memoir* is less by than compiled by him.

This is partly because so much of *Papa Hemingway* is so completely familiar, at least to people who have been reading much of anything on the subject over the years. Thus for the umpteenth time, but now in "conversation," we learn what Ernest said to Gertrude Stein, read about the early rejection slips coming to his room over the Parisian sawmill (which Hotchner has somehow moved from Montparnasse to Montmartre), discover what he thought about William Faulkner's ten-dollar words and his own more common ones. Once more we get the story of how he was wounded in World War I, how he always waked at dawn and wrote, and under what conditions he stopped writing. Once again here is an account of how all his early manuscript was stolen from his first wife on a French train, and of why he took Scott Fitzgerald out of "The Snows of Kilimanjaro," putting "poor Julian" in his place. And so on, and on, and *on*. It is easy to sympathize with the reviewer who said, "If I have to read one more account of Hemingway's writing methods, I shall break my pencils."

Discovering the many origins of this well-worn stuff would in most cases involve more trouble than the project is worth. But one example concerning Marlene Dietrich is relatively simple to illustrate. Early in the book Ernest and A. E. are talking after dinner one evening at the *finca,* and Papa asks, "You know how we met, the Kraut and me?" What follows is an account of a time when Miss Dietrich would not sit at a table where she would make the thirteenth at supper; Ernest nimbly inserted himself as the fourteenth and saved the party. This anecdote resembles very remarkably one she herself wrote up in a piece on Papa called "The Most Fascinating Man I Know," which appeared in *This Week* magazine on February 13, 1955. Here is Hotchner in *Papa Hemingway:*

. . . when I got to know Marlene quite well, she told me: "I never ask Ernest for advice as such but he is always there to talk to, to get letters from, and in conversations and letters I find the things I can use for whatever problems I may have; he has often helped me without even knowing my problems. He says remarkable things that seem to automatically adjust to problems of all sizes."

Compare Marlene in *This Week:*

I never ask him for advice, as such, but he is always there to talk to, to get letters from, and in conversation and letters I find the things I can use for whatever problems I may have; in that way he has often helped me without even knowing my problems. He says remarkable things that seem to automatically adjust to problems of all sizes.

That is only the first of nine paragraphs of this. (Is there a ghost in the house? If so, this is no way to exorcise it.)

A second example involves a truly berserk conversation with another movie star:

A hospital. Madrid, 1954.
Ava Gardner. "You've never had an analyst?"
Papa. "Sure I have. Portable Corona number three. . . . I spend a hell of a lot of time killing animals and fish so I won't kill myself. When a man is in rebellion against death, as I am in rebellion against death, he gets pleasure out of taking to himself one of the godlike attributes, that of giving it."
Ava. "That's too deep for me, Papa."

The second sentence of this most improbable pontification was quoted by Earl Wilson, a Broadway columnist, some fifteen years ago. And the third is a Graceful Improvement of some lines Hemingway composed on himself for Georges Schreiber's *Portraits and Self-Portraits* in 1936: "Since he was a young boy he has cared greatly for fishing and shooting. If he had not spent so much time on them . . . he might have written much more. On the other hand he might have shot himself." The last sentence of Papa's paragraph was obviously never spoken by anyone. But except for its second clause, Hotchner's helpful amendment, it was *written*, all right—for the first paragraph of Chapter Nineteen of *Death in the After-noon*, which is a book, published in 1932, by Ernest Hemingway. It is copied more or less correctly: "When a man is still in rebellion against death he has pleasure in taking to himself one of the Godlike attributes; that of giving it."

Ernest is not the only person Hotchner quotes on Hemingway, present company not excepted. A single instance, involving Papa's little army and World War II, will suffice:

Hotchner, in *Papa Hemingway* (1966):
Robert Capa . . . once told me about Ernest's Irregulars. . . . The

men had a hard time believing that Ernest was not a general, because he had a public relations officer, a lieutenant as an aide, a cook, a driver, a photographer and a special liquor ration.

As he works from a book of Capa's called *Slightly Out of Focus,* compare:

Young, in *Ernest Hemingway* (1952):
The French Irregulars who put themselves under Hemingway's wing . . . had a hard time comprehending the fact that the reporter was not a general. . . . He had a lieutenant as an "aide" and "personal-relations officer," and was assigned a cook, a driver, a photographer and a special liquor ration.

This *Personal Memoir* resounds with Remarks That Probably Never Got Made, and one of the most reverberant of them is something Ernest told A. E. over a drink in Madrid:

All good books have one thing in common—they are truer than if they had really happened, and after you've read one of them you will feel that all that happened, happened to you and then it all belongs to you forever; the happiness and unhappiness, good and evil, ecstasy and sorrow, the food, wine, beds, people and the weather. If you can give that to readers, then you're a writer.

This rendition leaves something to be desired, but the Hemingway section of *Bartlett's Familiar Quotations* (page 983, column b) has got it right:

All good books are alike in that they are truer than if they had really happened and after you have finished reading one you will feel that all that happened to you and afterwards it all belongs to you; the good and the bad, the ecstasy, the remorse and sorrow, the people and the places and how the weather was. If you can get so that you can give that to people, then you are a writer.

In a somewhat similar way it is surprising to discover that a line of Gary Cooper's that had a lot of currency at the time of Hemingway's death ("I bet [Ernest] that I will beat him out to the barn") was spoken to none other than A. E. Hotchner—when Mrs. Cooper "left us alone" in her husband's sickroom. And if we can stand one more surprise of this sort, examine what Papa, in the Alps in 1954, said to A. E. about that scandalous *New Yorker* profile of him by Lillian Ross:

After you finish a book, you're wiped out. . . . But all she saw was the irresponsibility that comes after the terrible responsibility of writing.

Then consider Lillian herself in that same profile, published some four years earlier:

Hemingway turned to me. "After you finish a book, you know, you're dead. . . . But . . . all they see is the irresponsibility that comes in after the terrible responsibility of writing."

Despite the reviewers, then, Hotchner's vaunted "ear" and his admirable "self-effacement" are not impressive. When his ear is not hearing what was written down in formal prose, Hemingway's monologues come out more or less effectively. Indeed, his ear hears capital letters, which is not easy. (Listen to Hemingway *talking:* "In comes Mike, his left hand swollen like the Pride of Your Garden if you were growing squash"; "Life at the *finca* got a little rough just before we left for the Dark Continent"; an Italian, "attached to an American naval unit in Norfolk, Virginia . . . has fallen in love with The Hamburger," and so on.) As for Hotchner's having effaced himself to the point of invisibility, even when, as in the case of contradiction, repetition, or whatever, his presence is stridently called for: is it possible that he just wasn't there? And as for the captured paragraphs of monologue: how hard is it to get them right if in another country all you have to do is open the mail, write "Ernest said to me," put the quotation marks where they should go, and correct the spelling as you copy? It would be hard for anyone who has read a few Hemingway letters—and quite a few are in print—to ignore their resemblance to

what this memoir prints as man-to-man talk. At one point
while they are supposed to be together in Cuba (and not on
the telephone) Papa tells Hotch, most convincingly: "Maybe
it's something you could handle. You're in New York. . . ."

Hemingway wrote thousands of letters, and Hotchner, who
admittedly was not around the greater part of the time, must
have been the recipient of quite a number. Why then are we
told directly almost nothing about what was in them? Could
it be that he wants not just Papa's sentiments but his words?
And knows he cannot have them if they came through the
post? He "owns" those letters, all right; may sell or burn them
with impunity. But print them openly he cannot.

Among the reviewers, whose hats, by and large, are in the
air, there are a few who have strong reservations, but only
two, John Kenneth Galbraith and John Thompson, have admitted to a reasonable doubt. Mrs. Hemingway has found
enough factual errors to make up a small book, but John
Mason Brown, a typical enthusiast, lauds particularly A. E.'s
"seismographic accuracy" and "phenomenal memory." Even
as Hotchner relates, a biographical piece by an actual friend
(Malcolm Cowley), which lit up its subject like the Lincoln
Memorial, made Hemingway "Truly *sick!*" Yet Brown thinks
"Papa himself . . . would have approved of" this book. Orville
Prescott is equally perceptive: Hotchner "deserves to be com-
pared to Boswell."

As if this were not enough, our biographer has the courts
behind him. When Mrs. Hemingway tried to stop publication
of Hotchner's book, her case was rejected *in toto* by State
Supreme Court Justice Harry B. Frank. When she appealed
his decision, he was unanimously upheld.

It appears that the judge's rejection of Mrs. Hemingway's
case was based on three arguments. First, he ruled that conversations are not protected by common-law copyright. Sec-

ond, he criticized her failure to realize that "random and dis-connected oral conversations are given some semblance of form only by virtue of their arrangement in the context of literary creation." Last, he objected to her legal silence during the three years that Hotchner was writing his book; when she did file suit it was so late that to stop the thing would have put a "disproportionate economic burden" on author and publisher.

Now, it is clear that critics are not judges. But judges are not critics, either, or any sort of Hemingway men. It would be interesting, then, to learn why it is the judge assumes Mrs. Hemingway knew about this book through three years of silence, and downright fascinating to know how he would go about proving it. (Far easier to believe her simple statement to the effect that "At no time did Ernest or I have any idea that Mr. Hotchner was taking notes, or had any intention of writing a book until last June [1965].") To think that she sat around for a couple of years waiting to do something about it is to suppose that she is an impractical, unintelligent woman, heedless of her husband's reputation or the condition of his estate. Evidence to this effect is not immediately available.

Ernest once complained to Hotch, "I've always had that problem—other writers pinching my stuff." What he did not realize is that he was talking to the future record-holder, coming on fast. In other words, how is Justice Frank so sure that the ingredients of each "conversation" were, before the unleashing of Hotchner's creative force, "a disoriented con-glomeration of unconnected expressions"? How would he go about establishing that? What if the famous notes *were* actually letters, and the tape was Scotch? And if all the burden of proof is on Mary, are we talking about justice or law?

Apparently there has been no place for testimony in this case. Too bad; it might have been worth watching if Heming-way's "young Sun Valley doctor, whom I shall call Vernon

Lord," should be called up and asked why his real name (which has appeared in print innumerable times, especially since Hemingway was registered under it at the Mayo Clinic) was not used. Hotchner has already answered that one: "To protect" the doctor. From what? He comes out looking very well. "Vernon Lord" is now in Vietnam, but as for another prominent pseudonymous character, "a young Glasgow girl I'll call Honor Johns," the fact that Hotchner is trying to protect himself seems obvious. And perhaps wisely, since this spirited young lady, who is not impossible to identify, states that she "can truthfully say that there is not a single statement having to do with me in the book that is really accurate."

The writer Harvey Breit argues most convincingly that the truth of the one scene involving him is "exactly reversed," so that Hotchner comes out the Only One Who Knows and Cares. Major General C. T. Lanham, possibly Hemingway's truest friend through the Hemhotch era and the recipient of more than three hundred letters from him (many of them of extraordinary length), writes that he is "saddened" and "enraged" at this "parody": "The Hotchner Hemingway is simply not the Ernest Hemingway I knew and loved." Lillian Ross points out that despite A. E.'s alleged success at getting Papa to denigrate her profile, she has some sixty letters from him that were written after publication of her "attack," and all of them friendly. "The American writer-photographer Peter Buckley," who shared a room with Hotch during the crowded Zaragoza *feria*, has found so much wrong with that section of the book that he has no faith in it as a whole: "I was with him 24 hours a day. *Notes?* He never took a goddamn *note*. Not unless when I was asleep."

Once at Carcassonne Hemingway says to Hotch, "Most of the wall and the towers of the city are faked, but the restoration is so wonderful, who gives a damn?" Doubtless some readers feel this way about *Papa Hemingway*. A few others, however, are known to give a very good damn. This portrait reveals only such sides of Hemingway as Hotchner was capable of seeing. It shows the half of the man that wrote none of his best stuff; what is permanent in Hemingway came out of depths and strengths a patient errand boy never glimpsed.

If in the guise of "sound and true friend" you are going to invade a man's privacy, then you have an absolute obligation to get and keep things as scrupulously straight and aboveboard as is humanly possible. The real failure of this book is not, in the end, either legal or factual, although along the way it may be both. Ultimately the failure is moral, and it is stupendous. There are quite a few people who would like to be around come that early morn when it dawns on Mr. Hotchner that he is going to have to live with this book for the rest of his days, and not just on it.

1966

LOCKED IN THE VAULT

Quite an experience, you might say, this having been most securely secreted, whenever I could get to New York, in the bottom of a bank Somewhere in Manhattan, elbow-deep in all those enormous safe-deposit boxes filled with practically all the manuscripts a legendary writer left behind. Heavy the keys to those boxes overnight, or out to lunch! A sight to bug and blur the eyes: unreal, another world, history. (Also a long, penetrating peep into the privacy Hemingway once accused me of invading.) The man kept practically everything, all the way from the 1919 Chicago days, before the Paris apprenticeship had ever begun, to the very end. On the other hand, except for work-in-process, he took little or no care of all this material—published or not. So there it was, with the clips and pins sometimes rusted quite through the pages where he'd stuck them long ago, the tiny teeth marks on the corners where mice had fed, the holes clear through buried texts where worms had tried that ill-preserved virginity. Yet for all their efforts, salt air, rodents, and insects that worked hard accomplished less than you'd expect. Mostly the papers are in good shape.

Not that I was so much interested in their condition. But I knew how widely scattered and carelessly stored much of this treasure had been, and like many I had heard those sick rumors: Mary Hemingway was taking no care of it, was even destroying manuscript. A good place here, to knock dead these particular pieces of literary gossip. The fact is that the sole executrix of her husband's estate has taken her duties most seriously, competently, and assiduously, as she continues to. Virtually alone, in a state of exhaustion following his protracted and desperate illness, still in the shock of a death that she was barely able to face at all, she managed some rather difficult maneuvers in order to gather and preserve with care an awful lot of hard-to-get-at stuff. And to the best of my knowledge she has not disposed of so much as a torn corner, with nothing on it, of a single sheet of manuscript. It couldn't have been easy either, in any circumstances, getting things, say, out of Castro's Cuba, or extricating them from the mice, cockroaches, and what have you that inhabited the boxes stashed in the back of Key West's "Sloppy Joe's."

What I was really interested in, of course, and like so many others, was what is written all over that paper. I suppose the first question, though, is what was I doing there, staring at it. The full answer to that goes back more than two decades, a long story involving Hemingway's opposition and subsequent reactions to a book on his work that I finally published in 1952. But the immediate reason for my sporadic occupancy of that vault was the result of a question his widow had asked me when, at the end of a fine, lively lunch in late December of 1966, she twinklingly remarked that if I didn't think I'd be bored she'd be happy to take me there. I replied that I did not think I'd be too terribly bored, so off we walked (she walked; I kind of floated), and though the institution had closed for the day we were hospitably admitted. A couple of those great boxes were hauled out and opened, and I confess to noting a bit of a rise in blood pressure. There it was, the real thing.

What else? But I had a very special as well as long-time

interest, remember. I gingerly fingered some of it, particularly
seven blue French schoolboy-notebooks labeled "L'Incroyable
—100 Pages—Cahier," each titled "Fiesta A Novel," with
"Ernest M. Hemingway" and the places of composition (Va-
lencia, Madrid, San Sebastián, Hendaye on Book II), his current address ("113 Rue Notre Dame des Champs Paris VI")
and the dates (various stretches of 1925), all duly inscribed.
The first draft of *The Sun Also Rises,* obviously, his first "real
novel." My second reaction knocked the pressure down: a
gold mine was here that had never been dug. Absolutely no
one knew or could know what all or exactly was in those
boxes. Not his widow, despite a valiant effort in that direction.
There is just too much; she is a writer herself, not a scholar
or bibliophile; she had met Hemingway and become his wife,
not an Authority on him, long after his work had become
famous. Not even he could have known, could have remembered everything, or that it had lived to be there. Drawing
strength from a couple of drinks and a deep breath I told Mrs.
Hemingway that she ought to know precisely what all this
was. She, however, scarcely needed telling; it had been
bothering her badly. But who could do it, and would? Adding
innocence of the magnitude of the job to my false courage, I
took a deeper breath and said, "Me." No, no; I was too busy
already and so forth; no, she couldn't accept. I dropped it, but
soon wrote one letter explaining that I really wanted the task.
She replied, thank you; yes.

Perhaps I really could have done it alone. But before I'd
got started, a wisely skeptical Dean of Research at my university volunteered assistance. Penn State is blessed with
Charles W. Mann, a friend and wizard out of Altoona, Pa.,
Chief of Special Collections in our library, and expert in such
matters as these. Mostly all I will say about Charlie directly
is that on our second or third visit, I forget, I began to wonder

who was assisting whom. The end product is a genuine collaboration.

So, what indeed is in those boxes? There had been a good deal of speculation and disagreement over that, much of it most inaccurate. The title to a published article which carefully brought together most of the reports as fact, "Up to 50,000 Hemingway Manuscript Pages Remain Unpublished," nicely epitomizes how far off was some of the guesswork that had appeared in print. Now, then, it must be understood that we produced an "inventory," not the fantastically complete and technical catalogue that will require years or teams. Notably, we did not make a scrupulous count of *all* the pages, scraps, and so on. But a very careful estimate is that there are approximately 16,000 pages of "manuscript"—meaning holograph, type, retype, carbon, proof—in those boxes or at the time in Mrs. Hemingway's apartment, carefully wrapped or boxed en route to the vault, of which about 3,000 pages are unpublished. Especially given the fact that, as oft-recorded, Hemingway wrote very slowly, that's a lot.

What we did find would take a book to describe. It did: *The Hemingway Manuscripts: an Inventory*, published in the fall of 1969 by the Pennsylvania State University Press to the tune of such astonishing publicity as a front page story in *The New York Times*. This despite the fact—Zeus forbid— that such a book, such a story, and perhaps even this piece may aggravate rather than alleviate the importunate requests for information from Mrs. Hemingway, who in the press of her many other labors endlessly writes polite responses to people who have absolutely got to see or hear about things which are simply unavailable until they may be published or else arranged, as she intends to have them arranged, when the Kennedy Library is built, so that scholars can peruse them in years to come.

Well, at least this much can be said here. Among the manuscripts not published is, in holograph, a very long "Sea Novel" which is scheduled to appear this fall with the title *Islands in the Stream*. There is also a substantial, mostly autobiographical "African Book," in which the author spends six weeks as a game warden—a sort of *Green Hills of Africa* Revisited. Another complete novel, set mainly on the Riviera in the Twenties and called "Garden of Eden," exists. And there is an early (1927) unfinished novel called "Jimmy Breen," twenty chapters of it, but apparently only just getting under way. Then there are quite a few unpublished stories, early and late, the latter set in World War II and lying somewhere between fiction and autobiography. Miscellaneous poems, some as early as 1919, others written in battle during World War II, others later, were found interspersed in the boxes. (How much of this material may eventually see print is undecided; that is up to Mary Hemingway in consultation with Scribner's and others. But there is decision on the general principles regarding publication. First, it is not contemplated that anything which would risk reducing the writer's stature will appear; second, cuts may be made in original or unrevised material, but nobody is going to add anything.) I also discovered, carefully folded and tucked deeply away in one of those "Fiesta" notebooks, a long, unsigned and rather harsh critique of that novel, scrawled by Scott Fitzgerald; this turned out to be a real bonus, since it exerted a considerable influence on the book as we have it even though Hemingway's final draft had already been sent to Scribner's before the stern but most friendly, encouraging critic got the chance to read it. (For this, see the *Fitzgerald/Hemingway Annual*, 1970.)

Most exciting to me personally was the turning up of several unpublished stories about Nick Adams, the youthful protagonist out of whose experience almost all of Hemingway's fiction was to spring. Among these the most substantial is not actually a story, but about half (a guess) of a novel in which Nick, as a runaway adolescent accompanied by his kid sister, is up in Michigan in escape of the game wardens, who, as is said, have got the goods on him. This long lyric fragment is unique in all Hemingway—pastoral idyll, a mythopoeic narrative with overtones (almost surely unintended) first of Huck and Jim on the Mississippi, last of Hansel and Gretel in the forest. Almost as exciting was the find, made during our first hour in the bank, of "Summer People," for I take it to be the first Nick story Hemingway wrote; the holograph shows him vacillating but finally deciding on his persona's name. Other items relating to Nick turned up—either in the vault or at Princeton, mixed in with the letters, stored there to aid Carlos Baker in his biography. Together *these* materials contribute a new—indeed a "missing"—and substantial chapter to *The Adventures of Nick Adams* (the working title for a collection I'm scheduled to edit for Scribner's). This book will present for the first time Nick's adventures "in order"—chronological order, that is, as he advances from child to parent. And the two new stories will both alter and considerably increase our understanding of the first and most important Hemingway "hero."

The last moment of peak personal excitement to be mentioned was the discovery of a long letter, half very grim and half simply hilarious, which Hemingway wrote me in 1952 and kept but never sent. This I came upon in a file beside a great rifle in a closet in Mrs. Hemingway's apartment—a most distinctive, storied penthouse she calls her "bubble." (These letters were sent to Princeton, where four more written me and unmailed were stored.)

Many discoveries, a few conclusions. One, Hemingway's repeated objection to my claim that his fiction was intensely autobiographical does not hold up well. His frequent practice was to use the real names of real people in early drafts of fiction. Particularly, for instance, he took exception to my identifying him with Jake Barnes, narrator-protagonist of *The Sun Also Rises*. But early in *Fiesta* there was no Jake, someone called "Hem" or "Ernie" instead. Another conclusion: the author often had to travel great distances from draft to draft. The magic of "The Snows of Kilimanjaro" is not really present in an apparently rather late version called "The Happy Ending." The distance from the first (?) shot at a crucial tale called "Indian Camp" to the final one is scarcely measurable; the ending of it is not changed but completely reversed, as Hemingway worked his way to what he "really felt, rather than what you were supposed to feel, and had been taught to feel." Charlie and I concluded as well that there was a great distance, which the author did *not* seem to feel, from when he was "going good" to when he was not; I could perceive no lack of confidence on his part in one long book which I simply could not read.

But the result of our effort, at least as of now for us, is not primarily all the information, discoveries, or the inventory. Feelings, and images, are first: the initial and prolonged excitement that became an unforgettable undertaking seems foremost. We started with two bad cases of the shakes, equally inept with simple knots of string. After working off and on for so many years with the finished corpus (my book was completely done before long and painful correspondence began) it was hard-pulsing to find oneself in the very arteries of it— sometimes in the coronaries, or so it seemed. The "immediacy" was nearly overpowering: you are there, in the mess and mystery of the "creative process." Toward the end, to be sure, the keys weighed less in pocket. We felt pretty cool and professional, like pathologists, I suppose, after they've performed a certain number of autopsies. But the deepest part of the feeling was the sense of living, even vicariously and fragmentarily, through the awesome struggle of a career to be remembered. To tell the truth, it was genuinely moving. Not new things so much; familiar things in early forms were even more compelling: the cruder the draft the deeper the tug.

And those pictures in the mind, which now anyway seem indelible. The top right corner, for instance, of something called "The Matadors," which became "The Killers," where forty-four years ago the author wrote "Madrid . . . for Uncle Gus; Written between 2:15 and 5:00 [?] P.M." Or one badly beat-up, yellow typing-paper box, into which he'd crushed a novel, the daily word count (so small) marked all over the cardboard, inside and out, the sweated numbers fashioned heavily, slowly, as if by a determined child who, already a master, was just learning how to form them.

1968

PART II *Second Thoughts*

CENTENNIAL, OR
THE HAWTHORNE CAPER

"As I have said, we are always finding new Hawthornes, but the illusion soon wears away, and then we perceive that . . . he had some peculiar difference from them."
— WILLIAM DEAN HOWELLS, 1900

T he great celebrations of literary 1964 are over. And at the rate we are using up the big names, we are before long going to run out of people to commemorate, though for now there are Dante (1265–1321), Yeats (1865–1939: Horseman, pass by!), and I suppose Kipling (1865–1936). Naturally last year belonged to William Shakespeare (1564–1616), and quite a year it was: *Festschriften* and all sorts of collections; stamps and innumerable new productions and recordings; Sampler Recitals and conferences of dedicated scholars (Crows in the Treetops); exhibitions, touring and stationary; White House performances: you name it. The clearest sign of how things have been going lately in the academies, though, was provided by the publication of Gordon Ross Smith's well-received but also frightening *Classified Shakespeare Bibliography, 1936–1958*. This volume is a sort of "supplement" to the standard Ebisch and Schücking bibliographies; and it is not that the tail is wagging the master (which is never going to happen) but that it is so large it largely obscures the dog. Herren E. and S. registered 3800 Shakespeare items; Smith, covering only twenty-two years, has some 20,000. His table of contents alone runs for thirty-five packed pages of small type, and itself contains nearly 1900 entries. (In an age of appalling statistics, one is vaguely conditioned to this sort of thing. But I had not thought Shakespeare had undone *so* many.)

Now the tumult and the shouting dies [*sic*], and it becomes clear that the man who was buried under by all this activity on behalf of a writer who hasn't been exactly hurting for some time was Christopher Marlowe (1564–93). (The Marlowe Dramatic Society, in another country, apparently devoted the year to making recordings of Shakespeare.) Nothing special was going for Nathaniel Hawthorne (1804–64) except his death. Anyway, the time was now propitious, as they guessed; exploring hands encountered no defense; and along came yet another assault on this modest, quiet talent, beloved of the universities. His "My Kinsman, Major Molineux" served as the basis for the first part of Robert Lowell's play, *The Old Glory*—a considerable *succès d'estime*, at least. And there were various exhibits and displays of relevant trophies and atrophies. But the event before us was the erection of yet another Scholarly Factory, this one located at Ohio State and operated by William Charvat, Roy Harvey Pearce, and Claude M. Simpson, editors—with Fredson Bowers (founding father and patron saint of the Higher Bibliography) and Matthew J. Bruccoli, textual editors. The offspring are to be the many volumes of the *Centenary Edition of the Works of Nathaniel Hawthorne,* which have been having rather a hard time getting born. *The Scarlet Letter* (Volume I) was delivered in 1962, but as the result of a printers' strike and attendant difficulties this loyal subscriber to the *Edition* is still pacing the floor for Volume II, *The House of the Seven Gables.* (It doesn't help to have your name at the bottom of the alphabet.)

The occasion of Volume I was auspicious enough, however, and on its appearance the *Times Literary Supplement* announced grandly, if ambiguously: "There cannot be another novelist in English to have been subjected so thoroughly and effectively to bibliographic science": *Lasciate ogni speranza, voi ch'entrate!*

"Subjected" just may be the word—a Freudian Slip not so much in meaning as tone—for that "bibliographic science" refers to nothing less than the awesome clutch of the Analytic and Descriptive Bibliographers. If one of these chaps encounters a broken serif on H_2 recto (possible evidence that Compositor C, *as* already suspected, had had trouble with his wife at breakfast that morning)—inexplicable splendor! Of course everybody and his brother is in favor of the Best Possible Texts, which are to professors of literature in any year as anti-Communism to politicians in the campaigns. And surely no effort to provide them has been spared at Columbus. Thus (it says here) Hawthorne's are "the first of a major American author to be established in accordance with modern collating editorial techniques, and the first, therefore, that can claim to be truly definitive." Well . . . all right, I guess. But it is bemusing that such microscopic attention has been focused on matter the author of which feared might be so pale, cool, allegorical, and so on, that "if opened in the sunshine, it is apt to look exceedingly like a volume of blank pages." And at least *one* question can be put: why *Hawthorne* (whose texts we had not supposed to be in all that bad a shape) instead of, say, Melville (whose are in a hell of a mess)? If that question has been dealt with the answer has attracted very little attention. Meanwhile, the Hinman machine, bless it, hums along. (A current picks his bones in whispers.)

The worthiest celebrations of this sort—bi-, tri-, quadri-, or whatever—are conceived in uncommon passion and call attention to mistakenly overlooked or underrated displays of talent. Hawthorne, prior to 1964, was not precisely lacking readers, scholars, and critics, any more than Shakespeare was. In all the years (115 of them) since publication of *The Scarlet Letter,* he never has been ignored. He had a few expert watchers before it; three editions of his romance came out in the year of its appearance; it has never been out of print. There was a heightening in 1904, the year of his "true" centenary, of interest that never had seriously flagged, and around 1940 there was a revival, which has gained in fervor, of the revival. We have explicated, allegorized, source-hunted, theologized, annotated, romanticized, deromanticized, decoded, psychoanalyzed, and mythologized Hawthorne until a chronic susceptibility to his work looks to have become endemic. It has not been necessary for a long time that any conscientious reader should grope his way, finding the stairs unlit, and it was a good decade ago when the editor of a certain professional journal announced that if he received one more damned article about Hawthorne and symbolism he was resigning from the board.

Where Is He Now? Dead by his own hand, no doubt, and his successor, too. The *MLA International Bibliography of Books and Articles on the Modern Languages and Literatures* lists Hawthorne publications (which, as a rule, will not be found in our obituaries) at the rate of nearly one a week since 1960 (sixty-one entries in 1963). (Ten for Marlowe.) And the prediction is: it will get worse. An operative with a channel to *PMLA* (I bring the horoscope myself; one must be so careful these days) transmits privileged intelligence to the effect that the 1965 *Bibliography* (for 1964) will contain seventy-two Hawthorne entries. (Thirty-seven for Marlowe.) Beginning (well, more or less) with a monograph by a young and not altogether perceptive critic named Henry James, there have long been more books on Hawthorne than even a specialist should ever want to read, and at last count (1962) there

were in addition 100 book-length doctoral dissertations—
which puts our man in a tie with Emerson, among American
writers, and second only to James himself. (And still the world
pursues: Emerson has not been a particularly hot property
for some time, and the James fever appears to have peaked
while concern for Hawthorne rises; he will be in first place
soon, if he is not already.)

Everybody wants a piece of the action. Thus, in 1964, to
"supplement" the *Edition,* there was issued a volume of
*Hawthorne Centenary Essays.** Part of the idea here is that
because the *Works* are confidently intended as a "permanent
edition" they are to contain introductions having to do with
textual and historical matters only—which are not expected to
"date," as criticism inevitably does. Presumably, then, these
Essays are the efforts that *could* get smelly—whether from the
hot breath of current affections or any other cause. So some
of them could, but it is doubtful that the Ohio text itself can
ever be superseded or seriously challenged, and perhaps the
editors, reminded that on attaining absolute perfection one of
Hawthorne's heroines promptly died, will think to toss in a
couple of typos before they are through.

I have not found any yet, but have instead been speculating
on how the *Edition*'s apparatus is going to look, say, in 2004,
when the bicentennial rolls around, if, as seems unlikely, it
ever does. Will the audience for *The Scarlet Letter* then really
care to know—does it now?—that for the second edition
"Copies collated on the Hinman machine are OU¹ (PS1868.A1.
1850a), OU² (copy 2), ViU¹ (Taylor [506614]), ViU² (Law-
ford [254970]), ViU¹ (McGregor [282796])"? The unfortunate
impression one gets from this volume is that our interest is
supposed to be divided about evenly between Hawthorne
and his texts. The obvious response to this complaint is utterly

---

* Roy Harvey Pearce, ed. Columbus: Ohio State University Press, $7.00.

simple: Hawthorne "is" what his texts make him. Precisely so. But after careful scrutiny one reader (this one, slow without doubt but redeemed, he has always felt, by a dogged sincerity and an eagerness to learn) cannot find a single really significant difference between the new text and that of the Riverside Edition (1883), regularly referred to in the bibliographies as Standard. (And, if that is simply a sign of his sluggish intellect, he can furnish—upon urgent request only—the directly quoted opinion of a Hawthorne critic and scholar distinguished beyond dispute to the effect that the differences between the Ohio text and that of the first edition, at any rate, are immaterial to any purpose *he* can conceive of.) So consider Constant Reader, who in his incredible innocence has been courting the Riverside lo these many years, only to see it now heartlessly dismissed by Professor Bowers as "notoriously corrupt." Obviously we have been traveling in different circles, Mr. Bowers and I. Thus one learns rather late that his object of fair repute is widely known to be a whore. (Sighs, short and infrequent, were exhaled.)

Well, now that's done and I'm glad it's over: it's more liberating than painful, this losing one's textual virginity. So the Riverside was no better than it ought to have been, as we say; our esteem of Hawthorne requires that even the faintest rumor of infidelity be put to rest. If the talent and the funds are available, let us have perfection.

Obviously, ability and money *are* at hand, but the price gives the prospect pause. At the front of the Ohio *Scarlet Letter*—in addition to Mr. Charvat's introduction, Hawthorne's own Preface to the Second Edition, and his introductory "Custom-House"—all necessarily or unobjectionably present—are A Preface to the Text *and* a Textual Introduction. At the back are Variants in the First Edition, also in the Second; Editorial Emendations in the Copy Text; Textual Notes; Historical Collation; Word Division (this department lists end-of-the-line hyphens in the present edition, the First Edition, and one of Special Cases); and a Special Collation List: Variants between the First and Second Editions. *This* business is not supposed to "date"? I will lay crisp new bills that in a few years it will prove as embarrassing to the experts as it now seems curious to the unwashed. Why all of it could not have been issued in a pamphlet for those who care (or on the divan piled with all the other stays at the end of the last volume) is impossible to say. Consider if you can an entry chosen as typical from very, *very* many: "168.2 sea-|weed] sea-|weed (*i.e.* sea-weed)." These are not fragments I intend to shore against *my* ruins.

The House of the Seven Gables, it turns out, is still a-binding, but now Volume III, which contains *The Blithedale Romance* and *Fanshawe* (long a "fitfully kept secret": Hawthorne's first anonymous romance, which he almost immediately regretted, and attempted to renounce), has arrived in the very nick of time. Once again, however, this reader must confess his failure to appreciate—quickly, at least—the significance of the textual revelations. It is alleged that Mr. Charvat was led to an excellent observation on the parenthetical nature of Hawthorne's style by reading both the manuscript and first-edition versions; apparently Hawthorne in manuscript was given to a redundant form of punctuation that makes him look just a touch more parenthetically antiquated than before— like this, (for example),—and, as Professor Bowers now more tolerantly, yet sternly, remarks, by the time the author wrote the *Blithedale* his "strong preference for 'farther' was beginning to weaken, and various indubitable 'further' forms appear, not always separated from 'farther' in respect to usage."

In short, where it first seemed that interest in Hawthorne and in his texts were running neck and neck, it now appears that the texts are galloping off with it. Yet another Textual Editor has been added to help whip the project home; in addition to much of the paraphernalia of Volume I we now have departments of: Rejected First-Edition Substantive Readings; The Ohio State University Leaf (collation of every variant in this treasure-sheet against the corresponding page in the Morgan ms.—with expensive illustration of both); Alterations in the Manuscript; Compositorial Stints in the First Edition (who set what); and an eighteen-page statement of the Editorial Principles of the Centenary Texts.

It has become impossible to feel that these are not, as the Church has it, Works of Supererogation. However, the texts themselves are coming along—even getting around, without apparatus, in paperback already. (A Bobbs-Merrill *Scarlet Letter* with the Ohio text appeared in 1963 for $1.25.) Honor, then, to the men who undertook this exhausting chore: already reputable scholars, they did not need the work for professional advancement, and can only have agreed to it as a labor of love.

The *Essays*, facing the possibility of ephemerality head on, are not excessively difficult to justify. We did not, honest to God, need eighteen new articles on Hawthorne. (But for one death, and the fact that several overworked people could not get the stuff in on time, it would have been twenty-some.) Nevertheless, there is sense in the stated reason for this induced labor: "To show him and his works as they presently confront us." It has been thoroughly done. Opening with a poem by Robert Lowell, and closing with an afterword by Lionel Trilling (both composed for the occasion), in between are six essays on the tales and the individual romances; six on matters not confined to individual works; three on aspects of Hawthorne's reputation; one on collecting his books, and one —yet again—on the texts. Here is, as Lowell's poem says (in an entirely different connection), "the merciless march of professional feet." But the verdict cannot in fairness be unfavorable. The professionals are, for the most part, in good shape;

the volume as a whole delivers what Trilling's essay promises: "Our Hawthorne."

There has fortunately been no editorial attempt, so common these days, at specious unification of the collection; indeed on occasion there is contradiction, and why not? There is, however, befitting the aim of the book, fairly frequent emphasis on Hawthorne's "modernity." Which seems the right emphasis, for under his quaint disguises he was indeed one of us. This is only partly because we had to learn to read modernly—later James, earlier Joyce, Kafka—before we could read him (a kind of learning James had not himself when he wrote his *Hawthorne*). It is more that his view of the world, enchanted to a stone to trouble the living stream, stood fast before the utopian drift of his age. There is no silly attempt anywhere in the book to make him out an existentialist; there is instead a consciousness that, as Hyatt Waggoner puts it, Hawthorne saw man as a creature who, "aware of his guilt and faced with the nothingness of death . . . knows anxiety and despair in any society." He understood very well what we mean by "irrational man"; deeply perceived "the radical incompatibility of world and mankind" (this is Lionel Trilling); was, like Kafka, preoccupied with "man's dark odyssey" and "alienation." He took over "the stock machinery of Gothic fiction" (Daniel Hoffman), which was "devised to reveal the demonic, libidinous, and anarchic energies of which rationalism took no account," and put it to serious work. Finally, as Messrs. Gross and Stewart don't mind saying, he profited when "a cultural sense of broken promises in the post-World War II world raised the literary stock of those authors who could be read as having a 'tragic vision' of life."

The fact that he often seems modern is only one reason, though, for continued and then renewed interest in Hawthorne over the past few decades. Another is that he asks so many critics home to dinner. The Marxists were pretty much unable to make it, and despite his firmly democratic political position Parrington foolishly declined, thinking him yet another enemy of the people (as Mr. Trilling naturally recalls). But so severely qualified a "romantic" was he, and so sobering a moralist, that the New Humanists had no need to eat their sorry fare alone. And as for most of the rest—psychological critics, new critics, myth critics—here, at his best, was a smorgasbord. (I see crowds of people walking round in a ring.)

No romantic in any ordinary sense, Hawthorne's choice of romance as a form also receives a good deal of attention in these *Essays*. By calling on Northrop Frye, Daniel Hoffman probably has got next to the heart of one important matter: close, that is, to an exact description of genre. Myth, writes Frye, is "one extreme of literary design; naturalism the other, and in between lies . . . romance," which tends to "displace myth in a human direction and yet, in contrasts to 'realism,' to conventionalize content in an idealized direction." "The romancer," Frye adds (and what did we do for Anatomy without him?),

does not attempt to create "real people" so much as stylized figures which expand into psychological archetypes. It is in the romances that we find Jung's libido, anima, and shadow reflected in the hero, heroine, and villain respectively. That is why the romance so often radiates a glow of subjective intensity that the novel lacks, and why suggestion of allegory is always creeping around its fringes.

Hawthorne employs a "symbolic architecture," Hoffman says, "building verisimilitude upon a structure of myth." "A divided man on every subject that claimed his deepest energies, [he] equivocates in *his* definition of romance"; and thus we get in him the "romance-novel or novelistic romance" (a nice equivalent in form—for me, anyway—to my notion that he is in content a psycho-moralist or moral psychologist). Hoffman may overplay the verisimilitude somewhat in order to bring romance and novel into balance in Hawthorne; it is doubtful, for an obvious example, that the sense of "realism" we get in the "Custom-House" really carries over into the romance that is the rest of *The Scarlet Letter*. But this is not much more than a quibble, and it is hard to see how the problem of "defining" Hawthorne's type of fiction has much of anywhere more to go.

Which brings us into the matter of the individual essays, or most of them, taken in order and beginning with Charles Feidelson, Jr., on *The Scarlet Letter*. Which, in turn, is to put one's worst foot forward, for this reader is on a different wave length, or something, from this writer, who operates at a very heady level of abstraction. (I have been told to say, when this happens, that I was too tired at the time.) There are lots of wheels spinning; after twenty-two pages Hester Prynne is still "Emerging from the prison. . . ." But one senses an exceptionally sharp, ambitious, and compact intelligence at work, and sometimes things are both packed and clear—as when the Puritans of Hester Prynne's world are described in a fine paragraph that begins:

These people have experienced a disintegration of God's world into God-and-nature, a collapse of the secular world into nature-and-man, a fragmentation of the human world into community-and-individual, and a division of the private world into body-and-mind.*

---

* On the same romance, equally exacting (though in a completely different way), and parenthetical beyond Hawthorne cubed, the one truly brilliant essay finished in time (but published just too late) for a centenary dateline was written by Austin Warren, in my judgment Our Hawthorne Critic beyond all others: a stylistically jagged—but elegantly, eloquently!—powerfully condensed, spiritually and aesthetically sophisticated, psycho-morally intricate piece called *"The Scarlet Letter:* A Literary Exercise in Moral Theology," which appears in the Winter 1965 issue of the revived *Southern Review* (there are already too many Reviews, but in this case, and even in such sad clothing,

Given our admiration for Hawthorne, it is astonishing how little of his work we actually esteem—eight or ten tales, and one short romance. Marcus Cunliffe presents *The House of the Seven Gables* as a good deal of a failure, chiefly because in "the interfusion of the three themes—Evil, Lineage, and Impermanence . . . the first two conflict with the third." This is so, yet all is not entirely well with this normally perceptive critic; by "Evil" he specifically means Hawthorne's "moral," as quoted from his Preface: "namely, that the wrongdoing of one generation lives into the successive ones." The trouble is that in taking this at face value Cunliffe, like so many others, has ignored Hawthorne's important reservation, made only a few lines later, that this is an "ostensible" moral; has ignored further the entirely perfunctory—if not downright ironic—tone with which Hawthorne introduces it. ("Many writers lay very great stress upon some definite moral purpose, at which they profess to aim their works. Not to be deficient in this particular . . . ") The *Seven Gables* is probably nearly as cluttered as the critic finds it, but small wonder he is confused when he starts out down the wrong hallway (in a direction that later on Mr. Pearce is careful to avoid).

Likewise, Robert C. Elliott pronounces *The Blithedale Romance* "tantalizing, slippery, finally unsatisfactory"—but

---

welcome back!). Impossible to reduce Warren's myriad *aperçus* to *précis,* but following on the opinion that "The Custom-House" is an "artistic blunder" (a heresiarchal stand to which I am discipled, and for the reason given) here is a sample sentence (though also a unique one, if—can you find it, or am I wrong?—there is subordination difficulty in the punctuation): "The enduring power of the book lies in its 'keeping so close to its point,' lies in its method: looking at the 'same idea' (loose word for situation or theme) from 'different sides' (loose phrase for 'different points of view'), itself a loose phrase primarily meaning, now from inside the consciousness of Pearl (chiefly to be inferred from her behavior), of Chillingworth (occasionally analyzed by himself, occasionally by Hawthorne) and, centrally, by Hester and by Dimmesdale."

for the simplest and most valid of reasons, that the setting of
the story "cried out for detailed, novelistic treatment" and
"the stringency of the satiric view," neither of which is provided. (Add to this a "radical incoherence" in theme—true—
and "unsatisfactory" seems rather mild.) Neither can Harry
Levin develop much enthusiasm for the last of the romances,
The Marble Faun. But he is not interested in arguing the book
down, and composes instead an allusive, gracefully learned,
perceptive and polished "discussion" of it. (He also mentions a
"striking thought"—that Hawthorne chose in the faunish
Donatello to celebrate "a natural . . . link betwixt human and
brute life" in the very year of Darwin's *Origin of Species;* however, what to *do* with the fact, once recovered from the blow,
has apparently not occurred to either of us.)

After the *Faun,* Hawthorne's failure was unrelieved, as he
watched each of four romances begin with a plausible concept
and collapse in a heap of broken images. Edward H. David-
son writes again on this subject, *Hawthorne's Last Phase* (the
title of his book, 1949), and offers entirely literary and intellectual reasons for the author's inability to complete any of the
stories, the chief one being that he was finally torn apart by
"the seemingly opposite imaginative poles of the Romance
and the Moral" he had once been able to combine. (Later on,
Trilling gives an equally ideological explanation: "Eventually
Hawthorne lost all power of belief in the other [*i.e.* "preter-
natural"] world, and with it all power of creation.") Well,
maybe so, either way. But it is never conceded or even mentioned that these difficulties might have been not so much
causes as symptoms, and no allowance whatever is made for
the effects on body, mind, and spirit of that "strange illness
which baffled Dr. Oliver Wendell Holmes."

Dealing with more general matters, Hyatt Waggoner is
excellent on "Art and Belief" which, since "the shaping force
behind Hawthorne's art is the special character of his religious

belief," are for him the crucial issues. The religious position is not easily described: neither traditional nor institutional, more nearly experiential; and at once "romantic, subjective, psychologically oriented . . . Christian." Waggoner finds more Belief than have many others less sympathetic to it, but he acceptably charts the religio-literary lineage—Dante, Spenser, Milton, Bunyan—and comes up with a proper tag when he invents for the last an appropriately corny name for his Salem admirer: "Mr. Shakyfaith." His essential point—that Hawthorne's "special quality as a writer is a function of his unique relationship to both the form and the content of traditional Christian allegory, on the one hand, and to modern symbolism, on the other"—is a blanket statement that will not fully cover all members of the corpus. (Isn't the most admired of all the tales nowadays, "My Kinsman, Major Molineux," somewhat out from under?) But, as generalizations go, that is a good one.

Daniel Hoffman's essay pursues Hawthorne along the trail marked in his *Form and Fable in American Fiction,* but explores new sections of the territory; he comes up with, among other things, an excellent reading of one of the trickiest of the tales, "The Artist of the Beautiful." And, perhaps tacitly following a suggestion made in these pages (for Winter 1962, in the course of a review of his book), he successfully tries his hand on "The Grey Champion." (My vanity requires no response. . . . I make no comment. What should I resent?)

The thesis of our editor's own essay—that a "major burden of Hawthorne's work . . . is that human existence is ineluctably historical; and an inevitable aim of his work is to put that burden on us"—contradicts or at least jostles some of the other pieces, especially Hoffman's and Waggoner's. Pearce speaks of his subject's "insistent rationalism," and claims the writer "derives his symbols not from myth . . . but from the facts of history itself." But he, too, is persuasive, and the truth is probably that everybody is right and wrong, depending on which works are uppermost in mind, and what one's immediate interest in them is.

With his usual clarity and penetration, R. W. B. Lewis takes a relatively easy target with the notion that in *The Bostonians* James "depended upon our having the novels of Hawthorne in mind": bull's-eye. Edwin Fussell's target, on the other hand, looks at first to be somewhere on the other side of the moon. He starts firing with: "Hawthorne was at heart a Western writer"; "Young Goodman Brown" is "about American advance to the West." Finally, the writer's "gradual and accelerating decline after *The Scarlet Letter* conceivably reflects the disappearance of the frontier." For a while it appears that Fussell, brooding about Salem away out there in California, and probably exposed to the treacherous winds of Frederick Jackson Turner to boot, has come down with *something* or other. But things eventually clear: we are being baited; he is talking (most of the time, at least, plausibly) about the influence of the frontier on the writer's imagination, hence his imagery. Thus one watches the object of such brilliantly sarcastic phrases as—close call!—he had almost used turn to fear in a handful of dust.

Edwin H. Cady's is a good account of the nineteenth-century reputation, and especially good on the extraordinary weaknesses (and strengths) of James's *Hawthorne*. And following this we finally confront the most curious aspect of this whole business: that in an Age of Criticism—how do you like it now, gentlemen?—the most vexed of all problems in Current Hawthorne Studies is our sense, not so much of the works (let alone the texts), as of the man who wrote them. The real argument today, involving but momentarily dislodging the critics, is biographical.

The thing of it is, to simplify a complex situation, that the picture we long had of the dark, melancholy Nathaniel—

estranged, aloof, secretive—was an impression we got from reading his books, with a few facts (principally the twelve-year self-imprisonment in his room after Bowdoin) thrown in. It was first sketched by James, who said (in short) that Hawthorne had "few perceptible points of contact with what is called the world." But gradually, as much more about his daily existence became known, the portrait blurred, and finally became difficult to recognize. After his father's death, the son Julian read his books and expressed his bewilderment: How could the man he had known have been the author of them? (At this point, we should recall what Julian's aunt Elizabeth told her nephew at about the same time: "Your father kept his very existence a secret, as far as possible.")

The most interesting transaction in the current Hawthorne market is this: that it has been precisely during the period when the critics have been coming up with a full display of radical ambiguity, paradox, irony, and a complexity rich to the point of impenetrability in his works, that his biographers, loaded down with fact and marching on flat feet in the opposite direction, have brought to press (howling, I think) a rather normal, ordinary, open, and well-adjusted sort of fellow. Several of their predecessors had a good deal of insight but not much information; these newer people have a depressing amount of information and practically no insight. Scraping the barrel for the most recalcitrant (because irrelevant) data, one of them—Robert Cantwell, a famous case—emerged with the theory that, far from being cut off from it, Hawthorne was so involved in his age that during the years when he was supposed to have been spooking it up in that room he was really performing secret duties for the U.S. Treasury.

Some of the speculation on the haunted, isolated Hawthorne seemed once to make sense of the man and his work, but subsequent research crazed and finally collapsed a lot of thin ice without providing a new base that modern theorists could comfortably perform on. The trouble with much of the research that has palmed the "normal" Hawthorne off on us is that it has ignored his own remark (preface to *The Snow Image*) to the effect that facts about a romancer's "external habits, his abode, his casual associates, and other matters entirely on the surface . . . hide the man, instead of displaying him." So well is he now hidden that we are privy to a simply marvelous triumph whereby is displayed to us the sort of fellow who could never possibly have written the fiction that is the sole justification of the time, energy, and ingenuity that have been expended on him.

The problem is frankly of special interest to the present writer because he suspects that of the theorists he is the way-outest yet. So far as he knows, he is the last, déclassé man alive who believes what Herman Melville told Julian *he* was convinced of: that "there was some secret in my father's life which had never been revealed, and which accounted for the gloomy passages in his books." One imagines it rather becoming to be standing with Melville against the world. Rather less attractive, however, to take the teetering position that he fancies he knows what the secret *was*. (*Further,* all a-stagger now, that it explains more than just the gloomy passages.) Never mind; mistrusting his tenure, he does not intend to reveal it here. They can always get you for Moral Turpitude (and the hypothesis could be construed so as to involve something like that). Thus he means to publish it posthumously—along with his iconoclastic, three-volume study of the prosody of Michael Wigglesworth (1631–1705) titled *"The Day of Doom" and the Morning After,* for which, as his rejection slips will testify, the literary world is not prepared. (Both manuscripts have been willed to the Harvard University Press.)

Another reason for bringing all of this up at this point is that if any one man is responsible for turning things toward the view of Hawthorne as Adjusted Citizen it is Randall

Stewart. Since that was back in the Thirties, and Stewart has lived to see his own efforts get entirely out of hand, one is curious to see what he will have to say. Praise and honor to *him* be: with the help of Seymour Gross he confronts the problem directly, confesses his complicity, and argues that in very recent biographies (one by Edward Wagenknecht, another by Hubert Hoeltje) the cause of demystification has gone as far as it can go (which is practically out of sight): "The 'white' myth of Hawthorne has supplanted the 'black.'" (And myth is the word.) So here, presumably, we go again.

In "Hawthorne Abroad" ("a case of imperfect sympathies on both sides"), the admirable Roger Asselineau gets into an uncharacteristic bind while attempting to deny that Hawthorne was "'deeply planted' in New England soil." ("He only floated over it.") From the start he tried to escape it, says Asselineau (forgetting that the escape was generally from the pan to the fire—the New England present, that is, to its past). Finally the argument is so contradictory one doubts his eyes: Hawthorne's "New England training" allowed him to go through life "with blinkers on"; thus his European experience was only "skin-deep": "His essence was left unchanged. He remained a staunch New Englander to the end"!

Next, Matthew Bruccoli provides information which will surely interest people who collect books—Hawthorne's in particular; then Fredson Bowers himself (who writes rather well, by the way) discusses the texts in general. He attempts to show that "accidentals" change meaning—which they do, but (as he also shows) not very *much*. He reveals that it is possible now to know—as, chilling thought, not even Hawthorne would have known—that "five different compositors set *Fanshawe*" ("and with tolerable accuracy . . . the exact pages that they set"). But the biggest things he mentions having turned up so far—lilacs out of the dead land!—are just a little short of overpowering: "In deference to the sensibilities of his wife," very likely, three passages having to do with liquor and sexuality (and only one of them at *all* "substantial") were deleted from the *Blithedale*. I believe it.

In the last essay, Mr. Trilling gets off to a shaky start in saying that "Henry James' monograph on Hawthorne [1879] must always have a special place in American letters, if only because, as Edmund Wilson observed, it is the first extended study ever to be made of an American writer." Wilson did say that, in his *Shock of Recognition* (though, by saying James's "must be" the first, he hedged a little). And the remark has had some currency. (I have made it myself.) But it is surprising to find it in a book composed for the most part by experts—particularly one in which George P. Lathrop's 1876 *Study of Hawthorne* ("a pioneering systematic examination and evaluation") is discussed at some length; and *it,* by the way, wasn't first, either. But Mr. Trilling soon shapes up, then comes on strong to show how "our modern Hawthorne, our dark poet, charged with chthonic knowledge, whose utterances are as ambiguous as those of any ancient riddling oracle, multileveled and hidden," is, first, a product of our criticism and, second, precisely the figure James was not only blind to but denied the existence of. (We, on the other hand, "have lost much of the charm and fragrance" to which James paid tribute.) But, in relating the two writers, Trilling is primarily interested in arguing that because of our "feeling about the world, alien from that of James," James "recedes," while Hawthorne comes to seem the modern writer. Which is approximately where we came in.

Well, *that's* done: and *again* I'm glad it's over. It's a little tiresome—you know?—to read so many entries on the same subject—perforce, given a deadline, without much interruption. Eventually it occurs to you that this necessity automatically puts you in a false position: your experience of the book, far from being representative, is virtually unique, for you are just about the only character around who has got to read it all. (Others can pick and choose, if you can't.) So one must make allowance for his high-risk status, and fight the delusion that he hears voices singing out of empty cisterns and exhausted wells—which he really does not.

R. W. B. Lewis says it for most of the contributors to the *Hawthorne Essays* when he notes that he is not going "to say anything very new . . . the occasion is ceremonial: a time for reaffirmation." It is true that some of the essayists are moving over traveled roads, once in a while encountering their own professional footprints. But *Frisch weht der Wind der Heimat zu:* here and there a contributor appears to be mistaken; seldom if ever does anyone seem stale.

Not to me. But perhaps that is because of another, compensating false situation: my own long and peculiar fascination with this strange writer, which remains a mystery. (Something he carries on his back, which I am forbidden to see.) I am convinced we really understand him now, and I rationalize the attraction by telling myself he is profoundly an American writer, relevant to us, and the Great Society and all, as seldom if ever before, and finally to be understood, perhaps, only by modern Americans. But in truth I have been decadently savoring all the while a remark about Our Hawthorne that I will at last put down: "There is something unhealthy about his writings which one does not notice at first, but which in the long run will work upon you like a very weak and very slow poison." The observation is Emile Montégut's; the translation from the French is M. Asselineau's; the date, 1852.

1965

MELVILLE'S EDEN,
OR *TYPEE* RECHARTED

'I'll carry you off
To a cannibal isle . . .
Nothing to eat but the fruit as it grows . . .
Nothing at all but three things.'
  'What things?'
  'Birth, and copulation, and death.'
  'I'd be bored.'
  'You'd be bored.'
      —T. S. ELIOT, *Sweeney Agonistes*

Nobody nowadays is going to draw much of a crowd
by setting up to debate questions of literary genre; anyway
the designation of *Typee* as Herman Melville's "first novel" is
pretty well established. But it should not hurt to mention the
fact that a segment of autobiography crossed with travelogue
is not quite what we usually have in mind when we speak of a
novel. If we had not got it straight from Mr. Capote that *In
Cold Blood* was the first "non-fiction novel" we might be
tempted to enter *Typee* under some such curious heading. But
if this should really not be called the first of Melville's novels
(or "romances"), which of his titles ought? *Mardi*, his third
book? *Moby-Dick*, larded with "non-fiction," his sixth? *Pierre?*
  The problem of how to classify *Typee* dogged it before it

ever saw publication, and that question, which is now academic, was in the beginning crucial. "I fear you abhor romances," Melville wrote to his first publisher. He was perfectly correct. The Englishman John Murray, from whom travel books for his Home and Colonial Library issued endlessly, was persistently unsure of *Typee's* credentials. Its narrative he found dramatic, and he liked the way the style kept things moving along. But he thought he detected the "taint" of fiction, and of fiction he published none at all, not knowingly. At that, Melville was doing better overseas than he had done at home; in New York *Harper's* had rejected him outright—on the ground that since his story could not possibly be true it was without value, Q.E.D. Temporarily placating Murray, the author inserted three chapters of amateur anthropology, and stolidly prefaced his title, *A Peep at Polynesian Life,* with *Narrative of a Four Months' Residence among the Natives of a Valley of the Marquesas Islands.* The book was published in England in 1846; then, later the same year, in America—with *Typee* leading off.

Washington Irving, who went through most of the proofs while in London, predicted success. And a success it was; immediate and substantial, critical and popular. That little-known writer of tales, Nathaniel Hawthorne, reviewed it favorably, and so did a virtually unknown newspaperman named Walter Whitman. By 1938 some fifty-nine editions of the book in English were tallied; and that was *before* the great surge of interest that elevated Melville to the place he now occupies with James and Faulkner in a triumvirate of American novelists had really got under way. A sort of prose Gauguin long in advance of the painter, who was to live, work, and die in the very same islands, Melville was able to summon up an air of primitive mystery, infused with broad hints (or better) of the erotic and the potentially frightening. They gave

Typee its considerable appeal, and brought "the man who lived among cannibals" instant fame.

Even so, skeptics and adversaries came along with the enthusiasts. Missionaries were angry; and poor Murray, though he was soon to publish *Omoo,* the sequel to *Typee,* continued to have misgivings so bothersome that he was to ask, more than once, for "documentary evidences" that Melville had ever so much as set foot in the Marquesas. The author could not (at any rate did not) supply them, and just as the suspicion that his bruited adventures were fictitious was threatening his newborn reputation, he was the beneficiary of what must have seemed an act of Providence (albeit, to the missionaries, a cruel one). Toby Greene, long-lost companion to most of his stay in the Marquesas, wrote to an unbelieving reviewer of *Typee,* revealing that he was found, and much alive, in Buffalo, New York. Further, that he was "happy to testify to the entire accuracy of the work" in those parts that involved him. To his second New York edition Melville added Greene's account of his disappearance—some compensation, at least, for the deletion of the sections on the missionaries and the French occupation of Tahiti. But even Toby was not enough for John Murray, who was feeling the pressure and asked yet again for "evidence." Applying a little rhetoric, Melville answered finally: "I will give no evidence—truth is mighty and will prevail. . . ."

So, what with the energies and ingenuities of modern scholars, raking the beach for the last shell, truth has done. And so, partly because that fictional taint Murray thought he detected was incontestably present, we now call the book a novel. In particular we prize those elements which head it in the direction of one. Times, we say, have changed. In such a way that the situation is exactly reversed, to the agreeably ironic point that if our view of *Typee* had been that of its publishers one hundred and twenty years ago, we might never have heard of the book. The prevalent truth today, based on a great deal of evidence Melville never supplied, is that the novel is a somewhat odd package, made up in unequal parts of fashion, fact, fancy, and felony.

The fashion of the age was, of course, for travel literature, which Murray was vigorously abetting and without which the book might never have been written, let alone published. Melville stood ready with the very mix his eventual readers favored: romantic diversion *plus* such plain instruction in strange manners and customs, flora and fauna, and so forth, as would alleviate any guilt that vicarious cultural apostasy might provoke. Further, it is unlikely that any area was so ripe for picking as the South Seas. Daydreams of noble savages and languorous paradises could seem there both adequately alien and sufficiently plausible for most. Others, to be sure, had sailed vigorously into the region and got books out of it. But dry, unimaginative books. However green the talent, the literary discovery of the South Seas remained for a young sailor with no known prospects to make.

Of fact there was abundance. Melville had assuredly not planned a sojourn in some enchanted island when he signed on the *Acushnet;* he was lucky. Before he got home he had accumulated experience enough for five books, and he wrote them. He also began in the right place—not with his whaling adventures; rather with the relatively simple and aesthetically undemanding experience of the Marquesas. To this, real events—desertion of the ship, residence in an island valley, and departure—provided a natural form and sufficient excitement. In actuality things were pretty bad on the *Acushnet.* Poor whaling and ill health made the captain so irritable and tyrannical that two mates jumped ship at the first good chance; young Melville, sensitive and proud, thought him a brute. The *Acushnet* put into port ostensibly to avoid scurvy and to look for recruits. (It is recorded elsewhere that the natives supposed "absolutely" that the real purpose of anchoring was "enjoyment of female favors.") Given the sickening possibility that home was "several years" away for this ship, it was not completely unnatural that a young man should plan to get off it. It is virtually certain that he knew there were supposed to be cannibals in those hills, but not in all of them, and it is likely that he had heard useful things about the place from a whaling cousin, Thomas Wilson Melville, who had spent a couple of weeks there several years before, and from whom he probably took the name "Tommo" for his persona.

For two weeks he made plans with Toby, a friend of like inclination. Best information was that the nearest valley was inhabited by the Happa, or Happar tribe, of good repute, and the central valley by Taipis, or Typees, deplored for dietary reasons by all. On what he and Toby guessed would be their last trip ashore they took off, badly underequipped, only to find themselves soon lost in a black, fruitless Eden, and Melville with chills and fever from a mysteriously damaged leg. They did evade the crafty *Acushnet,* which hid behind an island for twenty-four hours before sailing back in hope of catching them on the beach, but it took four days of torturous travel, with one of them sick, to reach precisely the valley they had calculated to avoid. Melville watched the cuisine closely, and found nothing at fault.

No serious doubt has been thrown on his account of some other matters, either; Toby's disappearance, for instance, was probably as given in the book. It is established further that a small Australian whaler was in such need of hands as to bother with Melville's rescue; he did get aboard the *Lucy Ann,* where things were substantially worse than on the *Acushnet.* But that is another story, called *Omoo: a Narrative of Adventures in the South Seas* (1847).

Life and the travel market had put the young Melville in a

most favorable position, but the exploitation of the South Seas for literary purposes required as well a little imagination and, most suitably to the times, his was then a Romantic one. He exercised it chiefly in playing up the idyllic aspects of "Happy Valley," bringing it as close to Eden as would seem credible, while at the same time thinking to manufacture a few shudders—notably with the discovery of some shrunken heads (which do not square at all with accounts given by other visitors to the region). Probably to help his readers accept his reliability, he increased his stay, actually a bit under four weeks, to four months. Given the topography of the area in which he made it, his escape appears to have been another invention, and the melodramatic postures assumed by the prose in that episode enforce the suspicion.

Melville's fancy played not only on his own experience but on that of other writers as well; he borrowed heavily from several people, without thought of repayment. It was a common practice, especially in travel literature, and no such stigma attached to it as would today. Even so, this traffic in secondhand merchandise must seem to us a curious business, particularly when writers rejected their own experience for someone else's. The famous instance in Melville is his taking the setting of Nantucket, which he had never seen, from a book on the history of that place for the opening of *Moby-Dick*, though New Bedford was perfectly available to him as the port he himself had shipped out of. So with the *Peep at Polynesian Life*, as C. R. Anderson's *Melville in the South Seas* (1940) demonstrates. *Typee* is indebted to five books, and to two in particular: Captain David Porter's *Journal of a Cruise Made to the Pacific Ocean* (1815) and Charles S. Stewart's *A Visit to the South Seas* (1831). Indeed Anderson's research has put John Murray's request for "evidence" in a new light, for this scholar speculates that, given a lively imagination and his sources, Melville could have written his book "without ever having seen the Marquesas." The point to be made is, of course, that we do not read Melville's sources, we read him, a young man on his way to becoming a writer. But plunder the others he did, even for description of things he had certainly observed firsthand, such as the bay and the physical beauty of the natives. Fayaway's "strange blue eyes" are in one source, and in others are to be found the precedents for his accounts of native activities, including religious observances and so forth, and even some of his scenes. The memorable opening assault of the females on the *Acushnet* is to be found in Porter (poor weather on the day of its arrival, according to the ship's log, also makes one doubt that Melville personally witnessed that invasion). Thus neither his coming or his going—or his stay—appears to have been quite as his readers were asked to believe.

Typee is, then, questionable autobiography; the modern reader searching it instead for signs of the Melville-to-come will not be rewarded extravagantly, either. As the writer himself was first to point out, his development was very rapid once begun, but slow to begin. "From my twenty-fifth year [1844] I date my life," he wrote to Hawthorne as he was about to finish *Moby-Dick* in 1851:

Three weeks have scarcely passed at any time between then and now, that I have not unfolded within myself. But I feel that I am now come to the inmost leaf of the bulb, and that shortly the flower must fall to the mould.

Evidence that he was still a novice in 1846 is conclusive in *Typee*, and nowhere clearer than in the style, which can be distinctly amateur: "I little thought . . . that in the space of a few weeks I should actually be a captive in that self-same valley. . . . How shall I describe the scenery that met my eye,

as I looked out from this verdant recess!" Some of the conversation with Toby is so artificial that one must hope (though
the purpose of it may elude him) that parody is intended:
"'You will have it to be Happar, I see, my dear fellow; pray
Heaven you may find not yourself deceived,' observed I. . . ."
Similarly inept, at times, is the structure: "I think I must en-
lighten the reader a little about the natural history of the
valley," begins Chapter 29. At other times it isn't even trying,
as in Chapter 31, which starts: ". . . I am about to string together, without any attempt at order, a few odds and ends of
things not hitherto mentioned. . . ."

It will not do to exaggerate it, but some promise of a future
is not *entirely* absent from this book. Melville could already
be consciously amusing, as in the early passage involving the
display of a royal lady's tattooed rump. And when shortly
thereafter the poor mermaids are debauched aboard ship,
there are signs of power. The style in its light formality can be
wordy, but also vigorous and spirited. Melville was already
developing a knack for "breathing life" into his prose, as we
say, and that ability was to carry him a long way.

So, too, he was beginning to hear from his mind. Thoughtful and outspoken, *Typee* inveighs credibly against disastrous
invasions of a primitive culture by Western political and religious interests; for its time it is remarkably frank, especially
in its coverage of sexual matters. But most important to *Typee*
is the question it implicitly poses: given the unmistakable
evils of our society, is an innocent, primitive state any better?
The answer seems to be that the natives are more virtuous
and happy than.we, but that their life cannot feed for long an
intellect set in motion by a more advanced culture. However
much he might wish to think so, "civilized man" cannot content himself with a near-animal existence—eating, breeding,
and (most of all by far) sleeping. As even D. H. Lawrence

allowed, we "cannot go back . . . towards the past, savage life.
. . . Whatever else the South Sea islander is, he is centuries
and centuries behind us. . . ." In short, those islands already
looked like the good place for a winter's vacation they are
becoming; otherwise, eventually, a bore. Besides, Melville's
Typees are emphatically *not* innocent, as Tommo's discovery
of fresh human bones makes abundantly clear. This revelation
is conceivably another invention: Melville needed to resolve
the suspicion he had created over the matter, and to conclude
that Tommo's fears were groundless would have just about
wrecked the book. Whether or not his natives were in actuality cannibals is still unclear; probably they were. What is
clear is that Tommo's had to be. That's what identified the
work; "Typee," Melville explains, *means* "cannibal" in the
Marquesan dialect.

Here, then, began his lifelong preoccupation with the
shadow that falls between what appears and what is—especially with the face of evil and the various masks it hides
behind. Tommo's departure is Melville's everlasting "No" to
an evil that was new to him, and to an existence that was not
only mindless but eventually catastrophic to the mind. Here
had already begun as well the development of what might be
called his basic metaphor: of life as a voyage—a search first
for a berth that would maintain a man in some tranquillity;
later (and equally doomed) a quest for an intellectual haven
among some fundamental truths he could believe in.

An anonymous "old salt" is reported as having said, "Well,
Typee was a good story: that is the way it really was out
there. But *Moby-Dick!* . . . All up in the air! Crazy!" What the
sailor had not detected was that even in *Typee* Melville was
making a few rudimentary attempts at getting off the ground;
the great symbolic, mythical powers of his masterpiece have
humble origins in the Marquesas. To cite Lawrence again,

Melville at his best always wrote "from a sort of dream-self." As an instance, the critic (*Studies in Classic American Literature*) describes Tommo first entering the valley:

Down this narrow, steep, horrible dark gorge he slides and struggles as we struggle in a dream, or in the act of birth, to emerge in the green Eden of the Golden Age, the valley of the cannibal savages.

Lawrence's "dream-self" is a kind of mythic "resonance" that became a full chorus in *Moby-Dick*. The little matter of that bad leg (surely an emblem of inner disorder as well), for instance. Tommo half-suspects he has been bitten by a snake, and in the vague context of the first Garden the admonition of the Lord to the reptile, "thou shalt bruise his heel," comes to mind very naturally. So might the heel of Achilles (though this is to exalt Tommo above his station) or the "swollen foot" of Oedipus, to which the name points, or even the limp of a most contemporary mythical hero, complexly related to Oedipus, the protagonist of John Barth's *Giles Goat-Boy*, who is carried pickaback about the campus by his brute slave, Croaker, precisely as Tommo is carried about the valley by his servant, the uncultivated Kory-Kory. In like fashion *Typee* corresponds roughly to several archetypal patterns, among them Joseph Campbell's hypothetical "monomyth": a withdrawal from a troubled world into prehistory; communion if not with a deity at least with his sacred grove; and return to a different life in the awareness that civilization can't go home again either.

In a period when American critics are compulsively attuned to the mythical overtones of literary works it is no surprise that several of them should have read *Typee* "mythically." Nor anything peculiar (since it is the author himself who frequently remarks the parallels) in the fact that several such interpreters have seized Eden (both pre- and post-lapsarian) for a handy grip on the book. In his first work as in his last, *Billy Budd*, Melville is very mindful of the Bible story. It is he who remarks that "the penalty of the Fall presses very lightly" on the natives, that it is not by the sweat of their brow that these men are condemned to earn their bread-fruit, that Fayaway (a convenient Eve in her affair with Tommo) wore the "summer garb of Eden," and so on. Thus R. W. B. Lewis will find yet another American Adam in Melville's tale, another search for a lost childhood, a vanished Eden, expressing a distinctly American resistance to the whole business of growing up. At the other end of a spectrum, Milton R. Stern will argue that Melville's version of the myth of Adam is an heretical inversion of the original story: the Fall in this book is not the expulsion from Eden but the fall *into* it; salvation for man cannot be found in pastoral; his only Grace lies in an escape from "innocence," which can be accomplished only by what is forbidden, eating of the tree of knowledge.

Between and beside such views of Tommo's Eden are numerous bypaths and way stations, but they all run out or collapse at the way the evidence of cannibalism Tommo happened on fails to accommodate itself to the story in *Genesis*. Structurally and thematically this discovery marks the conjunction of all strands of the book, but here exactly the trail is lost. Whatever the fruit of Eden, it was not human flesh that grew on that tree. Or was it?

The question now is whether, after sufficient sanity, safety and sobriety, a little speculation may not be permissible in the end. If so, the proposition would be that it is conceivable (no more is being urged) that where "*Typee* as Eden" appears to fall apart is precisely where it stands up best.

Lawrence, wild, fearless, crazy like a fox, may be summoned up one last time to remark that Melville "might have spared himself his shudder" at the thought and sight of cannibalism among those natives:

No doubt he had partaken of the Christian sacraments many a time. "This is my body, take and eat." And surely their sacred ceremony was as awe-inspiring as the one Jesus substituted.

"Substituted." Typically, Lawrence doesn't explain. Drop the bomb and let someone else pick up the pieces, that was his method (and a delight it is in the age of explication).

The pieces in this case were retrieved and reassembled by a man who was thinking of neither Lawrence or Melville but of Freud, the contemporary psychoanalytic writer, Theodor Reik. Though he did not work up his notions until 1957 (in *Myth and Guilt: The Crime and Punishment of Mankind*), they first struck him back in 1913 when he was directly associated with the master. His is, then, yet another Tale from the Vienna Woods. But he is working to our problem, and it would be foolish to dismiss without a hearing a relevant hypothesis as *it* takes the ancient story of man's first disobedience and the fruit whose mortal taste brought loss of Eden, and looks for "reality" in it. As he notes, sexual interpretations of the tale are old as pre-Christian, new as Otto Rank, and widely held. Yet for Reik the original sin of mankind was not a sexual but a "nutritional mistake," motivated by the wish to become God by eating a "special kind of food." In *Genesis* God the father appears as a tree-totem, and the origin of the grim story of its fruit lies in very primitive times when man ate his god, or despotic father, out of the wish to become that figure. ("Behold," said the Lord after Adam had eaten, "the man is become as one of us.") This immemorial tradition survives in the idea—fact, rather—of cannibals eating a missionary for the same, familiar reason, that they may possess the magic powers they attribute to him. In short, the Biblical injunction was to abandon on pain of death the practice of eating people.

Reik also extends this reading to connect with the "substituted" Eucharist, where the devout are united with Christ by "incorporating" his body and blood. Thus the myth of the fall of man, and the death and redemption of Jesus as Saviour, are a single, coherent story, the early church fathers having been correct when they said that the death-bringing tree of the Fall became the life-giving tree of the Cross. Christ offered himself as atonement for an ancient crime, harking all the way back to it.

If for a moment one is willing to suspend disbelief, the problem of what this interpretation might do for *Typee* is upon him. One thought would be that we gain from such a reading of the ancient symbols a more dramatic sense of the distance in time that Tommo tumbled as he was reborn into that valley, a sharper appreciation of the millennia erased by the minutes during which he fell captive to an age when the dawn had not yet broken on Western culture. As the natives cried "Taboo!" and Tommo glimpsed anyway "the disordered members of a human skeleton, the bones still fresh with moisture, and with particles of flesh clinging . . ." he saw more than he knew or we knew. He saw the heart of darkness, the leavings of Adam and Eve, evidence of what was to become man's first disobedience.

The Fall does not press lightly on *him,* so that what he saw is no more important than what he felt: the revulsion that may be said to have been the harbinger of the dawn of our history. Every bit as unwitting as Rip Van Winkle (who stumbled ignorantly into Valhalla), Tommo saw the fruit of the tree of the Garden unmasked of all *its* leaves. And though he has no way of seeing himself in such a role, he is a palsied messenger come from the dead to tell us all: not just whom we descend from, but what. Which is as good a way as Melville's to leave our ailing knight, alone and palely loitering, shaken by the smiles that hold him still in thrall, haggard on a cold hill, entranced in horror.

And no birds sing. "Birds," writes Melville,

—bright and beautiful birds—fly over the valley of Typee. You see them passing like spirits on the wing through the shadows of the grove. . . . Their plumage is purple and azure, crimson and white, black and gold. . . . They go sailing through the air in starry throngs; but alas! the spell of dumbness is on them all—there is not a single warbler in the valley!

1967

HAWTHORNE'S *GABLES*
un GARBLED

"No evil deed live oN."
—PALINDROME

T he House of the Seven Gables was written in a happy
time for Hawthorne: perhaps this helps explain why it is so
much more cheerful a book than *The Scarlet Letter.* He and
his family were now living in the Little Red House near
Lenox, in the Berkshire hills of western Massachusetts, and the
situation was as close to ideal as it gets for a writer. Hawthorne was no longer "dragging *Salem* at his ankles," as his
wife put it. He was enjoying himself with his children, Julian
and Una, in the country; their mother, Sophia, was anticipating
a third child, Rose. His social life was pleasant and active, and
there were well-known and lively visitors. For a change his
financial prospects were looking up, and *The Scarlet Letter,*
recently published, had made him famous. What is more, he
felt that his present work was going well. He had a very high
opinion of the *Seven Gables;* he expressed a repeated, however mistaken, preference for it over his recent triumph (this
was a preference in which the public and the reviewers were
shortly to concur); and he was having more pleasure in writing it than any other book. What was nearly as much: six

miles down the road lived a new friend and his greatest admirer, Herman Melville. This young man often negotiated the distance by horseback, and no visitor—when he could put aside his own work—was more exciting or more welcome to the Hawthornes. Melville was writing *Moby-Dick*. These were the golden years.

They were golden years for America: 1850–1855. During this short period Emerson, who had earlier done a good deal of the ploughing for the harvest, published his *Representative Men*. Melville published *White-Jacket, Moby-Dick, Pierre,* and *Israel Potter*. Thoreau published *Walden,* and Walt Whitman brought out the first edition of *Leaves of Grass*. These facts are not entirely unknown; the period is what F. O. Matthiessen called the *American Renaissance* (it was really more a *naissance*). But not so widely recognized is the fact that no man made a greater contribution to this splendid outburst than Nathaniel Hawthorne. During the period, in addition to several important prefaces, three full volumes of stories for children, and a campaign biography for his good friend Franklin Pierce (who was elected to the presidency), Hawthorne published *The Scarlet Letter* in 1850, *The House of the Seven Gables* in 1851, *The Snow Image and Other Twice-Told Tales* (which work includes a couple of his greatest short stories) in 1852, and in the same year *The Blithedale Romance*. Although he wrote on until his death in 1864, he had actually, after this spurt, only one important book left in him —*The Marble Faun,* which appeared in 1860.

I

It is remarkable how close the author must have felt to his *House of the Seven Gables*. Writers generally write from what they know intimately. But it is worth recording, as a matter of simple interest, how this book comes to be in many ways the most "personal" of Hawthorne's works. For one thing there is his relation to the "Pyncheon" family, and to that name itself, which, suggesting "truncheon," has appropriate overtones of cruelty, while the "pinch" befits their greed for money. Now "thorne" sounds as threatening as "pinch." ("Take my hand, Phoebe," Clifford would say, "and pinch it hard with your little fingers! Give me a rose, that I may press its thorns, and prove myself awake by the sharp touch of pain!") And it is also relevant to remember here that it was Nathaniel himself who inserted the "w" in his name, softening it from Hathorne.*

Why should Hawthorne have felt even the trivial degree of affinity for the Pyncheons which the small element of similarity in the names might seem to suggest? The answer lies with his Hathorne ancestors, or, specifically, with the two forebears whom he discussed in the famous "Custom-House" introduction to *The Scarlet Letter*. In the *Seven Gables* he compressed them into one ancestor. Consider the description of Colonel Pyncheon as he appears in the portrait that hangs in the gabled house—a threatening picture of a stern, bearded Puritan, with a Bible in one hand and a sword in the other. Isn't this the persecuting ancestor, Major William Hathorne by name, whom Hawthorne had already described in that introduction as his own "grave, bearded . . . progenitor,— who came so early with his Bible and his sword. . . ."?

It was this Colonel (promoted in rank from Major by the novelist) who in the novel brought down on himself and his line the "curse" that hovers over the house of Pyncheon—a

---

* When Hawthorne learned, from an excessively irate descendant, that there had actually been a Judge Pyncheon in Salem, he coolly explained that the name was chosen because it "had a certain indescribable [!] fitness to the tone of my work." The true model for the Judge was a man named Upham; he had been instrumental in losing Hawthorne his job in the custom house, some years before, when the Whigs came into power.

curse issued from a scaffold by a man about to be hanged, ostensibly for witchcraft. In the history of the novelist's own family it was the Major's son, Judge John Hathorne, who was supposed to have received that malediction.* This is the same curse which, in that introductory chapter of *The Scarlet Letter,* Hawthorne said "the dreary and unprosperous condition" of his family "for many a long year back, would argue to exist." A better argument for the existence of this curse, in fact, and for its operation specifically on Hawthorne, is that he suffered in his own conscience the guilt that these ancestors had incurred: "I . . . take shame upon myself for their sakes."

The other thorn in the side of the Pyncheons, the lands in Maine that represent a fortune lost to them (since the title bestowed by an Indian deed is missing), is parallel to a misfortune that put an equal pinch in the finances of the unprosperous Hawthornes: there was a tradition in his own family, on his mother's side, that it had been deprived of thousands of acres in Maine (deeded an ancestor in 1666 by an Indian) through the loss of the title. Not content with these connections to his book, the author put something of his family even in the Maules. When we read of Matthew Maule's descendants that they were marked off from other men "by an hereditary character of reserve"—that there was a "circle" around them, "insulating them from human aid," and no outsider could penetrate it—we are reading as well of the descendants of the Major and the Judge, or so, at least, people who knew the Hawthornes in the more somber Salem days believed.

Hawthorne also put a lot of himself, and his own, into the

---

* The curse was actually pronounced on the Judge's colleague, Nicholas Noyes. Sarah Good said at her trial, "I am no more a witch than you are a wizard;—and if you take away my life, God will give you blood to drink."

actors of this fiction. Most clearly he appears as the current
Maule—as Holgrave, that is—the man who can penetrate the
appearance of a person's face and read his soul, the man who
retreats from his grim and solitary study to walk, still alone,
along the seashore near Salem. As it develops, of course, Holgrave is even a bit of a writer. In a strong echo of Hawthorne's
own literary practice, he happens to know an incident of
family history, which he has put into "the form of a legend";
he means to "publish it in a magazine." (And when the story
meets our eyes, as it does immediately, it turns out to be unmistakable Hawthorne.)

To be sure, Holgrave is more a progressive and a reformer
—even a faddist—than his creator was. He is never more than
Hawthorne "in a liberal mood." In another, and perhaps more
characteristic mood, it is the conservative Clifford into whom
the author puts himself—or, to speak more exactly, Clifford
is Hawthorne's fear of what he might have become if he had
not been "saved": he is the man cut off from other men
(though not from children)—cut off, almost, from life itself.
The elaborate and touching passage in which the novelist describes Clifford ushered back to life from a long, dungeon
stay outside it, through the magic worked on him by a young
woman, Phoebe, is precisely parallel to Hawthorne's feeling
that all those years he spent alone in his room in Salem had
isolated him from life and the world: "I have made a captive
of myself, and put me into a dungeon, and now I cannot find
the key to let myself out." Then, as he wrote from Brook Farm
to his fiancée, Miss Peabody, her love had recreated and re-
stored him: "It is a miracle worthy even of thee, to have converted a life of shadows into the deepest truth, by thy magic
touch." (Consider also once again the similarity of names,
Phoebe and Peabody; actually "Phoebe" was one of Nathaniel's
nicknames for Sophia.)

The House of the Seven Gables was very close to Hawthorne

in other, and more significant, ways. Take the matter of hypnotism—or rather, mesmerism.* A significant evil in *The Blithedale Romance,* it plays a large role in the *Seven Gables* as well. Now it happens that the depths of Hawthorne's mistrust of mesmerism are very enlightening—not so much that his somewhat quaint opinions on the subject are interesting, but that in discussing it he once stated the quintessence of his personal morality, and this from a writer who was, perhaps above all things, a moralist. When Hawthorne was living at Brook Farm, Sophia wrote him that she was considering hypnotic treatment as a possible cure for ailments from which she suffered. Her future husband wrote back, on September 27, 1841, with firmness—his words are almost, and prematurely, an order—born of deep conviction:

Take no part, I beseech you, in the magnetic miracles. I am unwilling that a power should be exercised on you of which we know neither the origin nor the consequence. . . . Supposing that the power arises from the transfusion of one spirit into another; it seems to me that the sacredness of an individual is violated by it; there would be an intruder into the holy of holies. . . .

The view which I take of this matter is caused by no want of faith in mysteries; but from a deep reverence of the soul, and of the mysteries which it knows within itself, but never transmits to the earthly eye and ear.

---

* After F. A. Mesmer, who first postulated its principles in Vienna about 1775, mesmerism is not quite the same thing as hypnotism, a later concept which denotes a psychological phenomenon whereby through the power of suggestion one individual may influence another. Mesmerism, which "the mesmerizing carpenter" Matthew Maule practices on "Alice Pyncheon" in the chapter of that name, posited a physical "magnetic fluid" which pervades and unites mind and matter. Both terms were long subsumed under the heading "Magnetism," to which Hawthorne alludes with reasonable misgivings below. (It is probably worth noting further that somehow Maule is adept at mesmerism a couple of generations before Mesmer.)

"The sacredness of an individual." "The holy of holies." "A deep reverence of the soul." We are at the heart, the very center, of Nathaniel Hawthorne and his work, and it was his scruples about mesmerism (at the time about to give way to hypnotism) that brought his early but final moral message as clearly to light as anything he was ever to write.

But his personal horror of the violation that he felt magnetism might constitute is an important thematic element in the *Seven Gables*. So are many elements that are met with elsewhere in his writing, for this novel is a highly characteristic, as well as a highly personal, performance. One of the final pronouncements of *The Scarlet Letter,* for instance, is this: ". . . be the stern and sad truth spoken, that the breach which guilt has once made into the human soul is never, in this mortal state, repaired." *The House of the Seven Gables* has, or is said to have, as one of its "morals," the same lesson to teach: "It is a truth . . . that no great mistake, whether acted [*Scarlet Letter*] or endured [*Seven Gables*], in our mortal sphere, is ever really set right."

Except so far as Clifford is concerned, however, the *Seven Gables* seems to show how the past may indeed be redeemed, a great mistake corrected, a fresh start established. Curiously enough (because of the enormous differences between them), it is in this way almost a "sequel" to *The Scarlet Letter.* The earlier novel ended with Hawthorne's reluctantly stern judgment on Hester, his heroine. She learned finally that she could not, as she had earlier hoped, bring happiness into this world, because no one can who is himself "stained with sin, bowed down with shame, or even burdened with a life-long sorrow." But Hawthorne immediately held out the hope that the right person could indeed accomplish something of this sort. It would take "a woman indeed, but lofty, pure, and beautiful . . . showing how sacred love can make us happy. . . ." Inadequate as she may seem in so great a role, and however anticlimactic after Hester, this figure—so clearly foreshadowed at the end of *The Scarlet Letter*—is Phoebe of the *Seven Gables*.

II

The House of the Seven Gables is, however, like all works of art a unique one, and it must stand quite independent of connections with Hawthorne himself, and his other books—or fall. The question is what the qualities of this uniqueness are, and what distinguishes this novel.

Among its most striking features are the creaky old pieces of Gothic machinery Hawthorne has lugged down from the attic and arranged about the place. The Gothic novel, characterized by horror, blood, supernatural or "spooky" effects, and so forth—all functioning in an antique structure of Gothic design—had been popular in the late eighteenth century, and had begun to date in the midnineteenth. But Hawthorne did not scruple to help himself generously to its properties. The Pyncheon house, "miserable old dungeon," was conceived, the author says, "in the grotesqueness of a Gothic fancy"; its furnishings are so appropriate to that conception that one occasionally finds himself looking for illustrations by Charles Addams, or a part that Boris Karloff played. Items: a portrait with magic reactions, a secret spring behind it, a hidden document, a secret drawer, the rumor of a buried fortune in English guineas; ghostly music presaging death, a "strange Grimalkin" that haunts the garden, the sorcery of the Maules; a mysterious crime, a dark wrong, somewhere in the past; an hereditary curse—"blood to drink."

Even in America it would have been fairly normal (witness Poe, for instance) if this somewhat puerile design had been shaded with a few decadent strokes—some hints of depravity that would add a bit of special titillation to the pleasurable shudders that the Gothic materials were designed to produce. One might expect, after the fashion, that more would be made of the pretty, innocent but nameless brides who were led into the miserable dungeon of the Pyncheons. Or that more mileage would be got from the exotic, un-New-England Alice Pyncheon of Holgrave's story, symbolically seduced by the young Matthew Maule, and held in humiliating, perversely sexual bondage by him. Most of all, the convention would seem to demand that Phoebe, the essence of unspoiled and lovely maidenhood, should, if in any way possible, be diabolically persecuted. Indeed it is through the dewy Phoebe, in her relationship with the emaciated Clifford, that Hawthorne comes closest to fulfilling the requirements of this vogue. Clifford is described as by no mean insensible of her physical charm; she, as devoted to his pleasure. But the novelist says that he simply cannot find words to express the "beauty and profound pathos" of this affair. Contrasting sharply with the Judge, who had made Phoebe blush, he says that there was no need for the girl "ever to shudder at the touch of his thin delicate fingers," and having brought the matter up he lets it go.

This is a situation in which we cannot eat our cake, or have it, either. It is no longer possible to take pleasure in the Gothic trappings of this novel—precisely because they *are* "trappings"; and the decadent elements that often accompany them —and are frequently, as in Poe, of considerable psychological interest—are here too meager to be worth more than passing notice. This is by no means always the case with Hawthorne; witness "Rappacini's Daughter" and *The Marble Faun.* It is the case in this book because in his conscious mind, at least, Hawthorne was resolved *not* to write a Gothic novel, or even this time a really gloomy one; given the rather grim subject of the workings of an hereditary curse, he was bound that he would make it as sunny an affair as possible.

The Gothic elements and the subject, oddly combined with

a determination that the book would not be morose or melancholy, account for the highly distinctive tone of the *Seven Gables*. It is never either gloomy or cheerful for long, but first one and then the other. The evocation of shadowy wrongs and ruined lives combines with lively and even bantering attitudes. A typical instance, but an exceptionally clear one, juxtaposes the decayed and hopeless Clifford and Hepzibah with their fantastic poultry. The novel is a nice alternation, and finally a tension, between the twin attractions of the breezy and the murky, of the light and the dark, or heavy. So determined is Hawthorne to keep the unpleasant side of his tale in check that he stoops to repeating the most philistine and imperceptive of old saws about the reading of "sad" or tragic literature, which runs: There's trouble enough in the world already, without . . . For if Phoebe drops a tear while reading to Clifford, he makes her close the book: "And wisely too!" interjects Hawthorne. "Is not the world sad enough in genuine earnest, without making a pastime of mock-sorrows?"

After a spell of fresh air in the garden, however, the action retreats shyly back into the house, as the author likens "our story" to an "owl" (and he once spoke of himself in exactly these terms) "bewildered in the daylight, and hastening back to his hollow tree." Soon we are indoors again, "the twilight is glooming . . . the shadows . . . grow deeper." A "dark gray tide of oblivion . . . creeps slowly over the various objects" until all has faded, and we "go sighing and murmuring about, in quest of what was once a world." But Hawthorne will not stay in the shadows for long, either (cannot, in this case), and if there is more cloud than sunshine in the *Seven Gables* it is also a fact that—however the thematic impropriety may make us squint—the novel ends, for the young people anyway, in a blaze of sunlight.

A related distinguishing feature of the book is its "charm." As Henry James remarked, this charm is "vague, indefinable,

ineffable." But if James meant he could not describe it, he
could evoke it, calling to mind "summer afternoon in an elm-
shaded New England town." It is a matter of delicate colors
and shades, a patient refinement of moods, a subtle exactness
in atmosphere. These are matters, of course, of excellence in
technique, or style. The verdict on the matter of the prose
style in a narrower sense, however, cannot be unreservedly
favorable. The style of this novel is simply Hawthorne's style,
which from book to book is remarkably of a piece. At its best
it has a wonderfully lucid, balanced, formalized, even Latin-
ized, grace—the coolness and the sheen of old but untarnished
silver. Modern readers generally find it somewhat old-
fashioned, but by no means unattractive. At its worst it is a
travesty of its very virtues, is characterized by a sort of rhe-
torical fatuity. Take Alice Pyncheon's reply to the young
Matthew Maule when he says she will doubtless feel safe with
him as long as her father is present:

"I certainly shall entertain no manner of apprehension, with my
father at hand," said Alice, with maidenly dignity. "Neither do I
conceive that a lady, while true to herself, can have aught to fear
from whomsoever, or in any circumstances!"

To be sure, Alice is very proud, and the passage is attributed
to Holgrave—is from the interlude given to his pen. But its
equivalent may be found elsewhere in the book; and besides,
as already observed, when Holgrave writes he turns out to be
Hawthorne again. Ideally it would be Holgrave writing here,
and the story he tells would throw important light on the
book as a whole. At first glance one wonders if, instead of
having such a legitimate purpose, Hawthorne was not simply
tired of using flashbacks, and wanted to give still more background (some of it repetitive) than he had so far provided. A
second glance shows, however, that the story Holgrave is given
to tell lights up two of the novel's themes, and in doing so

really justifies itself. One of these has to do with the sin that is pride, the other with the related but more terrible sin involved in the control of other people. Pride is the "too haughty" Alice's sin; the violation of "a woman's delicate soul" (the "holy of holies") is Maule's.

Now this focus on pride does underscore one meaning of the novel's action. All the Pyncheons save Phoebe—the Judge, Hepzibah, and Clifford—are proud; so were the Maules, in their own way; so is Holgrave. And the sin of Matthew's constraining will, which debased Alice and finally destroyed her, points to the central principle of the book's morality. But the story's immediate function is still more important, and would in itself warrant the digression or device. Holgrave suddenly finds himself in the same position as his ancestor. In a second he could be master of Phoebe's "free and virgin spirit," as Maule was of Alice's. And he has reason for wishing to be; to his particular type, says Hawthorne (possibly from knowing himself), nothing is more tempting. But Holgrave has the saving grace: "the rare and high quality of reverence for another's individuality." He resists. Mesmerism was to Hawthorne in the nineteenth century as witchcraft to his ancestors in the seventeenth—a Black Art practiced on other people to wreck them. The knack of it was passed down to Holgrave from his forebears, as was the curse on the Pyncheons from theirs, but he will not exercise it.

Holgrave's story is, therefore, structurally sound. But its point, so important to the novel, would seem to show the reverse of what the novel, in its Preface, professes to argue: "the truth, namely, that the wrong-doing of one generation lives into the successive ones. . . ."

This is not the only place in the book where the action would seem to contradict the message. Indeed, the construction of the *Seven Gables* is somewhat jumbled. The novel starts with a kind of reluctance, and then picks up a slow and relaxed pace. The tempo is a very unmodern one, but not at all an unpleasing one if we will relax and adjust to it. By building up small things like Clifford's entrance and the matter of his identity, Hawthorne gets quite a large return from a very small investment. Sometimes he tries to get too much, as in the chapter on the dead Judge. But things go smoothly and pleasantly, for the most part, right up to the ending. At that point, and as though the author had become suddenly and unaccountably exhausted, the entire structure collapses.

One wonders what in the world Sophia was thinking of when she listened to her husband finish his reading of the *Seven Gables* and put it on paper that she found "unspeakable grace and beauty in the conclusion. . . ." The conclusion is unspeakably awkward. For thematic reasons, Hawthorne was absolutely forced to marry Phoebe and Holgrave—but with so little interest in the business that he could not bother to prepare for the event by showing them developing so much as a real interest in each other. All of a sudden they are going to marry, settle down in peace, happiness, prosperity, and Holgrave's career as a daguerreotypist. Worse than this, they have a new house, bigger and better than the seven-gabled one—and a most excellent new symbol of the very thing that had ruined the Pyncheons in the first place. If there is any sense at all in Hawthorne's moralizing about the old house, then it follows that the new one must in time exert an even more awful influence: it is built once again on ill-got gains (the Judge's wealth); it is even more "withdrawn from life." Then to cap the process whereby the demands of the "moral" part of the story succumb to the demands of another part for a happy ending, Phoebe and Holgrave have come into a fortune—the other side of the circumstance that caused the original trouble. No irony is intended in any of this; there is little here but a series of lapses. D. H. Lawrence must have been thinking along these lines when he wrote with a bit of a sneer: "The new generation is having no ghosts or cobwebs. It is setting up in the photography line, and is just going to make a sound financial thing of it."

If one stops to think about the problem, he may realize that it might have been a bit difficult to show Phoebe and Holgrave falling in love. This is because they are not especially real people. Holgrave is of considerable interest as a distinctly American type, a new man on the face of the earth, with a characteristically and uniquely American background. But he does not seem to be a person. Phoebe is simply a cliché. She is one of three pure, pale blondes in Hawthorne's romances—Priscilla (of *Blithedale Romance*) and Hilda (*Marble Faun*) are the other two. The real women of Hawthorne's romances are, alas, another trio: Hester (*Scarlet Letter*), Zenobia (*Blithedale Romance*), Miriam (*Marble Faun*). They are not so pure or so pale, and they are all brunettes.

The characterization is not one of the strongest points of this novel. The *House* itself is a bit of a character, but its people are static—are, as James said, "all pictures rather than persons." Hepzibah and Clifford, however, standing in pointed contrast to Phoebe and Holgrave, are most excellent pictures. In Clifford, Hawthorne had found a new way for a man to become, or almost to become, one of the recurrent sinners of his work. All these sinners—Chillingworth, Brand, Rappaccini, and the rest—have gone astray in having overdeveloped some faculty, usually the power of analysis, so that it has crowded out their affections. In Clifford it is the "sense of the beautiful and harmonious" which, if he had had a real chance to cultivate it, might have made him such a sinner, too. Not so closely related to other figures in Hawthorne, Hepzibah is just as well described as her brother. She is both an individual and the very type of decayed gentility—with only the delusion of the importance of her family, and her hatred of the Judge, to keep her afloat. The old order changeth, yielding place to

new, but it is the old people of this novel that readers remember when they have forgot the young ones, which may not
be exactly as Hawthorne would have wished.

The rest of the characters, in themselves, are not so important. The Judge is mechanical, and a bit stagey; the best
that can be said for him is that he makes his presence sufficiently felt. But although Uncle Venner and Ned Higgins, the
great eater of cookies, and Dixie and his friend, the two
laborers, are insignificant as characters, they have an important role in the novel. They tie the action in the house to
life outdoors. This is also the function of the shop Hepzibah
reopens, and it is all the function these people have. Hawthorne had been afraid that without a chapter of reality to tie
it to the ground, the symbolic, archaic world of his *Scarlet
Letter* would take off into space like a balloon; hence the introductory "Custom-House." He appears to have had the
same worry about this seven-gabled world; hence these minor
figures and the shop. Late in the novel he shows very clearly
this concern. Speaking of the shop bell, he says that it makes
one "sensible that there is a living world, and that even this
old, lonely mansion retains some manner of connection with
it." Lacking faith where he was strong, he was afraid that
without such ties what happens in the mansion would isolate
itself, lose contact with reality, and vanish. But it is not the
"living world" that interests us in Hawthorne's romances, or
interested him, and their real substance is never in that world.

III

The most substantial and remarkable thing about the *Seven
Gables* is probably the richness—and complexity, depth, and
subtlety—of its implications. The question of what Hawthorne
was trying to say of a general nature in this novel is a difficult
one, and the number of answers that have been given to that

question suggest both the impossibility of a simple response and a high degree of thematic interest in the book. This novel, we may read, is Hawthorne's study of the effects of original sin—or (not the same thing) of the past living in the present. It is a presentation of his notions about American democracy —or about the relation of pride to death. It is about history, whether it evolves in a cyclical or lineal (or some other) fashion. It is about isolation redeemed, about withdrawal and return. Or about the weakness of aristocracy and the virtue of youthful vigor and adaptiveness. Or about the power of the imagination, victorious over material force—and so on and on.

One could easily add to and expand on such a list. One thing that Hawthorne is surely trying to say (through Hepzibah and more clearly through Clifford) is that the most important thing in life is to be engaged in it—to be alive and functioning in the thick of it, to have a place in the stream, and not in some eddy. What the isolated Clifford needed most was a "deep, deep plunge into the ocean of human life. . . ." It is the very essence of his tragedy and Hepzibah's, as she says, that "We belong nowhere." Relating to this point is the notion, already mentioned, that it is love which best involves us in the world, that brings the world alive and makes it real. Love is what is supposed to save Phoebe and Holgrave, who are rescued from the past by it, and redemption by love is one of the novel's major themes.

But the principal fable of the *Seven Gables* should, and does, relate to the thesis, already quoted, that Hawthorne pointed up in the Preface: "the truth, namely, that the wrongdoing of one generation lives into the successive ones. . . ." Yet this "moral," announced in a curse and occasionally worked out in the action, has for various reasons long seemed itself one of the chief flaws in the novel. T. S. Eliot, while praising the book itself very highly ("Hawthorne's best novel after all"), was not unduly harsh when he dismissed the curse, many years ago, as "a matter of the simplest fairy mechanics." And much earlier, Henry James pointed to most of the rest of the trouble when he objected that "the subject . . . of the story does not quite fill it out." James added, however, that he had "an impression of certain complicated purposes which seem to reach beyond" the subject—of "all sorts of deep intentions, of interwoven threads of suggestion."

Although he did not describe this impression, or explain where he got it, James did well to entertain it. Hawthorne, on the other hand, was pretty insistent that his subject was the one he signaled at the start. He speaks further of "the little regarded truth, that the act of the passing generation is the germ which may and must produce good or evil fruit in a far distant time." He says the Pyncheons had "inherited a great misfortune." He refers to his novel as "our history of retribution for the sin of long ago." And he makes clear that he does not wish to be taken figuratively but literally in all of this when he records his suspicion that the "weaknesses and defects, the bad passions, the mean tendencies, and the moral diseases which lead to crime are handed down from one generation to another, by a far surer process than human law has been able to establish. . . ." It is not just that some Pyncheons repeated some of the crimes of their ancestor, but that in repeating them they showed that a moral weakness was alive in the genes.

It is not difficult to see why this narrow and perhaps indefensible thesis has long seemed one of the major weaknesses— possibly the most important one—of the *Seven Gables*. In the first place, it looks for all the world like an idea to "do up" in a romance, like a purely mechanical device for getting under way. Worse, it was an idea that Hawthorne was not prepared to defend or fill out. *The Scarlet Letter* offers spectacular anticipations of now-demonstrated psychological truths; but "human law" has still not been able to substantiate the claim that "moral disease" is hereditary in Hawthorne's sense. Neither could Hawthorne. The question is whether he really tried.

But Hawthorne was a very shrewd and subtle man; and to his stated "truth" he offered a reservation, almost invariably overlooked, that nearly cancels it as a thesis: "When romances do really teach anything, or produce any effective operation, it is usually through a far more subtle process than the ostensible one." This observation penetrates deep into literature; it is especially relevant to Hawthorne's own work, and most especially to this novel. Hawthorne's best writing came "against the grain"—or at any rate against the veneer. It came from some voice deep within him that he could not control. "The devil," he said, "gets in my inkstand." But he did not really think of it as a devil; he recognized it as the voice of a power "higher and wiser than himself, making him its instrument," and he often, and fortunately, gave in to it.

The House of the Seven Gables is the perfect case in point. It does not, indeed, teach the bald and dubious lesson that it purports to, and it is a much better novel—more complex, ambiguous, and absorbing—than if it did. The story of the descent of crime and guilt broadens, as Hawthorne begins to deal with it, to a consideration of the whole matter of descent. In the texture that clothes the alleged thesis, the novel branches out to examine many forms of heredity, and ultimately flowers in a persuasive expression of the enigma that is the relation of living things to their ancestry. The thesis turns even to antithesis, and the final impression is of the inscrutable mystery that is life itself.

One way of putting this is to say that Hawthorne, underneath, was too good a novelist to stick with what Hawthorne, on the surface, claimed for his subject. His mind was too interested, too curious. Actually the book investigates not one but three different kinds of inheritance: human, animal, and vegetable. The house is not the only setting for the action of the novel. The Pyncheons have also a garden, and what transpires there can be ignored, but at the cost of misunderstanding the book.

A good deal of space in the *Seven Gables* is devoted to vegetation, and first of all, bridging the house and the garden, are Alice's Posies. Springing from seed flung long ago into a cranny on the roof by Alice herself, these flowers blossom among the gables, where they grow melancholy in an effort to gladden the house. They are in themselves a bit of an enigma. Of ancient lineage, they were sown by a Pyncheon and a sinner; they are said to get water, on occasion, that is drawn from Maule's well in the garden, which is reputed to make people sick. But the flowers flourish.

The garden is a suitable place for the revelations that come about there. It is a region out of fairy tales, not Gothic. It is enchanted—the scene of Clifford's only happy hours; an "Eden," later, for Phoebe and Holgrave. It is a magic place, with the usual prohibition, this time on the fountain: "Be careful not to drink," says Holgrave; ". . . it is water bewitched!" Whereupon he vanishes.

This garden is also, significantly, a confusing place—so confusing that some of the very best of Hawthorne's critics have referred to it in such terms as "long-since exhausted." It looks that way at times. But it turns out that it has "rich, black soil," and there are, among other things, luxurious, rare, and beautiful white roses in it. These flowers Alice also planted, and they grow, there in the ground where they belong, out of two hundred years of vegetable decay and cultivation. At heart, however, they are blighted and mildewed. In addition the garden contains other "antique and hereditary flowers," these in "no very flourishing condition" either. But it has also an abundant vegetable crop, and once Hawthorne calls the place "that one green nook in the dusty town." Most enigmatic of all its produce are the bean vines. Holgrave had found beans in the garret of the house and, curious as Hawthorne in these mysteries, had planted them to see if there could still be life in "such ancient seeds." The result is spectacular: bean-vines with vivid scarlet blossoms, and hummingbirds dancing about the flowers.

What was Hawthorne trying to do here? The crude way to handle the garden would be to force the generations of plant life to parallel the generations of Pyncheons and thus somehow to supplement the thesis. At one early point it looks as if he will do precisely this. Speaking of the garden he says that, except for human interference, "the evil of these departed years would naturally have sprung up again"—in "rank weeds (symbolic of the transmitted vices of society). . . ." But once again, despite this cultivation, there *is* still a "sordid and ugly luxuriance of gigantic weeds" there, and neither the white roses nor the other "hereditary flowers" had profited from care.

It would be simplest to say that Hawthorne was just confused, or did not care, about what life in the garden added up to. And it could be that in his conscious mind one or the other of these things was so. But that "higher," or deeper, voice cared, and knew that confusion, and allowed it to stand and develop. That voice knew also what it made of the confusion. This becomes clear in the handling of inheritance in the animal kingdom.

Or, to speak more accurately, the poultry kingdom, for here the point is very clear, and it took only some hens in the garden to make it. Like the flowers and the beans, they are descendants of an ancient line; like the red Posies, they are said to find the water of the well most palatable, and like the white roses, they are in a debilitated state. They have the "traditionary peculiarities of their whole line of progenitors, derived through an unbroken succession of eggs . . .'"; or, for Hawthorne gets a little waggish with these chickens, maybe they are a bit "crack-brained" out of sympathy for Hepzibah. But the subject of inheritance has by now too much bemused Hawthorne; he cannot maintain the light touch, and he abruptly makes of this one of the most thoughtful passages of the novel.

It all comes out the day Phoebe is examining the "hereditary marks" of one of the chickens—its odd plumage, head, and legs; it keeps "giving her a sagacious wink." Holgrave tells her that the marks betoken "the oddities of the Pyncheon family," and that the chicken itself is "a symbol of the life of the old house, embodying its interpretation, likewise, although an unintelligible one. . . ." And here Hawthorne's own voice breaks in on the whimsy to make the point: "It was a feathered riddle; a mystery hatched out of an egg, and just as mysterious as if the egg had been addle!"

The final part of this argument is that not even the human generations of the house support very thoroughly what life in the garden has confused. If the sins of the fathers are passed to the sons and their sons, why didn't it work that way with the Maules? The original Maule was a wronged, but also a vengeful and vindictive, man. His grandson was worse, and destroyed Alice Pyncheon in cold blood. The original "witchcraft" survives in the mesmerism that Holgrave is adept at. But the whole point of that inheritance is that Holgrave (presumably because he had submerged himself in the world, and purged himself—though not of his magnetic talents) is benign and cheerful and will *not* act as his inherited guilt should dictate. As for the four Pyncheons we meet, only the Judge really fits the thesis. Or does he? Representing the dominant strain in the Pyncheon line as Clifford does the recessive, he is the current "representative of hereditary qualities," "a little diluted," that crops up in each generation. He is, in line with the dilution, less sturdy and more nervous than his ancestor. But this observation leads Hawthorne to wonder if there is a "great system of human progress, which . . . may be destined gradually to spiritualize us," with "every ascending footstep" diminishing "the necessity for animal force. . . ." Now this is an interesting speculation, but not entirely appropriate to the man who aroused it—if, that is, he is really to represent the inheritance of tendencies that lead to crime. At another point, while discussing further what characteristics the Judge might actually owe his Puritan ancestor, Hawthorne may have become conscious of this confusion, for he suddenly throws up his hands, saying: "It is too fruitful a subject, this of hereditary resemblances. . . ." Since that subject was to be, and largely is, the subject of the book, the author's behavior here is very odd. But to realize that Hawthorne found the basic meaning of his novel in the course of writing it, and found that this meaning was by no means so simple as he had thought when he started, is to explain these contradictions.

Now a part of the symbolism of the Posies and the chickens bears on the cessation of hostility between the Maules and the Pyncheons. To show the efficacy of love the hens begin laying eggs, finally, and the Posies blossom. But as for all the examinations of heredity in the *Seven Gables*, there is only one thing they can add up to and they do. The point is expressed very well by that grotesque chicken, when the mystery of the laws of its descent is probed. It cannot smile like a sphinx or a Gioconda; it looks up and winks. The secret is "unintelligible": a "feathered riddle; a mystery hatched out of an egg." We do not know what, for good or ill, makes the animals or the flowers what they are. We do not know what makes us what we are.

There is, however, a better picture to carry away from the *Seven Gables* than the one of the chicken, for that scene is a little marred by the author's insistent and occasionally inap-

propriate jocularity. The better picture is, ultimately, one of
Hawthorne—or first of Clifford, then of Holgrave, as Hawthorne. The memorable image of Clifford is registered on that
famous afternoon when he was standing over the brink of
a parade that passed under his window, and saw it, in the
finest line of the novel, "as a mighty river of life, massive in
its tide, and black with mystery. . . ." It is this passage which
does most to give force to Holgrave's remark, made in the
middle of the action: "I begin to suspect that a man's bewilderment is the measure of his wisdom." When Herman Melville
read *The House of the Seven Gables* and came across that, he
checked it in the margin.

1957

HUCKLEBERRY FINN:
THE LITTLE LOWER LAYER

Huck Finn's prenatal experiences were mostly in the nature of misadventures which date back to the moment of his conception by a curiously indifferent parent. The novel was written as a sequel to *The Adventures of Tom Sawyer,* at the completion of which Twain had said, "By and by I shall take a boy of twelve and run him through life in the first person." He began the book, got about half through it, disliked it, lost interest, and put it aside for several years. Then a visit to the Mississippi River restimulated him and he returned to the manuscript, finishing it at a speed which amazed even him.*
Involved all the while, however, in a thousand other projects, he then went off lecturing, quite uninterested in his book, his biographer tells us glumly, except as to its sales, and quite unaware that he had written what is by far his best novel.†

A lot of publicity was provided to the end that Huck should make a lot of money, though. The best move in this direction was taken shortly after publication in 1884, not by Twain, but

---

* Or so the story used to be. See, however, Walter Blair's *Mark Twain and Huck Finn,* Berkeley: University of California Press, 1962.
† Two years before he died Clemens wrote out a statement and signed it: "I like the Joan of Arc best of all my books; and it *is* the best. . . ."

by a Concord (Massachusetts) Library Committee which found the book morally dangerous for youngsters and banished it from the shelves. This aroused a considerable furor, most of the combatants favoring the Concord view, and some even to the point of finding an exposure to the boy "vicious" for adults. Other public institutions followed New England's lead, and it was in the present century that a Brooklyn library removed the novel from its children's department on the unimpeachable ground that the boy told lies, itched, scratched, and said "sweat."

Today, of course, the book is permitted the young and is even forced on them. Not that an interest in the morals is past: they are now approved. Various people have made a good deal of this. They praise Huck as a "child of nature" who has lived close to the simple facts of life, and is "unperverted by the tyrannies of the village that would make a good boy of him." This approach naturally makes much of the conflict in the boy over what to do with the runaway Jim. This is a conflict between the village code and the human code, which is climaxed by Huck's decision to protect the slave in his escape, and which climaxes the whole book with Huck's "I studied a minute, sore of holding my breath, and then says to myself: 'All right, then, I'll *go* to hell!'" Of course if Huck were the child of nature alone, and were really unperverted by the village tyrannies, there would have been no conflict. But he is not. Life in a household dominated by women, and adventures with the relatively bourgeois Tom Sawyer, have complicated his early empty-barrel existence. He gets his moral stature not because he is "scornful of everything but himself and what he regards as right," but because he has an uneasy and courageous struggle with the values of St. Petersburg, and wins.

He is really a wonderful boy in many ways, and the pleasure of getting to know him as a person has certainly had a lot to do with the book's popularity. Very colorful and yet very real, Huck is about as attractive a character as one will meet in print. And while he never loses his identity as a particular and unforgettable youngster, he has for some people taken on epic size as a symbol. Just as American life can be seen as a continual debate between the legendary figures of Paul Bunyan and Rip Van Winkle, so the arguments are epitomized by Tom Sawyer and Huck Finn. Paul Bunyan is the man who gets things done. He expresses our drive for power and leadership. But if we love power we also despise drudgery, and so we are partly Rip, who hated exertion although he'd walk all day hunting. Victories accomplished in Bunyan's name mean hard work and self-denial, repressions and frustrations. A vicarious rebellion against thrift and labor results, and in a rather wistful way we love Van Winkle. No less a personage than Winston Churchill (once with T. S. Eliot, George Santayana, and Charles de Gaulle a staunch member of the International Mark Twain Society) testified that Tom Sawyer and Huck Finn "represent America" to him. This is because the Bunyan–Van Winkle dichotomy is repeated in them. Tom, like Paul, is bold in spirit and inventive of mind. He is a doer, the idol of free enterprise. Huck is a loafer. Faced with material problems, petty or vast, he slips away in the night. There are no figures to show how many daydreaming victims of respectability have climbed aboard the raft with him.

Since it has often been claimed that the book's popularity results from the fact that it cooperates with an American desire to play hooky, some might not think it the ideal classroom favorite it has become. But the editors of one edition of the novel "for high school use" merely reinforce the point by capitalizing on this subversive aspect, and in Some Teaching Suggestions forgo the usual discussions of Style, Plot, and Characterization to remark: "In order to quicken the curiosity of boys and girls, it may be sufficient . . . to suggest that anyone who has ever longed to run away from home and civilizing influences . . . to be a tramp . . . should read the story of Huck's wanderings." There is a kind of finality here that defeats all criticism, and it is also to be found in a letter Clemens himself once received from a little girl:

I am eleven years old, and we live on a farm near Rockville, Maryland. Once this winter we had a boy to work for us named John. We lent him "Huck Finn" to read, and one night he let his clothes out of the window and left in the night. The last we heard from him he was out in Ohio. . . .

Huck's journey seems a kind of national dream. It keeps cropping up. There is, for instance, the newspaper columnist who testifies for himself and "about a million other guys" that "maybe a thousand times, as boy and man," he has resolved: "So help me, someday I'm going to take a boat clear down the Mississippi. . . . Gosh, just think of shoving off . . . where the river begins to give promise of being wide and long, sort of lazying all the way. . . ."*

The Adventures of Huckleberry Finn is one of the most widely read and reread novels in America, and a perennial wish for escape in the boy's image is based on the book about him in the firmest sort of way. Huck is forever lighting out. He was on the loose in *Tom Sawyer*. He was taken in by the Widow Douglas, but "when I couldn't take it no longer I lit out" again. Tom talked him into returning to the proper and pious widow's, but even during his incarceration he slipped out nights and slept in the woods. In the novel that bears his name he is always taking off—not only from St. Petersburg

---

* In *Dark Laughter* (1925) the protagonist goes down the same river, and Sherwood Anderson writes: "Since he was a kid and had read Huckleberry Finn, he had kept some such notion in mind. Nearly every man who had lived long in the Mississippi Valley had that notion tucked away in him somewhere."

but also from most of the other places where he has been involved. He is returned once more to respectability at the end, only to determine that pretty soon he will make for the "territory." Tom Blankenship, a boy Sam Clemens knew and in part based his runaway on, is said (though it is doubtful) to have settled down, finally, in the West. But for Huck himself the escape seems permanent.

Apparently there is something vastly suggestive about this boy's escapism. Whatever it is seems to start in the novel when Huck—trapped by his father in an isolated cabin, abandoned at one point for three days, and "all over welts" from the blows of a hickory stick—makes an epic decision that has a little of the tone and motion and a bit of the appeal of something very like "myth." He has got to get out, and he is going:

I thought it all over, and I reckoned I would walk off with the gun and some lines, and take to the woods when I run away. I guessed I wouldn't stay in one place, but just tramp right across the country, mostly nighttimes, and hunt and fish to keep alive, and so get so far away that the old man nor the widow couldn't ever find me any more.

The river changed all this, of course, when the June rise provided first a canoe and next a raft. Then finally Huck and Nigger Jim escape together down a river that is beautiful, powerful, solemn, and full of wonder. Most people sense that the Mississippi has something to do with the way the novel holds and stays with them and draws them back. Some of them have spoken of "poetry" in this connection—of a "wilderness of moving water . . . the mysteries of fog and night and current," of Twain's having given to the river its "elementary place in the American experience" and even of the mighty stream as a "source of spiritual power." A movie called *Huckleberry Finn* was produced in 1939 with a bungling Mickey Rooney as impersonator, and there was one startling moment in the script when Mickey, in a tight spot, looked piously at the river and began to pray to it. It is hard to believe that T. S. Eliot, who like Clemens grew up beside the Mississippi, brought Mr. Rooney into the large circle of the men who have influenced him, but he was soon to begin some lines on the same river with the same perception: "I do not know much about gods; but I think that the river/Is a strong brown god. . . ."

It was D. H. Lawrence who once said: "You *must* look through the surface of American art, and see the inner diabolism of the symbolic meaning. Otherwise it is all mere childishness." This is a hopped-up remark, characteristic of Lawrence, and it contains as usual a kernel of truth worth more than the usual expositions of several sober writers. It seems pretty clear that *Huckleberry Finn* is to Lawrence's point—that something or other lies beneath its surface. Whatever it is that lies there speaks richly to people, whether of dreamy rebellions from the everyday concerns of their ordinary lives, or of gods, in a language strange to the ear which needs translating to be fully understood. Some symbol lies beneath this surface. People speak of "levels of meaning" in the novel—of a "legend," of something "forever true," of something "mythic" and of a night journey which "the whole world shares." Bernard De Voto, for one, was especially sensitive to this quality in the book. He wrote that "Huck sleeping under stars, or wakefully drifting through an immensity dotted only by far lights . . . satisfies blind gropings of the mind"—that there is something here which lies "beyond awareness."

Of course this is not the most precise way in the world of speaking. But when people use words like "legend" and "myth" here, they are trying to describe their reactions to something about which it is very difficult, if not impossible, to speak clearly. Some scholars believe that the word "myth" comes from the word "mü," which is imitative of the lowing of a cow and therefore inscrutable in denotation. But there is something about Huck's journey by water that moves his friends deeply, and even if it is a mystery we can talk about it.

Somehow the mythic or legendary quality of the novel—its glamour and escape value, and the invocations of the gods—and the deepest of all its levels must be bound up together. The basic appeal of the book is surely not accounted for with Huck as just a latter-day Van Winkle. This would be Huck without the river, and a landlocked version of the story would drain off with the water a good deal of the magic. In the same way the Mississippi loses meaning if we subtract from it a boy and a raft. The symbol is of Huck on a river.

The Mississippi was in point of fact a pretty glamorous place a century ago. Twain deleted from the picture the floating brothels he calls "steamboats," but he did not have to betray his desire to be honest about the giant stream in order to make it seem a wonderful and amazing body of water—a whole mile broad, and "awful still and grand," with logs drifting by black and silent, with everything dead quiet, and looking late and smelling late, and Jackson's Island standing up out of the middle of the stream big, dark, and solid, like a steamboat without lights. It was a different but still haunting place when the heat lightning was "squirting around low in the sky," and the leaves were beginning to shiver; or by real lightning "bright as glory," with the treetops "a-plunging about away off yonder in the storm," and a glare lighting up the white caps for a half mile around, the islands "looking dusty in the rain." The river is a very strange place, too. The June rise goes so high that Huck and Jim find themselves paddling among the animal-crowded treetops of the island they had been living on. A house goes past, and in it all over the walls were "the ignorantist kind" of words and pictures made with charcoal, and a naked man shot in the back and dead for days. There is nothing unnatural about a steamboat at night: "She would turn a corner and her lights would wink out and her pow-wow shut off and leave the river still again; and by and by her waves would get to us, a long time after she was gone, and joggle the raft a bit." But it made you "feel crawly," as again when, in a fog, the rafts with the men beating tin pans to avoid collisions go by, invisible but loud.

Yet the river counts for most with us when Huck is riding it under the conditions which are more normal to him, and it is here that we should go searching the symbolic meaning, buried deep and yet most compelling, and perhaps even diabolical. The normal mode of Huck's existence is escape, and the flight downstream starts when—having got loose from his father—he shoves off in the dead of the moonlight for Jackson's Island. Here he joins Jim, and gets a raft, and then one night, fearing capture, they

got out the raft and slipped along down in the shade, past the foot of the island dead still—never saying a word.

There might seem to be nothing very remarkable or suggestive about that by itself. But this is only the first of a series of almost identical departures which, gradually, begin to add up. Three things characterize each one of them: ease, silence, and darkness. After a while these things begin to grow on you. The escapes become a consistent symbol, and here lies the key to the novel's least accessible compartment.

The escape after the fraud of "The Royal Nonesuch," for example, is described as briefly as the departure from the island, and in exactly the same terms:

We struck the raft at the same time, and in less than two seconds we was gliding downstream, all dark and still, and edging towards the middle of the river, nobody saying a word.

Once again: gliding, dark, still.

When you are on a river, and untied, there is nothing to it.

There is no rowing, downstream on a river. There is no machinery to start or tend and listen to. There are not even sails to set and trim: you just let go and you move away. Twice, all that is involved is the cutting of a rope, as for instance when the two companions flee the victims of another attempted fraud. Huck, reaching the raft in a very great hurry, yells to Jim,

"Cut loose and let her slide!"
So in two seconds away we went a-sliding down the river, and it *did* seem so good to be free again. . . .

There are appeals in this recurring process beyond the obvious ones. There is of course escape for Huck and Jim, and escape for the reader, which mingles with all the other escapes in the book. But here, too, there is a deeper appeal, the deepest of the novel. This strange journey, blurred and mythic, down a glamorous river, becomes a very special and supremely effortless flight into a dark and silent unknown: we escape more than we are aware of and to something from which— if this were not vicarious—we could not return.

There are more brightly lit passages in the novel about the way Huck and Jim spend their more relaxed hours that are wondrously attractive, and the source for many daydreams. Mornings, the runaways would hide and watch the daylight come—"not a sound anywhere—perfectly still—just like the whole world was asleep." They watch the river's "lonesomeness," and by and by lazy off to sleep. The night's running has the same quality of drowsiness, of nothing much happening. This works to break off the sharp edges of Huck's perception, to smooth the thing, to make it vague, general, magical, in some way portentous and in some sense "mythic":

It was kind of solemn, drifting down the big still river, laying on our backs looking up at the stars, and we didn't ever feel like talking aloud, and it warn't often that we laughed . . . nothing ever happened to us at all—that night, nor the next nor the next.

In this atmosphere of forgetfulness, we relax our defenses. We are without care, and the river is beautiful. We go ashore, occasionally, and when fleeing what invariably turns out to be some difficulty there we are relieved to return to the water, and ready to experience symbolically the process which takes us with such dreamy ease into the black and breathless silence. There must be Freudians who, with a suggestion of knowing smiles on their lips, would leap to explain this "mystery": These gliding escapes into the silent darkness are simply lyrical expressions of the "death instinct," or of that desire to "return to the womb" which is about the same thing as dying, with an added advantage in the possibility of being reborn. Water metaphors frequently have to do with birth, and we believe that the first life on land actually did come from the sea; we still come into the world from a kind of salt water called amniotic; the French have variations of the same word, *mer* and *mère*, for sea and mother. And there are notable precedents for this symbolism right in American literature. It is as a substitute for suicide that Ishmael takes to the sea in *Moby-Dick*, he specifically says; the ocean is really a death-symbol in that novel, and the *Pequod* offers a temporary passage out of human existence. When the sea spoke to Whitman it was the "delicious" word "death" that it whispered over and over. Here then, in another masterpiece, Twain has all unawares drawn up from his subconscious a metaphor for dying. It moves us because, diabolically, we do not wholly wish to live.

There must also be Jungians who would be quick to explain what is going on in this flight, for here seems to be a perfect example of a psychic reaction in readers which is out of proportion to its exciting cause, and must therefore—according to Carl Jung—lead us to suspect the presence of an "archetype," a pattern in the "collective unconscious" of the race, which has been stirred. Huck's escapes by water are vastly more suggestive than some of the *Archetypal Patterns in Poetry* investigated by Maude Bodkin. Here is one of those downward movements "toward quiescence or toward disintegration and death" that she wrote about. Or, not much different, here is a repetition of the archetype of rebirth, which she found in night journeys.

Of course there is no conclusive evidence for such claims as these. And yet the responses of countless modern readers to some "mythic," unknown quality in Twain's story of a boy escaping down a river keep one from closing his ears utterly to the "depth psychologists." There is no more need to accept the existence of a collective unconscious than of a death instinct in order to understand that the dream of a final flight from a very imperfect life could powerfully attract us. We do participate with Huck in a series of escapes made glamorous by a mighty river. Repeated over and over in the same terms, the process compels, and does establish itself as symbolic. This time the raft has broken loose from a wrecked ship. Huck plunges into a rowboat, and

I out with my knife and cut the rope, and away we went!

We didn't touch an oar, and we didn't speak nor whisper, nor hardly even breathe. We went gliding swift along, dead silent, past the tip of the paddle-box, and past the stern; then in a second or two more we was a hundred yards below the wreck, and the darkness soaked her up, every last sign of her, and we was safe, and knowed it.

Or ever the silver cord be loosed—cut with a knife. We, too, are released again from a noisy and difficult life. In a second we are free, and do not lift a finger. Motionless ourselves, the black stream moves us mutely and endlessly down. Darkness, silence and ease overwhelm us: we are safe, and we know it, in the shadow of the last escape of all.

It is even easier to understand the magnetism of this event if the life one flees is sufficiently frustrating, disgusting, and shocking. It is well known how the successful Clemens steamed under the pressures of the very respectability he sought and gained, and well known that by 1884 a corrosive despair for humanity, full of evil and duplicity, was beginning to oppress him. In writing Huck's adventures he expressed, among other things, his impatience with the middle-class status he had attained. But it is seldom remarked that in re-creating Hannibal and the river which flowed by it, he was extraordinarily conscious of the facts of hideous violence and death, and expressed a horror of them that he had learned as a boy and had never forgot.

The Adventures of Huckleberry Finn has so much about it that is hilarious or idyllic that our attention is easily diverted from the spill of blood that seeps through its pages, giving them a large part of their meaning. Life on the Mississippi around 1845 could be gory: Twain based the novel largely on experiences he himself had undergone as a boy or had known intimately of, and had never quite got over. We are often disinclined to consider how peaceful and restricted, aside from television, is the average recent American childhood compared to childhoods of other times and of other places today. Many people have become adults without ever having seen "live" a human being killed. Plenty of boys have never looked at a corpse, and very few of them have witnessed a murder.

Things were different with young Clemens and thus with Huck. The difference is profoundly important to the novel. Sam often looked hard at slaves chained together flat on the dirt in the baking summer sun, awaiting shipment to the market. He was a boy in Hannibal during a time when that town was terrorized by a lynching, murderous gang ludicrously called "The Black Avengers of the Spanish Main." A cave near Hannibal contained as a public amusement the body of a young girl preserved in alcohol; it was arranged so that one could seize the corpse by the hair, and drag it to the surface in order to study the face. When he was ten years old the boy saw a man take a lump of iron and crush a Negro's skull with it; then Sam spent an hour in fascinated horror watching the slave die. One night he heard a drunk announce that he was going to the house of a certain widow for the express purpose of raping her daughter, and Sam followed him, lurking close by while he bellowed his intentions outside the girl's house. The widow approached the man with defiance, counted ten, and then gave the swaying fellow a musket charge full in the chest. At this point the townspeople collected like ants, but Sam had had enough. He went home to dream of the murder and was not disappointed, he says.

One night it was not a dream. Trying to sleep in his father's office, he became aware of some awful presence, and shortly the moon revealed a naked corpse with a hole in the middle of its chest. On another occasion he was playing near the spot where a runaway slave had drowned days before, and by accident he jarred loose the body, which had not been located, but which now popped up at him headfirst half out of the water, and seemed certainly to be chasing him as he fled. He watched knife fights in Hannibal, and at the end of one of them the loser fell dead at the feet of the boy who had wormed his way in for a good look. He was also witness, at noon on Main Street, to the murder of a man named Smarr. Kind persons placed a large Bible on the chest of the dying man. As he wrote years later, Sam "gasped and struggled for breath under the crush of that vast book for many a night."

The murders of Mr. Smarr and of the drunkard who was shot in the chest by the contemptuous widow are the direct sources for the murder of a man named Boggs in *Huckleberry*

Finn. Of the shocks young Clemens was exposed to as a boy, many others found their way, years later, into the novel. These facts help explain what might otherwise seem a very curious thing: that with no exceptions but the rather irrelevant Tom Sawyer scenes which open and close *Huckleberry Finn,* every major episode in the novel ends in violence, in physical brutality, and usually in death. All along the way there is bloodshed and pain. There are thirteen separate corpses. All this despite the fact that Twain, in planning his book, made many notes for similar episodes which he did not use.

He used enough. There is a woman drowned so long her face is a face no longer, and there is Pap's face, which is not much of an improvement—"white; not like another man's white, but a white to make a body sick, a white to make a body's flesh crawl,—a tree-toad white, a fish-belly white." Until he escapes this face Huck is constantly being beaten. He is twice caught and thrashed on his way to school, and when Pap locks him in the log hut he is worked over whenever the man comes in drunk. Huck likes the hunting and fishing they do to stay alive, but after two months of regular pounding he cannot stand it any more. Before he is able to escape, however, he spends one night with a father who has at last drunk himself into delirium, who hammers the floor, feels snakes crawling across his face, and tries to kill the boy with a knife.

Then there is the naked man, shot in the back, with a face Jim describes as too ghastly to look at, and another man who is tied to the floor of a sinking boat, "sort of blubbering" for his life while his companions leave him to go down with the wreck. Still more brutal is the murder of Boggs, a harmless drunkard, "the best-natured old fool in Arkansaw." Boggs is shot down in cold blood in the middle of a town street by a contemptuous man whom he has been exuberantly insulting. He comes out of his alcoholic haze long enough to yell in terror, "Lord, don't shoot!" and his daughter runs to help him.

But Colonel Sherburn shoots anyway, a Bible is placed on the dying man's chest ("they tore open his shirt first, and I seen where one of the bullets went in"), and the screaming girl is pulled off him, and taken away. Then (in one of the great moments in fiction) a long, lanky man in the street re-enacts the event to the intense satisfaction of all those who have assembled at the scene, and a dozen people offer him a drink. Not even the Duke and Dauphin depart in the humorous way that is so often taken to be the way of the book. The last time Huck sees them they are, to be sure, tarred, feathered, and astraddle a rail. But this, Huck makes clear, is not a funny picture as far as *he* is concerned: it is "a dreadful thing to see."

The most violent episode in the book is, of course, the Grangerford-Shepherdson feud. In all the novel, this is the horror Huck finds hardest to stomach. The Grangerford family takes him in, and soon all four of its males are killed, as well as two or three Shepherdsons. The death of Buck—Huck's young friend—is the worst. He and his cousin, both already shot, jump in the river and swim downstream as two Shepherdson men run along the bank, firing at the boys and yelling out, "Kill them, kill them!" Later Huck pulls the bodies from the river, and covers the faces. This is the most terrible experience in the novel for Huck, first because he so admired Buck and his relatives, and second because the slaughter comes on top of so much more of what sickens.

It is absolutely essential to an understanding of either the boy or the novel about him to see what the effect of all this brutality has been. It is also very easy to see: an overexposure to violence has finally wounded the protagonist.

Each episode makes a mark. The conversation of the robbers on the *Walter Scott,* with the man on the floor blubbering for his life, takes all the wind out of Huck; he cannot help thinking about the drowning; it is "dreadful." The swindle of the Wilks family also bothers him a great deal, and when the King sold the colored servants, and they were all crying together, "it most made me down sick to see it." The departure of the King and the Duke also "made me sick."

Each mark leaves a scar: these are not passing upsets for Huck. About the picture of the slaves who are being separated he says, "I can't get it out of my memory." And the sight of Buck Grangerford and his cousin being shot to death as they swam along in the water, already hurt:

made me so sick I most fell out of the tree. I ain't a-going to tell *all* that happened—it would make me sick again to do that. I wished I hadn't ever come ashore that night to see such things. I ain't ever going to get shut of them—lots of times I dream about them.

The aspect of these brutal episodes that is most relevant to the main plot of a boy going down a river on a raft is quite simply this: they serve to *wound* him. His experience of violence has made him sick. Innumerable readers have tried it, but the plain truth is that Huckleberry Finn, boy or book, cannot really be understood without this clear perception. *Now* we may look at what has happened to this uncomplicated "child of nature." He may be still "unspoiled," but from having been knocked about so much he is very bruised. Better he had never come ashore that night to see such things, but he came. Now exposed to more bloodshed, drowning, and sudden death than he can handle, he is himself their casualty. And Twain—working from his own bitter experience—could predict with unhappy confidence: he isn't ever going to get shut of them. Lots of times he dreams about them.

There are other things besides bad dreams which interfere with Huck's peace. Among them are a very active mind which he cannot put to rest, and a growing bitterness about human nature. He cannot sleep, he tells us: "I couldn't, somehow, for thinking." His encounter with the frauds called the Duke and the Dauphin is supposed to be funny. But Huck is not amused; they disgust him with mankind in general. He is wounded, and bitter, and suffering from both insomnia and nightmare, and he rebels. His rebellion brings about the crisis of the novel when he, utterly perplexed and sickened by his experiences, tries to decide whether he will "steal a poor old woman's nigger" or protect him. He is all conflict, and tries to pray, but the words won't come. Finally, tortured, he decides. He will protect the slave, although to him this means taking up wickedness again, and eternal punishment in the hereafter. He has deserted the values of the society of his time.

This is of course his second desertion, really. Completely dissatisfied with his pious foster mother and the effeminate respectability which surrounded her, he had already run away from St. Petersburg. Now, off on his own, and exposed to the violence and evil of society as a whole, he renounces it. He goes on now outside its ways. If it is good, he is wicked. And if it aims for heaven, he will go elsewhere.

The fact that it is in the chapter immediately following this crisis that Mark Twain turns the story over to Tom Sawyer, abruptly transforming Huck into a simple narrator, a straight man who sets up jokes for the comedian, is not really so hard to explain. The rest of the novel is irrelevant to almost everything that has gone before, but the common explanation that Twain simply didn't know the difference is unacceptable. At this point in the story the boy is about as far from the carefree, laughing urchin he is almost universally mistaken for as it is possible to get. He is a wounded and damaged boy. He will never get over the terror he has seen and been through, is guilt-ridden and can't sleep at night for his thoughts. When he is able to sleep he is tortured with bad dreams. Wildly superstitious, his waking world is made fearful by the spirits that people it; he has broken with the morality he has been taught, and is so disgusted by the evil and duplicity of his fellows that he declares himself finally to be ashamed of them. This is a boy who has undergone an unhappy process of growing up—clean out of his creator's grasp. So cockily Twain was going to take a boy at twelve and run him through life in the first person, and so rapidly the boy got out of hand. Once Twain had planted in Huck the complications he suffered himself—they had seen the same horrors, dreamed the same nightmares, suffered blamelessly the same guilt, and developed the same distaste for humanity—it was easier to write comedy, and revert to the Huck that Tom Sawyer thought he knew. Precisely as Clemens could never solve his own complications, save in the unmitigated but sophomoric pessimism of his last books, so he could not solve them for Huck, who had got too hot to handle and was dropped. What the man never realized was that in his journey by water he had been hinting at a solution all along: an excessive exposure to violence and death produced first a compulsive fascination with dying, and finally an ideal symbol for it.

1952

AMERICAN FICTION,
AMERICAN LIFE:
An Address to the Peace Corps

I would like to approach my topic with a bit of autobiography, if you'll excuse it, for I have had a slightly strange experience which has a sort of relevance for you.

A few years ago I read a paper about literary criticism at one of the meetings of the Modern Language Association (the English professor's equivalent of a plumber's convention), held that year in Washington, D.C. When I was done there was the customary polite applause, and a couple of dumb questions; that, I thought, was the customary end of that (and just as well, too, by the way). But it turned out that a kind of spy for the State Department had sneaked into the Statler, and a few months later I found myself in India—not deported, exactly, but giving lectures on American literature to the faculties of a series of Indian universities. The idea, as I understood it, was to encourage them to see that there *is* an American literature, and to initiate courses in it. Behind this idea was the notion, I believe, that a wider knowledge and a deeper understanding of our writing would work toward a better understanding of us, and thus, in an honorable way, promote our interests in the Orient. And behind that was the notion—at least in my mind—that I was implying, though never stating, a message, which was: Don't judge us by Hollywood, and *Life* magazine (which Indians detested, incidentally); look for the true America in our serious writers; more specifically, look for at least a part of modern America in modern American fiction—in our best novels, which, I should add now lest you doubt it later, I very much admire.

It is obvious that I was bringing American literature to foreigners, which is not what you are about to be up to. But a part of my point is that if one doesn't bring it to them they will bring it to you. Intellectuals, that is, of all grades of competence and sophistication the world over, are intensely interested in the likes of Hemingway and Faulkner, and many of them are feverish to discuss the matter with a live educated American. Now this can be a curious—possibly an unnerving—experience for the likes of you and me, knowing as we do so many people who do not honor intellectuals in the first place, and couldn't tell William Faulkner from William Cullen Bryant and care less in the second.

Well, it was a rough trip, punctuated inauspiciously by Little Rock at the start and Sputnik I toward the end, with two weeks of Communist Kerala in between, and endless curry, constant traveling, unbelievably uninteresting hotels, and prohibition, and condiments that can take the top of your head off. Indeed, I ended in the hospital with nurses around the clock. But although I would gladly supply you with some colorful details about intestines, liver, and other parts in distress, my story has less to do with how *I* fared than with how an idea made out—the idea, that is, that non-Americans can learn a good deal that is true and valuable about twentieth-century American life by reading the best twentieth-century American literature. In short, does our literature reflect our life? More specifically, does our novel reflect it?

As it happens, this isn't a bad question to discuss, either. It has a highly significant history in this country, it is full of complexity, occasionally of irony, and it raises very large questions, both about the nature of literature (not to mention art itself) and about the nature of the country which *you* will soon be reflecting and representing.

Now the twentieth-century American novel began very conveniently, and precisely on time—with the publication in 1900 of a book by Theodore Dreiser called *Sister Carrie*. We say it "began" with this novel because there are attitudes in it which, though they had deep roots, came to a sort of American fruition in this work. Very loosely speaking, these attitudes are "Naturalistic." Naturalism is a pessimistic form of determinism which holds that there is nothing above or beyond nature (like a God), that man is essentially an animal (who does not possess free will), and that his life is a pointless struggle (in which morals are meaningless) against blind forces that pitilessly overwhelm him.

As for the novel itself, it tells the story, as many of you know, of an ordinary girl, Carrie, who comes to the big city, Chicago, has an affair with a salesman and then with the unhappily married manager of a fashionable restaurant. He, Hurstwood, steals money from his employers and he and Carrie run away together, are caught, released, and then he tries for a new career in New York. He is unsuccessful, eventually becomes a beggar, and then kills himself. Meanwhile Carrie, although she has no great ability, becomes a famous actress, remaining however as unhappy at the end of the book as she was at the start. She goes up in the world, then, as Hurstwood goes down, and there is no real accounting for that fact; she is not remarkable or talented or worthy. Nor, despite the theft—a momentary lapse of judgment, and freakish—is there any real explaining why Hurstwood goes into such a desperate decline. This, I think Dreiser is saying, is life. That is: there is no particular connection between virtue and reward. What you get has very little to do with what you deserve. In his other, best-known novel, *An American Tragedy*, Dreiser tells the story of a poor boy who, on his way up the social scale, somewhat passively murders his pregnant girl friend, is tried, and condemned to death—though, as the author persuasively argues and his title suggests, it was really America that was to "blame."

By the mid-Twenties, when Dreiser wrote his *American Tragedy*, two other important writers were intensively examining the national scene: Sherwood Anderson and Sinclair Lewis, who have been referred to, respectively, as the Village Mystic and the Village Atheist. Anderson is best remembered for his studies of what he called "grotesques": small-town Americans who have been thwarted in love, and terribly warped by the lack of it. Lewis, the first American to win world-wide recognition with a Nobel Prize, was a kind of iconoclast who denounced by satire the homely norm of American life as dull, stupid, narrow, and fatuous. One after another, and to vast applause, our small towns and their citizens, our businessmen and social workers, the ministry, the medical profession, and other aspects of our society, came in for his amusing but withering ridicule.

It is not so much of Lewis and Anderson, however, that most of us think today when we think of the Twenties, but more of a slightly younger group whose careers were beginning in that decade: Hemingway, Faulkner, John Dos Passos, and Scott Fitzgerald. Hemingway's best novels of this period (many would say his best novels, period) were *The Sun Also Rises* and *A Farewell to Arms*. The first told the story of the aimless, dissolute, expatriated members of a "lost generation" in general, and in particular the bitter, hopeless story of a man who had been emasculated in the war. The second is even more disillusioned and pessimistic. It deals with the war itself —with a man who is forced to desert the army in which he has been fighting, and who loses his mistress as well, when she dies bearing his child. Faulkner we recognize chiefly as the author of a many-volumed saga of the Deep South, a bitter comic-tragedy of the abysmal decadence of its old aristocrats, and the hilarious but horrifying rise of the absolutely unscrupulous newcomers who displace them. A violent, macabre, and Gothic saga of a land cursed by slavery and ravaged by the Civil War, the mansions are inhabited by the drunken, impotent, and helpless remains of the once-proud, and the rats are overrunning the mansions. "Hemingway's world," as one of his critics has pointed out, "is one in which things do not grow and bear fruit, but explode, break, decompose, or are eaten away. . . . [His] characters do not 'mature' in the ordinary sense, do not become 'adult.' It is impossible to picture them in a family circle, going to the polls to vote, or making out their income tax returns. . . . It is a world seen through a crack in the wall by a man who is pinned down by gunfire." And Faulkner's world is even more garishly populated.

If one were to make a prolonged visit to a hospital for the insane, talking at length to its inmates, one would have as balanced a view of a cross section of humanity as one receives from the fiction of Faulkner. . . . You may search his novels from end to end without finding a single family in which the relationships are not twisted either by perversion or insanity.

Now this is a very hostile (and a very inferior) critic speaking (one J. Donald Adams by name), but he is within smelling-distance of a point, and if a long-established and well-known American critic is unable to see what Faulkner is doing, what are non-Americans to make of him? At the center of his stage are a famous woman who lives for many years with the corpse of her lover ("A Rose for Emily"); a degenerate criminal who rapes a college girl with a corncob (*Sanctuary*—she enters a brothel where she and a new lover put on sexual exhibitions for his vicarious pleasure); a boy who elopes with a cow, and a young man who desires above all women his sister (a girl who gives herself to any man who wants her, and also desires her brother—*The Sound and the Fury*); a man who lets his daughter die in childbirth, a white nymphomaniac who gets herself into a delirium because she thinks of her sexual partner as a Negro (he later cuts her head nearly off, and then is lynched, and emasculated with a butcher's knife—*Light in August*).

I could go on like that, but there is less sensational business to attend to. The fact is, however, that when we turn to the other two most prominent novelists of this era in America, John Dos Passos and Scott Fitzgerald, the situation is not a whole lot more cheerful. Dos Passos' best work appears, of course, in his trilogy, *USA*. *USA* is an epic of monumental, national failure, is the tragedy of a modern industrial society in which the individual is simply wrecked. A flat, sour drabness pervades all three volumes. There is no joy, no happiness; success is empty and failure is pregnant; all the lives are toneless and dismal. But the whole thing seems intensely real, and so it follows that the indictment is overwhelming.

At first glance Fitzgerald presents a more attractive picture, but second glances into his better novels, *The Great Gatsby* and *Tender Is the Night,* begin to penetrate the superficial party atmosphere, and to correct that picture. Gatsby is an amiable, decent man of suspicious wealth who is murdered through the absolutely unscrupulous plotting of some self-important decadent aristocrats, while a giant ash dump serves as an eloquent commentary on the meaning of the lives of the characters. The latter novel reveals the appalling disintegration of a few apparently glamorous, expatriated aristocrats; the heroine is periodically insane as the result of an incestuous girlhood relationship with her father, and the hero is destroyed by his patient.

Nor is the picture much more pleasing when we trace the story of our fiction past this halcyon period and into the present—through Thomas Wolfe and John Steinbeck to the really brutal war novels like *The Naked and the Dead* and *From Here to Eternity,* or to the truly poisonous imagination of the likes of Truman Capote, or finally to the work of the most widely known young American writer, J. D. Salinger, in whose fiction the most appropriate response to the world his really worthwhile protagonists are forced to inhabit seems to be a nervous breakdown.

Now I would argue that I have given a fair—however sketchy—picture of what the ordinary non-American reader would find in the best fiction of our best twentieth-century novelists. Have I given a picture of life in America that is more valid than our trashy movies and our lady's magazines will give? "What," says the astonished foreign reader of our better novels, "is life so utterly grim and pointless in America as I read in Dreiser? Are people so isolated and misshapen as in Anderson? Such ridiculous and stupid hicks as in Lewis? So bitter, so desperate as in Hemingway? So depraved as Faulkner? So depressed and depressing as Dos Passos presents them? Is it as disheartening as Fitzgerald has it? Are there *really* no families in the United States? No homes? No heterosexual parents who love each other and their children? Not even any passably happy and decent citizens? No religion? No culture? No hope? I don't think I understand this country very well."

Just before I went to India a lot of people were pretty stirred up about this state of affairs—about the picture of life in America they have, as compared to the picture they fear others will get from reading our best books. Many of the foremost journals in the country—*The New York Times, Harper's, Life,* for instance—opened their columns to this discussion. What will the world think of us? It is bad for our prestige abroad. Here we are relatively happy, and the most prosperous nation in the history of the world, wishing for both political and psychological reasons to be liked abroad everywhere. And what do you find in our books? Misery, degradation, despair. "Is it right," one sympathetic foreign observer wanted to know, "that the great *flowering* of the American novel should hamper America's leadership of the free world?" Or let us consider the way the point is put by *Life* magazine, whose editorial committees do on occasion and however misguidedly concern themselves with important questions:

Ours is the most powerful nation in the world. It has had a decade of unparalleled prosperity. It has gone further than any other society in the history of man toward creating a truly classless society. Yet it is still producing a literature which sounds sometimes as if it were written by an unemployed homosexual living in a packing-box shanty on the city dump. . . .

And, after coming out strong for a novel by Herman Wouk called *Marjorie Morningstar,* they cap the argument with the impression that a French critic got of us by reading our fiction: "A hypocritical society based on the power of money, racial prejudice, sexual taboos. Exile, alcohol, suicide seem the only escape."

The notion here is, of course, that if our literature does not reflect the beneficent and bountiful facts of our life it is false, untrue to the country of its origin, and dangerous.

If we had time I think I could trace this argument back at the very least to Thomas Jefferson for you—back, that is, to his agrarian view of the country as the world's healthy answer to the decadence of urban Europe. But in our literature the argument classically begins with a man named William Dean Howells. Himself a novelist, Howells once reviewed a translation of Dostoevski's *Crime and Punishment,* and in the course of it he remarked that "whoever struck a note so profoundly

tragic in American fiction would do a false and mistaken thing.
. . ." Life is not so bad here: "Our novelists, therefore, concern
themselves with the more smiling aspects of life, which are
the more American. . . ." It is "the large, cheerful average of
health and success and happy life" which is "peculiarly
American."

Later Robert Frost reinforced this opinion in verse:

> It makes the guild of novel writers sick
> To be expected to be Dostoievskis
> On nothing worse than too much luck and comfort.

Just before this Frost had asked:

> . . . How are we to write
> The Russian novel in America
> As long as life goes so unterribly?

And I recall that more recently, during an investigation of
Communist activity in Hollywood, Mrs. Leila Rogers (the
estimable mother of Ginger Rogers) testified that a certain
movie was unAmerican because it was "gloomy."

Precisely Howells' point, if in a vulgar reduction; nor is the
Howells view of American experience the ignorant error it is
often taken for; it is a half- or partial truth. But most serious
fiction in our century is not exactly "smiling."

It is a happy fact for whatever coherence this discussion
may pretend to that Theodore Dreiser springs directly out of,
and in direct antagonism to, the Howells view. Modern American fiction was conceived—not born yet, but conceived—on
the very day (somewhere in the mid-1890's) when Dreiser sat
down and began "examining the current magazines." They
did reflect the smiling aspects of American life, and his dis-
satisfaction with them was epochal:

I was never more confounded than by the discrepancy existing between my own observations and those displayed here, the beauty

and peace and charm to be found in everything, the almost complete absence of any reference to the coarse and vulgar and the cruel and the terrible. . . . Love was almost invariably rewarded . . . dreams came true . . . with such an air of assurance, omniscience and condescension, that I was quite put out by my own lacks and defects. They . . . wrote of nobility of character and sacrifice and the greatness of ideals and joy in simple things. . . . I had no such tales to tell, and however much I tried, I could not think of any.

And so he wrote *Sister Carrie*, which was a tale he *had* to tell. And what happened? Although he did find a firm to print it, for a long time the book was not effectively distributed because the wife of one of his publishers, a lady somewhat like Howells, named Doubleday, stopped it.* And when it did get out and was generally read, one of the most distinguished professors in America, Stuart Pratt Sherman, put his stern, magisterial seal of disapproval on it: the book was unacceptable because it was "outside American life." More recently William Faulkner wrote *Sanctuary*, a wild and horrifying melodrama apparently far more open to that charge. Indeed Faulkner told us in a preface to that novel that in a deliberate attempt to make a quick dollar he had invented "the most horrific tale I could imagine." (A highly successful attempt, one might add, since this is the best-selling of his books; and a successful statement, too, since the professors and critics took him at his word, which is a bad habit they have when dealing with writers and what they say about their own books.)

But what of the truth? One thing we may say with confidence is that Professor Sherman didn't know as much as he

---

* This "myth" has recently been corrected by Donald Pizer in his critical edition of the novel (New York: Norton, 1970), but the basic point—Doubleday, Page's dire objections to the book—remains unchanged.

might have about American life, which Dreiser's story was very much a part of. Sister Carrie was Dreiser's own sister, and her unhappy story was substantially true; indeed where Dreiser changed things he brightened the picture, for in "real life" the tale was more depressing, sordid, and "Russian." In the same way, Faulkner did not "invent" a wild and horrifying tale in *Sanctuary:* substantially it, too, happened in America, and he knew the story well. His rapist was an actual Memphis gangster named Pumphrey; his coed was a real Ole Miss coed; and I am told by an expert on Faulkner that the almost incredibly offensive object in the book was in life "worse than" the one specified. These things are not at all "outside American life," though some professors are. But are they representative of it? Do they reflect it? Even to ask the question points up its absurdity.

Let me read to you a passage in which Robert Penn Warren, himself a novelist, confronts our problem. He starts this way, by backing off a little:

Once upon a time there was a nation, which we shall call X. At the time of which we write this nation stood at a moment of great power and great promise. A few generations earlier it had concluded a long and bloody civil war to achieve unity. More recently, in that unity, it had won a crashing victory over foreign foes. It had undergone, and was undergoing, a social revolution; there was unparalleled prosperity, a relaxing of old sanctions and prejudices, a widening of opportunity for all classes, great rewards for energy and intelligence. Its flag was on strange seas; its power was felt in the world. It was, even, producing a famous literature.

But—and here is the strange thing in that moment of energy and optimism—a large part, the most famous part, of that literature exhibited violence, degradation and despair as part of the human condition: tales of the old time of the civil war, tales of lust and horror, brother pimping for sister, father lusting for daughter, a head of the state doting on a fair youth, an old man's eyes plucked out, another old man killed in his sleep, friendship betrayed, obligations forgone, good men cursing the gods, and the whole scene drenched in blood. Foreigners encountering this literature might well conclude that the Land of X was peopled by degenerates sadly lacking in taste, manners and principle.

And then Mr. Warren came to the point. He was not, as some of you have guessed, talking about the situation in modern America. X is England in the great age of Elizabeth, the age that produced perhaps the greatest literature the world has ever seen. The idea that since America is enjoying a period of great prosperity our literature should reflect this success has obviously got something wrong with it. Indeed it is drowned in confusion.

Since it is entirely possible that some of you will one day be faced with a foreign friend of this country, who in order to learn more about us once made his way very painfully through, say, a Faulkner novel (for Faulkner is difficult reading even for Americans), and emerged wide-eyed with dismay, it might be useful if I tried to spell out what some of the chief misconceptions about the relationship of art and life seem to me to be. If you should happen to see any sense in what I say now, and happen to remember some of it then, you just might find opportunity to use it. For clarity and simplicity I shall enumerate my points in a one, two, three fashion. (Or so I tell my classes: the real reason is that this way I don't have to compose any transitions.)

I. Serious literature is never a reflection of life. If people want to employ this sort of terminology they should change the language: literature is a refraction of life, and it cannot do without that distinction. The good writer does not mirror what is around him. He presents what he has encountered in one way or another—if only in his dreams or nightmares—as its rays have been deflected through his own, individual eyes. It is the angle of refraction, which distinguishes the

quality of his vision, that we reject or esteem. (I am simplify-
ing wildly, but a certain amount of that is necessary for present
purposes, and I am not done yet.)

II. Art is not life, but an ordering and an intensification of
it. Nobody really wants "life" in literature, for life as we all
know is a mess, an affair of utter disorder and sprawl, and for
long and frequent stretches is so stupifyingly tedious that to
read about it as it "really is" would shortly drive us mad. This
cliché, "Art imitates Life," handed me and perhaps you in high
school, is generally pinned on Aristotle (who will survive it).
His thesis was not unguarded, however; he did allow for the
artist eliminating the accidental (which I called ordering) and
for heightening the essential (intensification) so as to get at
the significant. But this still may play down the role the
imagination enjoys in art, for as someone said a long time ago,
"Imitation will fashion what it has seen, but imagination will
go on to what it has not seen." The "pleasure of recognition"
in literature—seeing on the printed page what we have often
seen in life, but seldom or never before seen written down—
can be very rewarding and is quite generally available to
readers. But the pleasures of vision are deeper and more rewarding and enduring.

The fact that life is frequently boring and takes a lot of
working on before it becomes literature explains among other
things why literature is a form of escape. I know that "escape
literature" is a dirty term, but the fact is that in a sense all
literature is escape literature. It varies enormously to be sure
in quality, seriousness, and so forth, and it matters more what
we escape to than from, but there is that point again: nobody
really wants to read about life precisely and exactly as he
knows it. This helps to explain as well why tragedy is perhaps
the greatest of all forms of literature. It may seem odd that we
should relish tragedy in our books as we assuredly do not in our
lives, but it is the most exhilarating, and the most ennobling,

of all literary experiences, and it requires a very high degree of ordering and intensification. At a low level there is the shop-girl's well-known preference for a teary ending at the movies, or the housewife's addiction to the absolutely desperate situations of soap opera, but at the other end there is Ahab, in the stupendous tragedy of *Moby-Dick*, who cries out "My topmost greatness lies in my topmost grief." It is a remark worth pondering, if you never have. But to get on:

III. Serious fiction in America has generally operated, at least since Hawthorne, Melville, and Poe, as a reaction against the facile optimisms our country periodically produces. These important writers all are saying, as Melville said that Hawthorne did, "No! in thunder" to the cheerful, affirmative, and often commercial popular views of their times. As we have seen, Dreiser began both his career and modern American fiction in the identical reaction, and it still goes on. However obvious, it is too often forgotten that our writers live in a society where a kind of idiot optimism is popularly and commercially insisted on. Surrounded as they are by magazine fiction and movies, "family" television, Madison Avenue, and all the rest, they are incessantly driven to try to right the balance—driven by a completely human perversity that reacts in disgust from the piety and cant of an inescapable diet of fake satisfactions and sentimental sorrows. This is an important and often ignored partial accounting for all the misery and sickness you find in our best writers today. How can they do other?

IV. America is too big, too paradoxical, complex, diverse, and heterogeneous to be reflected *or* refracted in any single work, or group of works, or even perhaps in the whole of serious contemporary literature. There are a dozen, or a hundred, or a thousand Americas! And from what point of view, or angle of refraction, should any one of these be seen? The intellectual's? The man in the street's? The woman of the street's? Or the home? The poet's? When you multiply the number of possible Americas by the number of possible approaches you come up in that region where figures begin to cease to convey much, at least to me.

V. The people who bewail the fact that our fiction does not now reflect the large, cheerful average of health and success in American life seem invariably to forget that there is nothing especially new about this situation. Writing about the American novel from its start to the present, one of the best critics of our fiction, Richard Chase, has pointed out, "The imagination that produced much of the best and most characteristic American fiction has been shaped by the contradictions and not by the unities and harmonies of our culture." Mr. Chase does not do much to explain why this is so, and he is forced to leave out of his discussion a good many books I would think it necessary to include, presumably because they do not fit his thesis very well. But he is on to something. Our novel is not the English novel, which "has followed a middle way. It is notable for its great practical sanity, its powerful engrossing composition of wide ranges of experience into a moral centrality and equability of judgment. . . . The profound poetry of disorder we find in the American novel is missing, with rare exceptions, from the English." The American novel "has been stirred, rather, by the aesthetic possibilities of radical forms of alienation, contradiction, and disorder." I suspect that this is essentially true, and that people who attack our modern fiction for being unreflective of the country that produced it are dodging a deeper question (which for present purposes I, too, must dodge), which is, why has this been basically true from the very beginning?

VI. This is the last one, and in the nature of a very narrow concession. I suppose that in a way a writer like Hemingway or Faulkner does, in some highly subtle fashion, speak profoundly of the American experience, and thus, by a very difficult route, give a picture of us that rings of truth. But it takes real effort, real understanding, and even vision, as well as a great deal of experience of this country, to see how and why this is so. Very few Americans have what it takes. Then how can we expect someone who is not an American to see the point? We cannot. (And it is very easy, by the way, to expect more of foreign intellectuals than they can produce; a sense of cultural and intellectual inferiority has afflicted almost all of us ever since Sinclair Lewis—or maybe Mark Twain; some of you will be discovering before long, I will venture to predict, that you are a lot smarter than you thought you were. It is easy, too, to expect more knowledge of your country abroad than one will find; I will predict further that the number and the depths of plain misconceptions some of you will encounter will take your wind away.)

Let me lift a little something more from Robert Penn Warren—this time a sort of anecdote he told. He once talked, he says, with an Italian Fascist who had deserted Mussolini in the Second World War and had come over to fight on our side. Why? Warren asked him. Because of the American novelists, the man answered. "The Fascists used to let us read American fiction because it gave, they thought, a picture of a decadent America. They thought it was good propaganda for fascism to let us read Dreiser, Faulkner, Sinclair Lewis. But you know, it suddenly occurred to me that if democracy could allow that kind of criticism of itself, it must be very strong and good. So I took to the mountains."

Well, I think that is very fine indeed. But note that this soldier was a highly perceptive fellow—and besides, he couldn't have had much of a picture of America yet, either, though he was on the right track.

Really to begin to find America in its modern books you would need to realize all the things I have mentioned, I think, plus a good many things I am not taking time to mention (fortunately for you), and a good many more I haven't the wit to mention (unfortunately for me). It happens that there are valuable and essential insights to be got from such nineteenth-century writers as Whitman and Twain, and you will be hearing about that later in this series of lectures. But as for finding us where we have been looking tonight, I doubt it.

Where then is America to be found? Perhaps because the country is so complex and huge, there have been very few attempts to capture it whole. Indeed only two of our really notable modern novelists have had the intention: Thomas Wolfe and John Dos Passos. And both attempts were seriously vitiated—Wolfe's by his failures of discipline, and by the fact that by the time he had truly discovered his purpose he was soon to die, Dos Passos' by the fact that *USA* was written out of the depths of a depression, and by a bitter man, and therefore presents a more sour, or jaundiced view of the country than most people are willing to accept.

Dos Passos did, however, try impressionistically to capture the country. For instance:

U.S.A. is the slice of a continent. U.S.A. is a group of holding companies, some aggregations of trade unions, a set of laws bound in calf, a radio network, a chain of moving picture theatres, a column of stock-quotations rubbed out and written in by a Western Union boy on a blackboard, a public-library full of old newspapers and dogeared history-books with protests scrawled on the margins in pencil. U.S.A. is the world's greatest rivervalley fringed with mountains and hills. U.S.A. is a set of bigmouthed officials with too many bankaccounts. U.S.A. is a lot of men buried in their uniforms in Arlington Cemetery. U.S.A. is the letters at the end of an address when you are away from home. But mostly U.S.A. is the speech of the people.

That, finally, is a very indirect way of putting my point: a true and rounded picture of America cannot be found in contemporary fiction if only because America is everyplace and no place. It is in our goods, and our arts, and our land and people. In Emerson's essays and Charles Saunders Pierce and Norman Vincent Peale; in our courthouses and ranchhouses and churches; in ginmills and cotton mills and General Mills; in Samuel Barber and Joe the barber and John Cameron Swazey; in the Declaration of Independence and Pogo and Peanuts and Little Orphan Annie; in pool halls and dance halls and halls of ivy and Robert Hall's—everywhere and nowhere.

Well, this is approximately and very protractedly what I wrote in a final report to the U.S.I.S., composed on my bed of pain, concerning my experience in India. "The idea that serious modern American literature is an accurate and valuable reflection of the country that produced it needs careful re-examination": my very, professorial words, as I recall them. But although I do know that a good many Indian universities now offer work in American literature where only one did when several others and I were promoting the cause, I don't know that anyone ever did really read that report. And so, frustrated for an audience, I have submitted you to my sentiments. It is nice that *someone* had to listen and I thank you for doing so.

1962

PART III *American Myth*

THE MOTHER OF US ALL:
POCAHONTAS

"Were there two sides to Pocahontas?
Did she have a fourth dimension?"
—ERNEST HEMINGWAY

. . . having feasted him after their best barbarous manner they could, a long consultation was held, but the conclusion was, two great stones were brought before *Powhatan:* then as many as could layd hands on him, dragged him to them, and thereon laid his head, and being ready with their clubs, to beate out his braines, *Pocahontas* the Kings dearest daughter, when no intreaty could prevail, got his head in her armes, and laid her owne upon his to save him from death: whereat the Emperour was contented he should live to make him hatchets, and her bells, beads, and copper. . . .

Of course it may never have happened at all, and even if it did we think we may be a little tired of it. Yet three and a half centuries have elapsed, and this interminable sentence about an incident from the travels of Captain John Smith still lives. Americans, their literature swarming with its offspring, still without revulsion can summon up the old image: Smith pinned down by savages, his head on a rock, all those clubs about to smash it; and the lovely Indian princess, curiously moved out from the crowd and across all the allegiances of her family, home, and land, her religion and her race, lowering her head to his. Why can this commonplace, even banal, picture absorb us yet?

Shopworn by sentimentality, Pocahontas endures and stands with the most appealing of our saints. She has passed subtly into our folklore, where she lives as a popular fable— a parable taught children, who carry some vague memory of her through their lives. She is an American legend, a woman whose actual story has blended with imaginary elements in time become traditional. Finally, she is one of our few, true native myths, for with our poets she has successfully attained the status of goddess, has been beatified, made holy, and offered as a magical and moving explanation of our national origins. What has happened to her story, why did it happen— and in fact what really was her story? It may be that our very familiarity with Pocahontas has kept us from looking at her closely enough to see what is there.

I

Even in the sketchiest of outlines, the story from which all the folklore and legends take off is a good one. As every schoolboy knows, the English arrived in Jamestown in 1607. During December of that year, while exploring the Chickahominy River, Smith—who had worked his way up from prisoner to leader of the expedition—was captured by men of Chief Powhatan, and two of his companions were killed. It was at this time that he reputedly was rescued from death by the chief's favorite child, a young girl—no more than twelve or thirteen—called Pocahontas. Then, after what struck him as some very odd behavior on the part of the Indians, he was allowed to return to Jamestown, a place where—the great majority of its members dying within a year of their arrival— one of the most appalling casualty rates in history was being established. By placating the Indians and planting corn, and with the help again of Pocahontas, who is said often to have brought supplies, and once to have come through the forest on a dark night to warn of an attack by her father, Smith is usually credited with having temporarily saved the colony. He gave the credit to her, however, as having done most, "next under God," to preserve the settlers.

The Captain returned to England in 1609, and in that year ships under Sir Thomas Gates brought relief to a group of people so desperate that one man had eaten his wife. The *Sea Venture*, flagship of the fleet, was wrecked in Bermuda, but its survivors somehow built a new vessel, and with it made Jamestown. One of its passengers was an Englishman named John Rolfe. Some time elapsed before he saw Pocahontas, because for a while she had no connection with the vicissitudes of the colonists. But in 1613, while visiting the chief of the Potomacs, she was tricked into captivity by an Indian bribed with a copper kettle, and taken as security for English men and equipment held by Powhatan. Now she met Rolfe, whose first wife had died in Virginia, and soon they expressed a desire to marry. Powhatan gave his approval, but Rolfe had to get permission from his own superiors and wrote Sir Thomas Dale a passionate, tedious letter protesting that he wished to marry Pocahontas despite, as he put it, her "rude education, manners barbarous and cursed generation," for the good of the plantation, the honor of England, the glory of God, and his own salvation—not "to gorge myself with incontinency" but, according to God's wish, to convert the girl. Even Smith had said that conversion was the first duty of the settlers; permission was granted. Dale gave the girl a good deal of religious instruction, christened her Rebecca—it was the first such conversion by the colonists—and in April of 1614 she and Rolfe were married.

Rolfe, it is generally believed, was primarily responsible for the production of the tobacco—detested by both King James and Smith—which made the colony permanent, and in 1616 he and his wife and their son Thomas were taken abroad by Dale to publicize the success of Jamestown. Thus it was that Pocahontas, less than six weeks after the death of William Shakespeare, arrived in England. In the party, too, was an Indian named Tomocomo, whom a thoughtful Powhatan had sent as a scout. He had a sheaf of sticks in which he was to place a notch for each white person he encountered, and some equally troublesome instruction to see this "God" about whom the English talked so much.

Pocahontas fared better, for a time. She was honored by the church and feted by the King and Queen, to whom Smith in glowing terms had commended her as his savior. James Stuart demanded to know if her commoner husband had not committed a treasonable act in marrying a princess. The Lady Rebecca became the toast of London, where alert pubs changed their names to "La Belle Sauvage." But not everything went well. She saw Smith again and was mysteriously displeased. Then while preparing for her return to Jamestown she was taken sick, very likely with smallpox, and died. She made a godly end, according to Smith, at the age of perhaps twenty-two, and was buried on the 21st of March, 1617, at Gravesend, on the banks of the Thames.

Her father survived her by only a year. Her husband returned to Virginia alone, married once again, and was killed four years later by Indians led by her uncle. Her son Thomas grew up in England, and then came back to this country to start the line of proud Virginians—of Jeffersons and Lees, of Randolphs, Marshalls, and an estimated two million other people—who to this day trace their ancestry back to the Indian girl. Smith transferred his affections to New England, which he named, but was never able to get the colonial job he wanted and died in bed in 1631. As for Pocahontas, the exact place of her burial is unknown, and the only tangible remains of her are a pair of earrings and a portrait, done in 1616, showing a dark and handsome if uncomfortable young lady, incongruously overdressed in English clothes.

There are other details of a more or less factual nature that have been added to this story by people who knew Pocahontas, or who wrote of her during her lifetime. Smith himself supplies some of them. It is he who describes that day in England when he somehow so upset her, and she "turned about, obscured her face," on seeing him—an event which, since Smith either could not explain it or did not wish to, has tantalized generations of romantics.

There is also the testimony of Samuel Purchas, who was present when Pocahontas was received by the Lord Bishop of London with even more pomp than was accorded other great ladies of the time, and who records in *Hakluytus Posthumus* or *Purchas his Pilgrimes* (1625) the impressive dignity with which the young lady received her honors. And in his *True Discourse of the Present Estate of Virginia* (1615) Ralph Hamor put down the pious details of her conversion and marriage.

But not all these additions conform to the somewhat stuffy reputation that has been built for her. Smith, for instance, coldly comments that he might have married the girl himself —or "done what he listed" with her. He also supplies a colorful but usually neglected incident relating how she and "her women" came one day "naked out of the woods, onely covered behind and before with a few green leaves . . . singing and dauncing with most excellent ill varietie, oft falling into their infernall passions"; and also tells how, later, "all these Nymphes more tormented him than ever, with crowding, pressing and hanging about him, most tediously crying, Love you not me?"

In addition, William Strachey, in his *Historie of Travaile into Virginia Britannia,* written about 1615, supplies information which does not appear in Sunday School versions of the story. The first secretary of America's oldest colony and the friend of great poets, including Donne, Jonson, and probably Shakespeare, Strachey disturbs the tenderhearted by noting that Rolfe's future bride is already married, to a "private captaine, called Kocoum." Even worse is his description of Pocahontas in earlier days as a "well-featured but wanton yong girle" who used to come to the fort and "get the boyes forth with her into the markett place, and make them wheele, falling on their hands, turning their heels upwards, whome she would followe and wheele so herself, naked as she was, all the fort over."

These are all the important sources of the Pocahontas story. Strachey's intelligence was not published until some 234 years after he wrote. Smith's swashbuckling accounts of his own adventures were taken as gospel for even longer, though for quite a while the story of Pocahontas had very little circulation, and was seldom repeated outside a couple of books on Virginia. But when about the start of the nineteenth century Americans began to search intensely for their history, the romance was resurrected, and Pocahontas began to loom large as the guardian angel of our oldest colony. Exaggerating even Smith's accounts of her, historians entered into a quaint struggle to outdo each other with praise, concentrating, of course, on the rescue story. Considering the flimsiness of the evidence, it is odd that for a long time no one seems to have entertained the slightest doubt of its authenticity. On all sides, instead, sprung up the most assiduous and vigilant defense of the lady. Here the case of the Honorable Waddy Thompson is instructive. Poor Thompson, who had been our minister to Mexico, published in 1846 his "Recollections" of that place, and in his desire to praise a girl named Marina, "the *chère amie* and interpreter of Cortez," he let slip a remark he must have regretted the rest of his days. He said that Pocahontas was "thrown into the shade" by her.

The response to these imprudent words was dreadful; an anonymous Kentuckian rushed into print a whole pamphlet Vindicating her Memory. He appealed to all Virginians, to all Americans, and finally "to the admirers of virtue, humanity, and nobleness of soul, wherever to be found," against this Erroneous Judgment. Pocahontas had every gift Marina possessed, and—no *chère amie*—she had also, he added, her "good name." Indeed, it is not possible to improve on her, and to demonstrate either this or his scholarship the gentleman from Kentucky appended long accounts of her from the work of twenty-six historians, including French, German, and Italian representatives. Her character is "not surpassed by any in the whole range of history" is one estimate.

The author of this pamphlet also spoke of "proof" that Pocahontas rescued Smith, which he called "one of the most incontestable facts in history": "The proof is, the account of it given by Captain Smith, a man incapable of falsehood or exaggeration . . . hundreds of eye-witnesses . . . and to this may be added tradition." Here the gentleman defends, somewhat ineptly, what no man is known to have attacked, despite the fact that there have always been excellent reasons for contesting the rescue. For one thing, the Captain had a real inclination toward this sort of tale. His *Generall Historie* of 1624, which tells the full story for the first time, reveals a peculiar talent for being "offered rescue and protection in my greatest dangers" by various "honorable and vertuous Ladies." Most striking of these is the Lady Tragabigzanda, who fell in love with him when he was in bondage, not this time to her father but to her husband, the powerful Bashaw Bogall of Constantinople. She delivered him from this slavery, and sent him to her brother, "till time made her Master of her selfe"—before which, however, Smith made a fantastic escape.

Then, much worse and apparent from the beginning, there is the well-known fact that Smith's *True Relation* of 1608, which tells of his capture by Powhatan, and speaks also of the chief's kindness and assurances of early release, contains no mention at all of any rescue. He had plenty of other opportunities to tell the story, too, but neither he nor anyone else who wrote on Jamestown is known to have referred to the event until 1622, when he remarked in his *New England Trials*, which includes his third version of his capture: "God made Pocahontas the King's daughter the means to deliver me." Then in 1624, when his *General Historie* was published, he told the story as we know it, and also printed for the first time his letter of eight years before to Queen Anne.

The obvious inference here is that if the rescue was actually performed Smith would have said so in the first place or, if he had not, would have told the story to others who would have repeated it. His *Historie* is boastful; it is hard to know how much of it he may have made up or borrowed from other travelers of the period. And there was a historical precedent for the Pocahontas tale: the story of a soldier, Juan Ortiz, who was lost on an expedition to Florida in 1528 and was found there by De Soto about twelve years later. Ortiz said he had been captured by Indians, and saved at the last second from burning at the stake by the chief's daughter, who later came at night in peril of her life to warn him of her father's plot to kill him. This story had appeared in London, in an English translation by Richard Hakluyt, in 1609, the year of Smith's return to that city.

Despite all grounds for suspicion, however, Smith's tale went unchallenged for well over two centuries—until about 1860, that is, when two historians, Edward D. Neill (who became known as the scavenger of Virginia history) and Charles Deane, began to make what now seem the obvious objections. These men were quickly joined by others, and in order to publicize Deane's case there entered the cause no less an intellect than that of Henry Adams. Writing anonymously in the *North American Review* in 1867, Adams lowered his biggest guns and patiently blasted what he called "the most romantic episode" in our history into what must have seemed to him and his crushed readers total oblivion. Henry Cabot Lodge concurred that the rescue belongs to fiction. Many other great men expressed themselves on the question, and quickly it became the custom to speak of the Pocahontas "legend."

Other historians, however, rushed to the defense. Chief among these were John Fiske, the philosopher and historian, and William Wirt Henry. Fiske in 1879 flatly dismissed the dismissals, and went on to champion the story. Why is it not in the *True Relation* of 1608? Because the editor of that work had obeyed an injunction against printing anything that might discourage potential colonists, and in a preface had explained that Smith had written "somewhat more" than was being published. Certainly the Captain was not allowed simply to go free, after having killed two Indians. The rescue by Pocahontas was quite in accordance with Indian custom. Any member of a tribe had a right to claim a prisoner as son or lover—but how could Smith have known enough about this to invent the tale? That scene in which he describes the weird behavior of his captors following his rescue was clearly a ceremony of adoption into the tribe, the natural consequence of Pocahontas' act. Why didn't Smith tell the story to his compatriots? Because he feared that if they knew the favor of an Indian woman was possible they would desert.

And so the battle, which continues to the present day, was on. There is a rebuttal. Why, for example, censor from Smith's first book a charming rescue story (which might cause desertions) and include, as the editor did, an excessively discouraging description of one of Smith's companions, "John Robbinson slaine, with 20 or 30. arrowes" in him? There is no easy answer to that. But, after the short period of the story's disrepute (conveniently passed in time for the Jamestown Tercentenary of 1907), wide acceptance ruled again—especially with proudly celebrating Virginians, who appeared to have forgotten that by their rules the girl was colored. Credence in the story, however, is of course not limited to the South. Indeed by 1957, when the 350th anniversary of the founding was elaborately solemnized, most Americans, including a majority of the published authorities, seemed to subscribe to the tale as fact. For the celebrations Paul Green wrote a "Symphonic Outdoor Drama" called *The Founders,* in which the key events of the young lady's life took on the force of ritual observance in performances at Williamsburg. Since the evidence is not decisive, perhaps everybody has a right to believe as he wishes.

II

Exactly what happened would not seem to make any enormous difference anyway. What counts more is the truly extraordinary way in which the story—despite the profound awkwardness of a climax that comes in the very opening scene—pervades our culture. Pocahontas is represented in countless paintings and monuments; she gives her name to ships, motels, coal mines, towns, counties, and pseudonymous writers, to secret orders and business firms. There are histories of her and Smith by everyone from poet (John Gould Fletcher) to politician ("Alfalfa Bill" Murray, a descendant). But all other signs of her fade before the plays, poems, novels, and children's books which for the last 150 years have flooded our literature. Dramatizing the story from the alleged facts, and filling gaps or inadequacies with invented material usually presented as fact, there are so many different treatments, ranging from the serious to the absurd, that they begin to look numberless.

But they fall into patterns. The first person to make literary use of Pocahontas was no less a writer than the rare Ben Jonson, who included an obscure reference to her in his *Staple of News* of 1625. Then, much later, she was treated at length in a little novel called *The Female American* (1767). Here the story as we know it is, however, simply a rehearsal for far greater events, and the really memorable thing about the book is that its author was an English lady known as Unca Eliza Winkfield, who changed Pocahontas' name to Unca, and Smith's to Winkfield, and gave her a daughter called, once more, Unca.

The writer who really started things, by first romanticizing the story in a proper way, was still another Englishman—an adventuresome fellow named John Davis, a sailor who came to this country in 1798 and spent nearly five years traveling about on foot. Very young and romantic, hyperthyroid, chronically tumescent, and rather charming, Davis wrote a book about his journey called *Travels of Four Years and a Half in the United States of America*. As a part of this work he "delivered to the world" the history of Pocahontas which, he announced, was reserved for his pen. Possessed of a lively and libidinous imagination, which he seemed unable to distinguish from his written sources, Davis tore into the story with hearty masculine appetite.

He begins with Smith in the hands of Powhatan, who keeps offering his prisoner a woman. The squaws fight fiercely for the honor, but to Pocahontas' "unspeakable joy" Smith is stern and turns them all down. After she has rescued him she comes to Jamestown, weeping "in all the tumultuous extasy of love." In order to cure her Smith slips off to England, instructing his compatriots to tell the girl he has died. She prostrates herself on his empty grave, beats her bosom, and utters piercing cries. One night while she is strewing flowers about his resting place she is come upon by Rolfe, secretly in love with her and of late much given to taking moonlight walks while composing love poems. ("Of these effusions I have three in my possession," says Davis, and he prints them.) Surprised by Rolfe's appearance, Pocahontas inadvertently falls in his arms, whereupon he seizes his opportunity and drinks from her lips "the poison of delight." A woman is "never more susceptible of a new passion than when agitated by the remains of a former one," is Davis' dark but profitable explanation, and thus it is that hours later, come dawn, Rolfe "still rioted in the draught of intoxication from her lips." Eventually they marry ("nor did satiety necessarily follow from fruition," the author adds anxiously). They go to England, and Pocahontas dies there.

Davis made it clear that he wrote as a historian: "I have adhered inviolably to facts; rejecting every circumstance that had not evidence to support it," he insisted, speaking of "recourse to records and original papers." The man was too modest, for of course these were, like Rolfe's poems, original enough but with him. And he should be given credit, too, for having seen the possibilities of uniting richly embroidered history with a mammary fixation (habitually the bosoms of his Indian women are either "throbbing" or "in convulsive throes"). That he did see the promise of this combination, and in advance of his time, is indicated by the fact that he himself soon wrote what he called a "historical novel" on "Pokahontas." The book is formally titled *First Settlers of Virginia* (1806), but it simply pads the previous account of the girl's adventures to novel length. Dropping Rolfe's claim to the poetry, Davis managed to add a couple of mildly pornographic native scenes, to use Smith's story of the enamored Indian girls ("Love you not me?") twice, and to present Pocahontas as "unrobed" in her first scene with Rolfe. He also prefaced a second edition with a letter from Thomas Jefferson to the effect that the President of the United States "subscribed with pleasure" to this Indian Tale.

After Davis, the deluge. This began with a vast number of plays now mostly lost, but including four prominent and commercially successful ones which are preserved. To James Nelson Barker, ex-mayor of Philadelphia and future first controller of the Treasury in Van Buren's cabinet, goes a series of firsts: his *Indian Princess* of 1808 (although anticipated in 1784 by the little-known German *Pocahontas* of Johann Wilhelm Rose) was the first important Pocahontas play and the first to be produced of the Indian plays which soon threatened to take over our stage completely; it is generally cited also as the first American play to appear in London after opening in this country. Hugely popular, and rather deservedly so, Barker's success was followed by that of George Washington Parke Custis, step-grandson of our first president, with his *Pocahontas* of 1830, and by Robert Dale Owen. The latter, son of the more famous Robert Owen, founder of the radical Owenite communities, and himself a very early advocate of birth control, the free discussion of sex, and the rights of women, made his Pocahontas (1837) an anachronistic feminist. His play, though over-long, is not incompetent and reads very well beside *The Forest Princess* (1844) of Charlotte Barnes Conner. Mrs. Conner, an actress, stuck close to the worst nineteenth-century concepts of theater and produced a series of unlikely postures which are epitomized in her final scene, where a pious Rebecca dying in England, hand stretched heavenward, speaks her last iambics:

> I hear my father—Husband, fare thee well.
> We part—but we shall meet—above!

after which the hand drops with the curtain.

John Brougham's *Pocahontas* (1855) was honorably designed to stop this sort of thing, and his travesty did stop the
production of "serious" Pocahontas plays for quite a time,
greatly diminishing the popularity of the Indian drama to
boot. But today his play is, to speak politely, "dated," for the
humor depends mainly on puns ("What *iron* fortune *led* you
to our shores?" "To now ill-use us would be base *illusion!*")
(italics his), line after line for two long acts.

Brougham's burlesque was extremely well received, however, and it performed a service for our drama that nothing
has adequately performed for our poetry. Pocahontas poems,
produced in the nineteenth century by the carload, are almost
uniformly dull, tasteless, and interminable. The efforts of
Lydia Huntly Sigourney and William Makepeace Thackeray
stand out only a little from the average. Most nineteenth-
century Pocahontas poems seem to begin either with some
silly sylvan scene or with "Descend O Muse, and this poor
pen . . . " Smith always arrives as expected, but the Muse
invariably has other things to do.

Equally forbidding are the Pocahontas poems written in the
manner of Henry Wadsworth Longfellow. Longfellow neglected to produce any Pocahontas items himself, but there
are a great many poems, and several plays in verse, which
have sought to rectify his oversight. These pieces are all distinguished by lines of unrhymed trochaic tetrameter ("By the
shore of Gitche Gumee / By the shining Big-Sea-Water")
which produce a stultifying effect the poets seem to equate
with an Indian atmosphere; they suffer from what might properly be known as the Curse of Hiawatha. Of course Longfellow got his famous Hiawatha line from a German translation

of a national epic of the Finns, but this is not known to have
stopped anyone, and on they go:

> Then the maiden Pocahontas
> Rushes forward, none can stop her,
> Throws her arms about the captive,
> Cries,—"Oh spare him! Spare the Paleface!"

What burlesque and abuse cannot destroy will just have to
wear itself out. Although the machinery that mass-produces
low-quality Pocahontas literature has long shown signs of collapse, the end is not yet. As recently as 1958 a Pocahontas
novel by one Noel B. Gerson, with nothing to recommend it
but the story, was smiled on by a very large book club. And
so still they come with the story, juggling the climax or devis-
ing a new one, and trying to make up somehow for the fact
that Smith never married the girl. Both problems can of
course be solved at once by ending with the scene from Smith
in which he and Pocahontas meet in London. Here Rebecca is
overcome at the sight of her lost Captain and dies in his arms,
usually of a broken heart; indeed it has become a convention
to do it that way. But that has not helped, and it is the plays,
particularly, which indicate that an industry really is exhausted. The best written and most interesting parts of their
scripts are those that deal with such matters as the construction of campfires with electric fans, logs, and strips of red
cloth.

One last sign of the popular Pocahontas drama's waning
was the appearance (once Brougham was well-forgotten) of
an Everything But the Kitchen Sink School. There exists, for
instance, an operetta in which Smith has a "regulation negro"
servant, comically named Mahogany, who plays a banjo. A
better sample is the *Pocahontas* (1906) of Edwin O. Ropp.
Mr. Ropp named three of his Indians Hiawatha, Minnehaha,
and Geronimo; and there is a rough spot in the action when a

man named simply Roger (Williams?), insisting on the freedom of religious thought, disappears for good in the Virginia forest. As for Pocahontas, she is taken, through her marriage with Rolfe, to England and back again to Virginia, where she lives out her days in the wilderness with her husband, two children, and their Christian grandpapa, Powhatan, singing the praises of home sweet home, as the play ends with lines lifted from the poem of that name. Mr. Ropp dedicated his play, it should be recorded, to a Moral Purpose, to the Jamestown Exposition of 1907, and to Those Who Construct the Panama Canal. The world was ready for another burlesque when, in 1918, Philip Moeller published his *Beautiful Legend of the Amorous Indian*. In this play only one character, the senile mother of Powhatan, speaks Hiawathan, and there is a heart-warming moment in the dialogue when Powhatan's wife says of her aging mother-in-law: "When she talks in that old manner it nearly drives me crazy."

III

It is not hard to find reasons for the low quality of a large part of our Pocahontas literature: the writers had no talent, for instance. A less obvious difficulty has been that most of the poets and playwrights have prided themselves that their works were founded firmly on "historical sources." This impeded the imaginations of most of them, who tried to romanticize history instead of letting the facts act as a stimulus to fiction. As a result of sentimentality and inaccuracy, there is little or no historical value in their products. And because the works are based so solidly on "history," often footnoted, they seldom have any value as fiction, for invariably events are related not because they are dramatic but because they happened—which is aesthetically irrelevant. If the story is to satisfy a modern audience, it must be treated imaginatively.

Properly told it could be a truly epic story. This is indicated by the fact that elements in the relationships of the characters are so like those in other epics of other countries—the *Aeneid,* for instance. Aeneas, we recall, was an adventurer who also sought a westward land and finally anchored at the mouth of a river. The country there was ruled by a king, Latinus, who had a beautiful daughter, Lavinia. Latinus had dreamed that his daughter's husband would come from a foreign land, and that from this union would spring a race destined to rule the world, so he received Aeneas and feasted him. Later tradition goes on to record the marriage, the birth of a son, and the founding of the city in which Romulus and Remus were born. Other parallels—with the stories of Odysseus and Nausicaä, and of Jason and Medea—likewise suggest the epic possibilities of the American tale.

To be sure, a few writers, usually in a far more modest fashion, have tried to make something of Pocahontas. Fewer still have succeeded, but even some of the failures are interesting. Working from the probability that a letter by Strachey, who was on the wrecked *Sea Venture* with Rolfe, provided Shakespeare with material for *The Tempest,* John Esten Cooke wrote a polite novel called *My Lady Pocahontas* (1885) in which he made Shakespeare dependent on the lady and Smith for his characters Miranda and Ferdinand. At the climax, Pocahontas recognizes herself on the stage of the Globe.

Much of this invention has been blithely repeated as history, but such an attempt at legend fails anyway for being too literary. Other attempts have failed for not being literary enough. Mary Virginia Wall in 1908 wrote a book on Pocahontas as *The Daughter of Virginia Dare*—the child, that is, of this first native-born "American," who mysteriously disappeared, and Powhatan. Thus it is the spirit of Virginia Dare which accounts for the Indian girl's compassion. Now this could be a fruitful merger, uniting two of our best stories and giving Americans a kind of spiritual genealogy. The fact that to have been Pocahontas' mother Virginia would have had to bear a child at eight does not really matter much. But such scenes as the one in which the daughter comes to her end matter a good deal. On her deathbed, a place that has proved scarcely less fatal for authors than for their heroine, Pocahontas stoutly carols "Hark the Herald Angels Sing" (the Amen "begun on earth and ending in heaven"), and what started with some small promise has backed all the way out of it.

Another, but much better, novel which tries to do something with the story is the *Pocahontas* (1933) of David Garnett. This is a good historical novel with a thesis. In scenes of hideous but authentic brutality, Garnett shows the Indian women torturing their naked prisoners to death in orgies of obscene cruelty. These lead directly to orgies of sexual passion which act as a purge. To this sequence he contrasts the cruelty of the whites, which they sanction with self-righteousness and piety and follow with guilt. Garnett's book is a romantic and primitivistic performance after the manner of D. H. Lawrence which uses Pocahontas, more tender than her compatriots, as a vehicle for a lesson on the superiority of uncivilized peoples. Doctrinaire, and intellectually a little sentimental, this is still probably the best Pocahontas novel.*

---

* It is not nearly so good as John Barth's *The Sot-Weed Factor* (1960), but this unprecedented novel is only incidentally about Pocahontas. Included in it, however, are John Smith's *Secret Historie,* parallel—but far superior—to John Davis' discovery of John Rolfe's poems, and the *Privie Journall* of a rival character. In the course of these extended tours de force a tribal custom is revealed that requires a prospective suitor to take the maidenhead of his bride before marrying her. In the case of Pocahontas no man has been successful in fracturing this membrane (indeed "most had done them selves hurt withal, in there efforts"). But with the aid of a fantastically invigorating vegetable

Equally good, or maybe better, are two twentieth-century plays, Margaret Ullman's *Pocahontas* (1912) and Virgil Geddes' *Pocahontas and the Elders* (1933). More interesting than the plays themselves, however, are prefatory remarks their authors made about their material. In an introductory quotation Miss Ullman speaks of her heroine as a "Sweet-smelling sacrifice to the good of Western Planting." Geddes writes that his play is a "folkpiece" and his characters "part of the soul's inheritance." Both writers, in other words, were pointing to some pregnant quality of the story which goes beyond its facts. This was a direction which an informal group of modern poets was taking too. The result was the elevation of Pocahontas to myth.

It is Vachel Lindsay who was primarily responsible for this development. In his "Cool Tombs" Carl Sandburg had asked a question:

> Pocahontas' body, lovely as a poplar, sweet
> as a red haw in November or a pawpaw in May—
> did she wonder? does she remember—in the
> dust—in the cool tombs?

About 1918 Lindsay quoted this passage, answered yes, she remembers, and went on to explain in a poem which transforms the savior of Jamestown into a symbol of the American spirit. He supplies a magical genealogy whereby the girl becomes, as in his title, "Our Mother Pocahontas." Powhatan is the son of lightning and an oak; his daughter is the lover and bride of the forest. Thus

> John Rolfe is not our ancestor.
> We rise from out the soul of her

---

device Smith publicly accomplishes the feat. In its review of the book, entitled "Novelist Libels Pocahontas Story," the *Richmond News-Leader* demanded to know if, in view of the respectability of the lady's descendants, all this was not "actionable."

Held in native wonderland,
While the sun's rays kissed her hand,
In the springtime,
In Virginia,
Our mother, Pocahontas.

Though she died in England, Lindsay acknowledges, she returned to Virginia and walked the continent, "Waking, / Thrilling, / The midnight land," and blending with it. We in turn are born not of Europe but of her, like a crop, and we are sustained by our inheritance.

One statement does not make a myth, but this concept was passed to other poets, notably to Hart Crane. First, though, came William Carlos Williams. A part of his prose study of the national past, called *In the American Grain* (1925), was devoted to an excoriation of the Puritans, after the fashion of the Twenties, and to praise for the sensual joy of the Indians, who are again taken over as an element of our spiritual ancestry. Williams gave only brief notice to Pocahontas, but he quoted Strachey's description of a naked, wheeling Indian girl.

These are the materials from which Crane, in *The Bridge* (1930), raised Pocahontas to full mythic stature. In some notes he made for the poem, Crane saw her as "the natural body of American fertility," the land that lay before Columbus "like a woman, ripe, waiting to be taken." He followed his notes, and the part of his long poem called "Powhatan's Daughter" develops them. Starting with the quotation from Strachey (which he took from a *transition* review of Williams by Kay Boyle) the poet in a waking dream at the harbor dawn finds someone with him ("Your cool arms murmurously about me lay . . . *a forest shudders in your hair!*"). She disappears, then, from his semiconsciousness to reappear later as the American continent, most familiar to hoboes who "know a body under the wide rain," as the poet himself is familiar with trains that "Wail into distances I knew were hers." The land blooms with her, she becomes a bride (but "virgin to the last of men"), passes herself then to a pioneer mother, a living symbol of the fertility of the land, and makes her last appearance as the earth again—"our native clay . . . red, eternal flesh of Pocahontas. . . ."

Like these four poets, Archibald MacLeish in his *Frescoes for Mr. Rockefeller's City* (1933) was discovering his own land and his faith in its future. Dedicating his book to Sandburg, and deriving a symbol from Crane, MacLeish describes a "Landscape as a Nude"—the American continent as a beautiful naked Indian girl, inviting lovers. With this repetition the concept has taken hold. Thus we have a sort of American Ceres, or Demeter, or Gaea, developed from Pocahontas—a fertility goddess, the mother of us all. We, by our descent from her, become a new race, innocent of both European and all human origins—a race from the earth, as in ancient mythologies of other lands, but an earth that is made of her. We take on a brave, free, mythical past as our alternative to the more prosaic, sordid explanation of history. And the thing is alive, as an image of the beautiful Indian girl is set in perpetual motion, and comes cartwheeling through our veins and down our generations.

IV

For all our concern with Pocahontas, one of the most interesting facts about her seems to have escaped everyone: the story John Smith told, which we have embraced so long, is one of the oldest stories known to man—not just roughly speaking, as in the Odysseus and Aeneas myths, but precisely in all essential parts. The tale of an adventurer, that is, who becomes the captive of the king of another country and another faith, and is rescued by his beautiful daughter, a princess who then gives up her land and her religion for his, is a story known to the popular literatures of many peoples for many centuries. The theme was so common in the Middle Ages that medieval scholars have a name for it: "The Enamoured Moslem Princess." This figure is a woman who characteristically offers herself to a captive Christian knight, the prisoner of her father, rescues him, is converted to Christianity, and goes to his native land—these events usually being followed by combat between his compatriots and hers.*

This is, for instance, the substance of a fifteenth-century French story about *un siegneur de Jagov* who went with a German army to Turkey, was imprisoned and sold as a slave to a *grand seigneur Turk*, whose daughter intervenes in the usual fashion and is converted to Christianity. There is also a medieval story, with roots in the legends of Charlemagne, called *The Sowdone of Babylone*—of Laban, the Sultan, and his daughter Floripas.† In the tenth book of Ordericus Vitalis'

---

* See, for instance, F. M. Warren, "The Enamoured Moslem Princess in Orderic Vital and the French Epic," *PMLA, XXIX* (1914), 341–58. It is a mistake, however, to speak of this theme as if it were wholly a matter of the distant past. For instance, the Enamoured Moslem Princess figures prominently in the Fourth Canto (1821) of Byron's *Don Juan*. Here she is Haidée, whose mother was a Moor; her father is Lambro, a pirate leader who holds the Christian Juan captive. The chieftain is about to kill his prisoner "When Haidée threw herself her boy before; / . . . 'On me,' she cried, 'let death descend. . . .'" Juan is saved, but is taken off, and Haidée withers away and dies.

† The same story, dramatized, is still performed once a year in Portugal, and has its own historical parallel in Brazilian history. See Vianna Moog, *Bandeirantes e Pioneiros, Parelelo entre Duas Culturas*, Pôrto Alegre: Globo, 1955, pp. 97–103. For that matter, there is an Oriental historical analogue: during the seventeenth-century Hindu-Muslim wars around Delhi, the Muslim princess Zebunnisha saved, in 1664, the rebel Hindu prince Shivaji from her father, Alamgir. They never married. Like the Pocahontas rescue, this incident is frequently used in historical romances of India.

Historia Ecclesiastica, whose origins are in the twelfth century, the story is the same—this time about a Frenchman,
Bohemond, his Turkish captor, Daliman, and his daughter
Melaz. It is the same in a romance in which Elie de Saint
Gille, a Frank, is carried from Brittany, captive of the amil
(prince) Macabré, to the land of the Saracens, where Rosamonde, the amil's daughter, betrays her father, saves Elie, is
converted and baptized. There are many other similar old
stories: one called "The Turkish Lady and the English Slave";
another, a Balkan ballad, called "Marko Kraljević and the
Arab King's Daughter"; still another involving *two* Magyars
who are shut in a dungeon by a sultan, then freed by his
daughter. The popularity of the tale is further indicated by
its inclusion in the *Arabian Nights,* whose origins fade into
ancient folklore. Here it appears as an interlude in the longer
"Tale of Kamar al-Zaman." Bostán, the beautiful Magian
daughter of Bahram, rescues As'ad from her father and is
converted to Mohammedanism. Another version, once popular, is in the *Gesta Romanorum,* a collection of "Entertaining
Moral Stories" compiled about 1300 from much older but
obscure sources. These Latin anecdotes, which contain the
germs of plots used by Chaucer and Shakespeare, were widely
read in translation in late sixteenth-century England (hence
Smith may have known them). Tale V, called "Of Fidelity," is
about a youth wasting away as a prisoner of pirates. Their
chief has a lovely and virtuous daughter who frees the young
man and, being promised marriage, goes to his country. The
origins of this version may be in Seneca the Elder, who at the
beginning of the Christian era formulated precisely the same
situation in his *Controversia* as an imaginary legal case for
debate. It is possible that he, in turn, got the story from the
Greek Sophists, who had a lively interest in literature and
disputation. There is no telling where they may have learned
it, but something very like it is in the ancient Greek myth of

Ariadne, the daughter of Minos, king of Crete, who rescued an Athenian named Theseus from a labyrinth where her father had imprisoned him to be eaten by the Minotaur, and then went away with him.

It has always been an uncomfortable fact of the Pocahontas story, and an apparently formidable obstacle to its survival, that after appearing to offer herself to Smith, the heroine never married the hero. It is a startling fact, and bewildering, that this curiosity has been an element of the story from the beginning. Though Ariadne had deserted her parents and motherland for Theseus, he for some unknown reason abandoned her by the shore of the sea and sailed away; she later married Dionysus. Orderic's Melaz did not marry Bohemond, but his younger friend Roger. In the tale of Kamar al-Zaman, Bostán marries not As'ad but his brother. Floripas, the Sowdone's daughter, also marries someone other than the man for whom she betrayed her father. Elie de Saint Gille never married Rosamonde; since Szilágyi Niklas says he has a love at home, that Sultan's daughter has to settle for the other Magyar, his companion; though he was later remorseful, Marko neglected the Arab king's daughter after his escape. In a few versions one is left to supply his own denouement, and may presume if he wishes that the hero and heroine marry and live happily ever after. But it is extremely curious that there appear to be no accounts in which we are told specifically that what we might expect invariably to happen actually happens.*

---

* The widely known and excellent ballad called "Young Beichan" seems an exception, but only because a new element, the motif of promised marriage, has been grafted on. Beichan is London born, and longs strange lands for to see, but is taken by a savage Moor whose daughter, Susan Pye, steals her father's keys and releases him from a prison, after which he goes back to England, having promised to marry the girl in seven years. Later she abandons her country for England, is converted

The presence of a disturbing element in a popular story is hard to explain. The notion that melodies unheard are sweetest and cannot fade, that the lover who has not his bliss then can love forever and she be fair does not seem to account for this peculiarity; it was never that way at all. Yet there must be something obscurely "right" about an apparently unsatisfactory ending, or over the many centuries we should have succeeded in changing it. And the durable popularity of the story also urges the presence of some appeal that is not on the surface, some force that has given an advantage in the struggle for survival which we should make out if we can. The notion that the story is symbolic of something is not new. The monks who used it for religious instruction hundreds of years ago sensed this and had their own reading: the young man, they said, represents the human race. Led irresistibly by the force of original sin into the prison of the devil, he is redeemed by Christ, in the form of the girl. But this interpretation incongruously makes Jesus the daughter of Satan, and seems also a little arbitrary. It is too utilitarian—but in that it offers one clue to the story's longevity.

Nothing survives indefinitely without filling some function, and the usefulness of this story is clear: the tale approves and propagates the beliefs of anyone who cares to tell it. An informal survey of the children's sections of two small Midwestern libraries disclosed twenty-six different books on

---

to Christianity, and gets a new name. She arrives in England to discover that Young Beichan has just married. But the ceremony is not yet consummated ("of her body I am free") and Susie Pye, now Lady Jane, is able to marry him after all. F. J. Child prints fourteen versions of this ballad in his *English and Scottish Popular Ballads,* while mentioning many related items in Norse, Spanish, Italian, and German. In its various forms it may have been affected by a fairly well-known legend on more or less the same theme, originating in the thirteenth century and concerning Gilbert Becket, father of St. Thomas à Becket. This also has the happy ending.

Pocahontas—and no wonder. Quite apart from the opportunity she presents to give children some notion of self-sacrifice, she is, in addition to all her other appeals, perfectly ideal propaganda for both church and state. The story has long been, among other things, a tale of religious conversion, and in its American form is so eloquent a tribute to accepted institutions that there is no need to deflate its power by so much as even mentioning the obvious lesson it teaches. Of course the thing is a little chauvinistic. It is always either indifferent to the attitudes of the betrayed or unconscious of them. Indeed it is a tribute to the high regard we have for ourselves that Pocahontas has never once been cast as a villainess, for she would make an excellent one. From the point of view of her own people her crimes—repeated acts of treason, and cultural and religious apostasy—were serious. But one does not resent a betrayal to his own side, and we can always bear reassuring: love exists, love matters, and we are very eligible, Pocahontas tells us.

The story will work for any culture, informing us, whoever we are, that we are chosen, or preferred. Our own ways, race, religion must be better—so much better that even an Indian (Magian, Moor, Turk), albeit an unusually fine one (witness her recognition of our superiority), perceived our rectitude. But it nicely eases the guilt we have felt since the start of its popularity over the way we had already begun, by 1608, to treat the Indians. Pocahontas is a female Quanto, a "good" Indian, and by taking her to our national bosom we experience a partial absolution. In the lowering of her head we feel a benediction. We are so wonderful she loved us anyway.

And yet the story has an appeal which easily transcends such crude and frequently imperialistic functions—especially in the rescue scene, which implies all the new allegiances that follow from it. There is a picture there, at least in the American rendering, which has compelled us for so long that it must certainly contain meanings that go beyond the illustrations of it in the children's books. It is characteristic of all hallowed images that they cannot adequately be put into words, and no single rendering would articulate all that might be stated anyway. But these are feeble excuses for total silence, and it does not take any great sensitivity to perceive that Pocahontas' gesture—accomplished not by any subterfuge, but by the frank placing of her own body between Smith's and death—is fairly ringing with overtones. This is because we see her act as a rite, a ceremonial sign which bestows life. A surface part of that symbolism has always been clear. The Indians understood it as we do, and immediately Smith was alive and free. But what we have not been conscious of, though the modern poets sensed something like it, is that her candor was that of a bride. That is one thing, buried beneath awareness, that has dimly stirred us. Unable to put it into words, we have let the girl keep her secret, but the ritual that we feel in her action is itself an unorthodox and dramatic ceremony of marriage, and we are touched. We see Pocahontas at the moment of womanhood, coming voluntarily from the assembly to the altar, where she pledges the sacrifice of her own integrity for the giving of life. This is an offering up of innocence to experience, a thing that is always—in our recognition of its necessity—oddly moving. It is an act which bespeaks total renunciation, the giving up of home, land, faith, self, and perhaps even life, that life may go on.

Perhaps this helps to explain why it is that what, in its flattery of him, is at first glance so much a man's story should also be greatly promoted by women. Apparently it is a very pleasant vicarious experience for us all. Yet in the depths of our response to the heart of the story, the rescue, there is something more profoundly wishful than a simple identification with persons in a touching adventure. All myths have an element of wish somewhere in them. But there is something about this one that is also wistful, as though it expressed a wish that did not really expect to be gratified. It is as though something in us says "If only it were true. . . ."

We surely ought to know what it is we wish for. In our fondness for Pocahontas can we make out a longing that is buried somewhere below even the affection we bear for our fair selves and white causes? This yearning might be for another kind of love entirely, a love that has forever been hidden under the differences that set countries, creeds, and colors against each other. From the freedom and noble impracticality of childhood, we as a people have taken this Indian girl to heart. Could we be hinting at a wish for a love that would really cross the barriers of race? When the beautiful brown head comes down, does a whole nation dream this dream?

But it is still only a dream. And that fact helps to explain why it is that from the very beginning the story has had what looks like the wrong ending, why the wedding of the protagonists remains a symbol that was never realized. To be sure the girl eventually married, and the groom was usually the hero's compatriot, but by then the event has lost its joy and its force—seems a substitute for the real thing, and not at all satisfactory. But the story might have died centuries before us, and we would have made much less of Pocahontas, if the substitution were not in some way fit and right. We sense that the adventure has to end the way it does partly because we know the difference between what we dream and what we get. We are not particularly happy with the denouement, but we feel its correctness, and with it we acknowledge that this is all just make-believe.

To understand the rest of our dim and reluctant perception of the propriety of the story's outcome, Americans must see the Indian girl in one last way: as progenitress of all the "Dark Ladies" of our culture—all the erotic and joyous temptresses, the sensual, brunette heroines, whom our civilization (particularly our literature: Hawthorne, Cooper, Melville, and many others) has summoned up only to repress. John Smith is the first man on this continent known to have made this rejection; his refusal to embrace "the wild spirit" embodied in the girl was epic, and a precedent for centuries of denial. Prototypes, too, and just as important, were the arrogantly hypocritical Rolfe and the rest of the colonists, who baptized, christened, commercialized, and ruined the young lady. With censorship and piety as tools, American writers—a few poets, far too late, aside—completed the job, until Pocahontas was domesticated for the whole of our society, where from the very start any healthy, dark happiness in the flesh is supposed to be hidden, or disapproved. Pocahontas is the archetypal sacrifice to respectability in America—a victim of what has been from the beginning our overwhelming anxiety to housebreak all things in nature, until wilderness and wildness be reduced to a few state parks and a few wild oats. Our affection for Pocahontas is the sign of our temptation, and our feeling that her misfortunes in love have a final, awkward fitness comes from our knowing that all that madness is not for us.

1962

FALLEN FROM TIME:
RIP VAN WINKLE

"Black wing, brown wing, hover over;
Twenty years and the spring is over;
To-day grieves, to-morrow grieves,
Cover me over, light-in-leaves . . ."
          —T. S. ELIOT, *Landscapes*

Washington Irving is reported to have spent a June evening in 1818 talking with his brother-in-law about the old days in Sleepy Hollow. Melancholy of late, the writer was pleased to find himself laughing. Suddenly he got up and went to his room. By morning he had the manuscript of the first and most famous American short story, and his best single claim to a permanent reputation.

Nearly a century and a half have elapsed, and the name of Rip Van Winkle, one of the oldest in our fiction, is as alive as ever. The subject of innumerable representations—among them some of the country's finest paintings—America's archetypal sleeper is almost equally well known abroad. Nor is his fame simply popular, or commercial. The most complex of poets, as well as the least sophisticated of children, are attracted to him.

But there is something ironic here, for at its center Rip's

story is every bit as enigmatic as it is renowned, and the usual understanding of Rip himself, spread so wide, is shallow. Very few of the millions of people who have enjoyed his tale would be comfortable for long if pressed to say exactly what "happened" to him, or if asked to explain what there is about the "poor, simple fellow" that has exerted so general and deep a fascination. Thanks to Irving, the thunder Rip heard is still rolling out of the Catskills. And it is pregnant thunder, charged with meaning. Perhaps it is time someone tried to make out what it has to say.

Irving's story may not be an easy one, but it can easily be told in such a way as to refresh the memories of those who have not encountered it of late. The hero of the tale was a good-natured, middle-aged fellow, and a henpecked husband, who lived with his Dutch neighbors in a peaceful village in the Catskill mountains along the Hudson River in the period immediately preceding the American Revolution. The trouble with Rip was that although he would hunt and fish all day, or even do odd jobs for the neighborhood women, and entertain their children, he was "insuperably averse" to exerting himself for his own practical benefit. He had lost an inheritance, his farm was in the worst condition of any in the vicinity and, worst of all, his termagant wife was always upbraiding him about these things. He had only one "domestic adherent," his dog Wolf, and one comfortable retreat, a bench outside the local inn, where under the sign of His Majesty George the Third met a kind of "perpetual club." But he was driven eventually even from this refuge, and forced to the woods for peace. On a fine fall day it happened.

Rip was shooting squirrels in a high part of the mountains. Tiring in the late afternoon, he rested on a green knoll beside a deep glen, with a sleepy view of miles of forest and the Hudson moving drowsily through it. Suddenly he heard the distant sound of his name. He saw a crow winging its way across the mountain, and Wolf bristling, and then he made out an odd figure, a short old fellow in antique Dutch clothes, coming up from the ravine with a heavy keg on his back. Rip quickly gave him a hand, and as they labored he heard distant thunder coming from a cleft in the rocks. They passed through this crevice, and came into a kind of amphitheatre, walled by precipices. Stunned with awe, Rip saw in the middle of the space a group of odd-looking men playing at nine-pins. They had peculiar, long-nosed faces; all wore beards; one man, stout and old, appeared to be their commander. "What seemed particularly odd," however, was that "although these folk were evidently amusing themselves, yet they maintained the gravest faces, the most mysterious silence, and were, withal, the most melancholy party of pleasure he had ever witnessed." The only sound was the thunder of the balls as they rolled.

When the men saw Rip they stopped their play and stared at him as if they were statues. His heart turned within him; trembling, he obeyed his guide and waited on the company. They drank from the keg in silence, and then went on with their game. Soon Rip was trying the liquor, but he drank more than he could hold, and passed into a profound sleep.

When he woke he was back on the green knoll. It was morning and an eagle wheeled aloft. His gun was rusted away, Wolf was gone, and there was no sign of the opening in the cliffs. He called his dog, but the cawing of crows high in the air was the only answer, and he headed lamely for home. As he approached his village he saw no one he knew. People kept stroking their chins when they looked at him, and when he picked up the gesture from them he discovered that his beard was now gray and a foot long. As he entered town he saw that the village itself had grown. But his own house was in ruins, and a half-starved dog that looked like Wolf skulked about the wreckage and snarled at him. In town the inn was gone, replaced by an ugly building called Jonathan Doolittle's Union

Hotel, and on the old sign King George's portrait had new clothes, and beneath it a new legend: George Washington. Even the nature of the people seemed changed: their drowsy ways had become disputatious. Rudely challenged to state his affiliations, "Federal or Democrat," Rip can only protest that he is loyal to his king, whereupon he is taken by some for a spy. No one knows him, the friends he asks for are dead, and he comes to doubt his own identity, until his daughter Judith's recognition confirms it. Now he is welcomed home, learns that his wife is dead ("in a fit of passion at a New England peddler"), and that he has unaccountably been gone for twenty years. The oldest and most learned member of the community is able to throw a little light on the story he tells: it is every twenty years that Hendrik Hudson, the river's discoverer, keeps a sort of vigil in the Catskills with the crew of the *Half-Moon,* and playing at nine-pins they make the mountains ring with the distant peals of thunder. And so Rip—idle, revered and happy—retires to his place on the bench at the door of the inn.

To be sure this story, though a fine one, is not perfect. For one thing, although Irving's Federalism enables him to jab in mildly amusing fashion at the shabby and pretentious republicanism of Rip's new village, such pleasantries come at the expense of our being wholly convinced of what he is trying to tell us—that Rip at the end is in clover. But the village is no longer entirely the place for him, and the fine old inn where he sits is just not there any more.

That this is, however, the rare sort of story that both satisfies and stimulates is shown by the fact that it has been so often retold, chiefly for the stage. There have been at least five plays—beginning with John Kerr's, which first appeared in Washington in 1829—and three operas, and several children's versions. But none has added anything important to our understanding of the story. Joseph Jefferson, who played the role of

Rip for forty-five years in his own extraordinarily popular interpretation, had a few sensible ideas about the material, but
he also failed to throw out much of the nineteenth-century
baggage handed down from Kerr.

Though Joyce and Dylan Thomas have punned elaborately
on Rip's name, most of the poets who have invoked him have
done nothing much either to interpret the story or the character, and only Hart Crane has given him serious and extended
attention. *The Bridge* (1930) has a section called "Van
Winkle," whom Crane thought of as "the muse of memory"—
or, as he put it to his sponsor, Otto Kahn, "the guardian angel
of the trip to the past." Here Rip is a figure evoked from
recollection of the poet's childhood and the nation's; since this
is to introduce Rip in a thoughtful and promising way, it is
too bad that very little is really done with him in the poem.

This is unfortunate partly for the reason that Rip is, potentially, a truly mythic figure. He is conceivably even more:
ur-mythic. At any rate a primal, primeval myth has been postulated (by Joseph Campbell in his *Hero with a Thousand
Faces*), and has been described—as "a separation from the
world, a penetration to some source of power, and a life-
enhancing return." And this is a most excellent description of
what happens in "Rip Van Winkle." But no one has elevated
the story to this status. As Constance Rourke wrote of it
twenty-five years ago, the tale "has never been finished, and
still awaits a final imaginative re-creation." If, then, we are
to be helped to understand the story more deeply by considering what has been done with it, we had better consider
what had been done with it before Irving wrote it.

II

In 1912 an eminent Dutch historian, Tieman De Vries by
name, published under the title of *Dutch History, Art and*

Literature for Americans a series of lectures he had delivered
at The University of Chicago. A large part of this book is
devoted to a monumentally inept attack on Washington Irving
for having, in "Rip Van Winkle," characterized the Dutch
people as stupid, lazy, and credulous. For his overwhelming
blow the author, protesting great reluctance and sadness,
brings forth the revelation that "Rip" is not the "original" story
that Irving is "generally given credit for," anyway. The bitter
truth, he discloses, is that the tale had been told before: its
embryo is a myth about an ancient Greek named Epimenides,
and this germ was "fully developed" by Erasmus (a citizen of
Rotterdam) in 1496. In the myth Epimenides was sent to look
for a sheep, lay down in a cave, slept for fifty-seven years and
waked to find everything changed and himself unrecognized
until a brother identified him. Erasmus used this story, then,
to attack the Scotist theologians of his day (whom he thought
asleep) as Irving used it on the Dutch. The fact that Irving
never admitted knowing Erasmus's story, says De Vries,
"touches too much the character of our beloved young author
to be decided in a few words," and thus, having written the
words, he drops the subject.

Quite aside from the foolishness about the Dutch, who are
fondly treated in the story, there are two real blunders here.
First, Irving's indebtedness was so widely recognized when
the story first appeared as to be a subject for newspaper comment and, second, his source was not Erasmus, whose tale is in
no sense "fully developed," but an old German tale published
by Otmar, the Grimm of his period, in his *Volke-Sagen* of
1800. Actually Irving was on this occasion very noisily accused
of plagiarism. At the end of his story he had appended a note
in which he hinted that Rip's origin was "a little German
superstition about Frederick *der Rothbart* and the Kypphauser
mountain," but this has always been regarded as a red
herring—so freely had he borrowed from another, and ad-

jacent, story in Otmar: the folk tale of Peter Klaus. About the only thing Irving could do when this was pointed out he did: threw up his hands and said that of course he knew the tale of Peter Klaus; he had seen it in *three* collections of German legends.

There were probably still other sources for "Rip Van Winkle." We know, for instance, that in 1817 Sir Walter Scott told Irving the story of Thomas of Erceldoune ("Thomas the Rhymer"), who was bewitched by the Queen of the Fairies for seven years. "Doldrum"—a farce about a man's surprise at the changes he found after waking from a seven-year slumber—was played in New York when Irving was fourteen. It is almost certain, moreover, that Irving knew at least a couple of the other versions of the old tradition.

The idea of persons sleeping for long periods is, of course, very common in myth, legend, and folklore. So sleep Arthur and Merlin and John the Divine, and Charlemagne and Frederick Barbarossa (or Rothbart, or Redbeard) and Wilhelm Tell, and Odin (or Woden), the Norse (or Teutonic) god, and Endymion the shepherd, and Siegfried and Oisin and several dozen other heroes of many lands, as well as Sleeping Beauty and Bruennhilde and other mythical ladies—and also the protagonists of many novels, who wake to their author's vision of utopia, or hell. And there are several myths and legends about these sleepers which come pretty close to the story Irving told. Probably the best known of these concerns the Seven Sleepers. These men, natives of Ephesus, were early Christians persecuted by the Emperor Decius. They hid in a mountain and fell asleep. On waking they assumed that a night had passed, and one of them slipped into town to buy bread. When he got there he was stunned to see a cross over the gate, and then to hear the Lord's name spoken freely. When he paid for the bread his coins, now archaic, gave him away, and he discovered he had slept for 360 years.

This myth has spread widely, and found its way into books so different as the Koran, where Mohammed adapted it and introduced a dog who sleeps with the seven men, and Mark Twain's *Innocents Abroad,* where Twain tells the story at considerable length (and says he knows it to be a true story, as he personally has visited the cave). Somewhat similar myths are also known in the religious literature of the Jews. In a section on fasting in the Babylonian Talmud, to choose a single instance, appears one of several stories about Honi the Circle Drawer, lately thrust into prominence as a candidate for identification with the Teacher of Righteousness of the Dead Sea Scrolls. One day Honi sat down to eat, the story goes, and sleep came; a rocky formation enclosed him, and he slept for seventy years. When he went home nobody would believe he was Honi; greatly hurt, he prayed for death and died.

The thing that is really vital to "Rip Van Winkle," but missing from all these other stories, is a revelation—some kind of mysterious activity witnessed by the sleeper. But such tales also exist—for instance, the Chinese story of Wang Chih, who comes upon some aged men playing chess in a mountain grotto, is given a date-stone to put in his mouth, and sleeps for centuries, finally waking to return home to practice Taoist rites and attain immortality.

More akin to Rip's is the misadventure of Herla, King of the Britons. He is approached by an ugly dwarf, somewhat resembling Pan, who tells him that he will grace Herla's wedding to the daughter of the King of France, and that Herla will in turn attend the wedding of the dwarf-king. At the Briton's marriage ceremony, the dwarf-guests serve food and drink from precious vessels. A year later, at the wedding of the dwarf-king in a mountain cavern, Herla takes a bloodhound in his arms, and he and his men are enjoined not to dismount until the bloodhound jumps. Some who try are turned to dust, but the hound never jumps and Herla thus wanders hopelessly and "maketh mad marches" with his army for the space of two hundred years. At last he reaches the sunlight and meets a shepherd who can scarcely understand the language the king speaks.*

Closer still, in one way, is the story of a blacksmith recorded in the Grimms' *Teutonic Mythology*. While trying to find wood to make a handle for his hammer, he gets lost; there are the familiar rift in the mountains, some mysterious bowlers, and a magic gift—this time a bowling ball that turns to gold. (Others who have entered this cliff have seen an old man with a long white beard holding a goblet.)

The most detailed precedent for Irving, however, and beyond a doubt his principal source, is the tale of Peter Klaus, which appeared in Otmar's collection.† This is a story of a goatherd from Sittendorf who used to pasture his sheep on the Kyfhauser mountain in Thuringia. One day he discovered that a goat had disappeared into a crack in a cliff and, following her, he came to a cave where he found her eating oats that fell from a ceiling which shook with the stamping of horses. While Peter stood there in astonishment a groom appeared

---

* This is the only story of its kind, except for "Rip," that can be attributed to anyone—in this case to Walter Map, author of the early thirteenth century *De Nugis Curialium* ("Courtier's Trifles"), in which it appears. An intolerant but witty feudal aristocrat, probably Welsh, Map is best known for his "Dissuasion from Matrimony," long attributed to a Latin writer of a thousand years before him. In this essay he counsels young men that women are monsters and vipers (do not look for exceptions, he says: "Friend, fear all the sex"). Thus Map provides a precedent both for Rip's adventure and for Irving's whimsical antifeminism. It is very doubtful, however, if not impossible, that Irving knew of him; Herla's story has been cited as the true source of "Rip Van Winkle," but Map's book was not available to Irving until some three decades after the Irving story had been published.

† Otmar's book is very hard to come by, but Henry A. Pochmann's "Irving's German Sources in *The Sketch Book*," *Studies in Philology*, XXVII (July, 1930), 489–94, prints the most relevant portions of it.

and beckoned him to follow; soon they came to a hollow, surrounded by high walls into which, through the thick overhanging branches, a dim light fell. Here there was a rich, well-graded lawn, where twelve serious knights were bowling. None of them said a word. Peter was put to work setting pins.

At first his knees shook as he stole glimpses of the silent, long-bearded knights, but gradually his fear left him, and finally he took a drink from a tankard. This was rejuvenating, and as often as he felt tired he drank from the vessel, which never emptied. This gave him strength, but sleep overcame him nonetheless, and when he woke he was back at the green spot where he grazed his goats. The goats, however, were gone, and so was his dog. There were trees and bushes he couldn't remember, and in bewilderment he went into Sittendorf, below him, to ask about his herd.

Outside the village the people were unfamiliar, differently dressed and strange-spoken. They stared at him and stroked their chins as he asked for his sheep; when involuntarily he stroked his own chin he found that his beard had grown a foot long. He went to his house, which was in decay, and there he saw an emaciated dog which snarled at him. He staggered off, calling vainly for his wife and children. The villagers crowded around him, demanding to know what he was looking for, and when he asked about old friends he learned that they were dead. Then he saw a pretty young woman, who exactly resembled his wife, and when he asked her father's name she answered, "Peter Klaus, God rest his soul. It is more than twenty years since . . . his sheep came back without him." Then he shouted, "I am Peter Klaus, and no other," and was warmly welcomed home.

Since this elaborate parallel with Irving epitomizes the process whereby a national literature adapted foreign materials and began to function, it is somewhat appropriate that our first short story should owe so large a debt to a European source. But it is not at all clear why this *particular* story should have come down to us across a span of some twenty-five centuries—from the time, say, of Epimenides. Some of its charm is obvious; the idea of falling clean out of time, for instance, must be universally fascinating. But the very heart of "Rip Van Winkle," and of "Peter Klaus"—the strange pageant in the mountain—is still, from whatever version of it may be the earliest on down to the present time, enigmatic.

In the scene with the "dwarfs"—to focus again on Irving— it is not even clear what is going on. When the silent men of outlandish appearance and their leader go through their motions, the feeling is very strong that their actions are intended to convey something. But what? They are bowling, of course, and producing the sound of thunder, but why are they doing this? Why are they so sad and silent as they do it? Why so odd-looking? And why does Rip's participation cost him a generation of his life? The action is fairly pulsing with over-tones: the men are speaking in signs; their motions cry out for translation as vigorously as if this were, as it seems, some strangely solemn charade. The question, which seems never even to have been asked, is what are we to make of this thundering pantomime? What have the gods to impart?

The notion that somewhere in the story lurks a secondary, or symbolic, meaning is by no means new. Walter Map, for instance, intended the latter part of his story about Herla to be a satire on the court of King Henry II, which he thought unstable. Erasmus, as already noted, attacked the Scotists through his; and the Talmud draws a moral from Honi's lonely end: "Either companionship or death." More interesting, however, is Arnold Toynbee's interpretation of "Rip Van Winkle" in the third volume of his *Study of History*. There is likely to be, he feels, something "old-fashioned" about any given colonial ethos, and his theory comes to a generalization: "Geographical expansion [of a civilization] produces social

retardation." Toynbee thinks Rip an expression of his principle, the long sleep symbolizing the slumber of social progress in a newly settled place. Irving "was really expressing in
mythological imagery the essence of the overseas experience. . . ."

The trouble with the interpretations of Map, Erasmus, and
the Talmud is that they are forced and arbitrary, and the
trouble with Toynbee's is that the story doesn't fit the theory
it is supposed to express. If we ever had a period during
which social progress was not retarded then it was exactly the
period Rip slept through. In that generation we were transformed from a group of loosely bound and often provincial
colonies into a cocky and independent republic with a new
kind of government and—as the story itself makes clear
enough—a whole new and new-fashioned spirit. In order to
fit the thesis Irving must have had Rip return to a village where
nothing much had happened or changed, and thus he must
have written a different story. But he chose instead to write
a story on the order of the myth about Honi the Circle
Drawer who, according to one tradition, slept through the
destruction of the First Temple and the building of the
second, or like the one about the Seven Sleepers, who slept
through the Christian revolution.* In all these tales the startling developments that have taken place during the sleep are
a large part of the "point." And even if to Toynbee nationalism

---

* Indeed Irving may have got some specific ideas from the Seven
Sleepers myth, for there the surprising changes in the speech of the
people, and the prominent new sign over the gate of the town, are
precedents for two of the very few important details to be found in
"Rip" but not in "Peter Klaus." Elsewhere there is an exact precedent
for the form Irving's change of signs took. In the famous *New England
Primer,* with its alphabetical rimes ("In Adam's fall we sinned all"),
a woodcut of King George that appeared in early editions eventually
became very smudged; when this happened the portrait began to carry
the name of our first President ("By Washington, great deeds were
done.")

is—and was even in eighteenth-century America—a thoroughly deplorable thing, it was not a sign of social retardation.

Since such explanations as these will not help much more than the poets and playwrights have done to show us what is going on in "Rip Van Winkle," and since there is nowhere else to look, we are forced at long last to squint for ourselves through that crevice in the mountain. There, in the shadows, lurk figures and images which take us back, along a chronological line, to a time before the beginnings of recorded history. And if we could identify and understand these figures and images we should have, finally, the answers to most of our questions.

Many editions of Irving's story carry as an epigraph some lines he took from the seventeenth-century poet William Cartwright:

> By Woden, God of Saxons,
> From whence comes Wensday, that is Wodensday,
> Truth is a thing that ever I will keep
> Until thylke day in which I creep into
> My sepulchre—.

The most plausible reading of these lines is: "By God it's a true story I'm telling." But this makes Irving's two notes—in which he calls this a true tale—redundant. Less simply read, it might be the story itself saying, "By God, I'll keep to myself the truth about this thing as long as I live." At any rate, it is either a curious coincidence or an obscure clue that, in swearing by Woden, Irving has pointed to the remotest origins of his story that can be uncovered. To bare these origins would be to force the story, at last, to give up its secrets.

Here is a grab bag of traditional elements—folk, legendary, and mythic. The green knoll on which Rip sits when he hears his name has behind it the Green Mounds of Irish fairy tales—often prehistoric burial mounds. It is an appropriate spot for his bewitching and approximate to the "buried men" he is about to visit. Magic potions and sacred drinks are so standard in mythology, folklore, and religion as to suggest parallels automatically as Rip plays Ganymede, wine-pourer to the gods. A less familiar little tradition lies behind those dogs, which Rip and Peter find barely and implausibly alive after so many years—this takes us all the way back to Odysseus, returning after a generation's absence to find his dog Argos in Ithaca, still half-alive and lying on a heap of dung.

But the most important recognition in Irving's story concerns the identity of the men Rip meets in the mountain, and of their leader. These are "Hendrik Hudson" and his crew.* The blacksmith and Peter Klaus never identify their strange mountain men, and the unnamed leaders never appear. Nevertheless, it is not hard to guess with considerable assurance of being right both who they are and by whom they are led. It was the Odensberg that the blacksmith entered, and the Kyfhauser that Peter wormed his way into; it is in the Odensberg, according to legend, that Charlemagne and his knights are sleeping, and the Kyfhauser where sleep Frederick Barbarossa and his.† Hudson, then, is playing the role of the great kings of

---

* It should, of course, be "Henry": Hudson sailed from Holland but was English. Of all the people Irving could have put in the Catskills, however, Hudson was a fine choice, not only because the river below him was named for him and discovered by him, but because he was (in 1611 on another trip) the victim of a mutiny near Hudson Bay, was abandoned there, and disappeared for good. Thus he is like the heroes of myth and legend who sleep in mountains; no one knows where, or if, he was buried, and it is easier to think of him as not entirely dead.

† This is clear in the story that lies, in Otmar's collection, adjacent to the one of Peter Klaus—the "little German Superstition about Frederick *der Rothbart*" that Irving claimed as the origin of "Rip." It is almost certain, then, that Irving knew who led the knights Peter saw, and who Hudson's most immediate ancestor was. How much more he may have known about the origins of the materials he was borrowing is very difficult to say.

European countries, as Arthur plays it in England, and is a survival of this tradition. This recognition opens the door.

Part of the Barbarossa legend, which is better known and more detailed than the one of Charlemagne, concerns the conditions under which he can return to active life. Around the Kyfhauser a flock of ravens is said to fly, and each time the king wakes he asks if they are still there (they are, and this means the time has not come). Another important detail of the story is his beard: it is extraordinarily long already, and when it has grown three times around the table where he sits, his time will have come. It is very likely, then, that the black wings hovering over Rip just before he enters the mountain, and just after he emerges into consciousness, are the ravens of Barbarossa—just as the beards which are prominent in his story and Peter's (although the natural enough consequences of not shaving for twenty years) come down to us from this legend.

But the most important detail of all is a game, common to so many of these stories—the Chinese and Japanese versions, and Peter Klaus and the blacksmith and Rip. And the fact that the game in the stories that primarily concern us here is always bowling, which makes the sound of thunder, gives the whole show away: we are dealing, ultimately, with the gods, and in the farthest recess of this cave the figure with the red beard (to represent lightning), that helped to identify him with Frederick the Redbeard, is the god of thunder—Thor, God of Saxons, whence comes Thorsday, that is, Thursday.

More clearly the prototype of all these sleeping heroes, however, is the magnificently white-bearded Woden, or Odin, the god of the dead whom Cartwright swore by. In the legend about Charlemagne, the people who saw the king described him as a man with a white beard, and the name of the mountain Charlemagne inhabits, the Odensberg, suggests all by itself his ancestor. But the fact that the blacksmith on the

Odensberg is in search of wood for a handle to an instrument of power which was the very emblem of the god of thunder, a hammer, suggests Thor just as strongly. So thoroughly have the two gods been confused in these myths that the king who is buried in Odin's mountain has in some stories the red coloring and the red horse that are really appropriate to Thor. On this horse the god issues from the mountain with his men, every so-many years, and in this activity he is again Odin, the leader of the Wild Hunt.

These confusions between Thor and Odin are not surprising, since the two figures are confused in Norse mythology itself. Although Thor was the son of Odin, he was also sometimes an older god than Odin; often he was a god superior to Odin, and sometimes they were thought of as exactly the same god. The direct ancestor of the Hudson Rip saw, then, was a Thor who has many of the attributes of Odin, and recognizing this takes us to the source of the traditions out of which Irving's scene is principally compounded. Recognizing these traditions, in turn, enables us to understand the subliminal richness of its materials, buried under the detritus of centuries.

The ravens which fly about the Kyfhauser, and the crows and eagle of the Catskills, are lineal descendants of the ravens Thought and Memory who sat on Odin's shoulder and kept him informed, or of the eagle that hovered over Odin's own retreat, or of the flight of ravens, "Odin's messengers" (without whose message Frederick cannot emerge)—or of all three. The dogs in the stories, mixing Greek myth with Teutonic, are progeny of the wolves Geri and Freki who sat at Odin's feet, or of the totem wolf which hung over the west door of his residence—in honor of which ancestry Rip's dog gets his name, Wolf. The drink which both invigorated and overpowered Rip is the same drink Barbarossa's knights gave Peter; it belongs also in the goblet Charlemagne was seen holding, and, despite all the magic drinks of folklore and myth, it is ultimately

"Odin's mead," from which Odin got wisdom, and inspired poets; it was a magic draft related to the drink always available in the Abode of the Blest, the drink that rejuvenates, and obliterates all sorrow.

In a like manner, the odd appearance of Hudson's crew, those ugly, drab, short and curious creatures (one fellow's face is comprised entirely of his nose) are echoes of the dwarfs Herla met—although those dwarfs also looked like Pan, mixing Greek and Teutonic (and probably Welsh) mythology again. But Hudson's men get their appearance from the Night-Elves who made Thor's hammer—those ugly little long-nosed people, dirty-brown in color, who lived in caves and clefts. Beneath this effective disguise the crewmen of the *Half-Moon* are really the knights of Barbarossa and Charlemagne, who are the brave dead warriors brought back from the battlefields by the Valkyries to Odin's hall of the dead: Rip has really been in Valhalla and seen the slain collected around their god, who by the old confusion is now Thor, whose men they have become. The reason for the oddness of their behavior—their melancholy and their lacklustre stares—has become completely obvious, if indeed it was not before: they are dead. And one of Odin's chief characteristics, his extreme aloofness, accounts for the fact that Rip got but a glimpse of their leader, while neither Peter nor the blacksmith ever saw him at all.

Why such pagan gods should have been imagined as sleeping in mountains can be plausibly explained. When converted to Christianity, the people who had worshipped these figures could not quickly and completely reject the faith of their fathers. To them the outmoded gods lingered on, wandering, sleeping, and appearing infrequently. Later, vanished but actual heroes like Charlemagne, Frederick, Sir Francis Drake, Prince Sebastian of Portugal, and Arthur, were given attributes of the earlier gods. It was most common as well to place them in a mountain, where they were in earth, like the dead, but not under it—not under level ground, that is—like the really dead. Here they are sequestered in their slumbers, but the gods can be thought of as not entirely departed, and the heroes as in a position to return.

Occasionally mortals get to visit the legendary heroes who have taken over the attributes of vanished gods. When this happens, the visitor suffers a magic sleep and a long lacuna in his life: he has lapsed into a pagan world, got himself bewitched, and trafficked with a forbidden god. The punishment is severe. Thus Herla lost everything and Peter lost his flock, wife, home, and twenty years of life—though Rip, to be sure, in Irving's half-convincing happy ending, doesn't suffer so badly. The reason for the punishment is nevertheless clear: it is Christianity's dire objection to traffic with such cults as attached to those gods, as with any intercourse with fairies. This centuries-old element of the story is an historical, symbolic, and didactic expression of the church's long struggle with paganism—and has nothing to do with any social retardation of progress in colonies. Look what happened to Herla and Peter, Christian instruction could say. They were kind and ingenuous men. What then could happen to you? And then because the story is compelling in its own right it survives past the need for it, even after the knowledge of its purpose is centuries forgotten.

Is there any other connection between the visit and the great changes that follow in the life of the man who made it? And what are these visitors doing where they are not supposed to be? The sleeping gods and heroes could be described, and have been, without any mortal to intrude on them, and it doesn't look as though the mortals had just happened in: most of them appear to have been approached and led. And Rip was called by name.

Almost all of the protagonists of these stories, if they witnessed anything within the mountain, saw some kind of game. The fact that the origins of many games fade into ritual and ritual dance suggests that the games in these legends and myths might have their origin in some rite. And some authorities (Jane Harrison and Lord Raglan are notable examples) believe that all myths have their origin in ritual—that a myth is never a folk-explanation of natural phenomena, or anything of the sort, but a narrative that was once linked with a ritual—is the story, in other words, which has outlived the ritual, that the ritual once enacted. Frazer had a more moderate view, and felt that there is a *class* of myths which have been dramatized in ritual, and that these myths were enacted as magical ceremonies in order to produce the natural effects which they describe in figurative language. This hypothesis has it further that the core of such a myth traces back, finally, to the divinity who is imagined to have founded the rite. The actors are simply impersonating an activity of the originator and worshipping him in this way, his acts being the prototype of the rite. Gradually, then, the rite may be performed more out of piety than from any belief in its efficacy, and finally may be forgotten while the myth endures.

Whatever the merits of this theory one thing seems fairly sure: if it explains the origins of any myths, Rip descends from one of them. The bowlers of the Catskills are impersonating a disguised Thor, in a figurative or symbolic way, in his principal role as God of Thunder, and the actions of these resurrected men are the means of their worship. The solemnity Rip and Peter felt, in the presence of a mystery, is entirely appropriate to so sacred and secret an occasion. "Rip Van Winkle," then, is our version of a myth that survives as a description of a nearly forgotten ceremony in the worship of Thor for the production of rain. It proceeds by a symbolic imitation of how rain is made. The ritual is of the magical sort, and is intended to influer. nature through the physical sympathy, or resemblance, between the ceremony and the effect it is supposed to produce.* Indeed the story is an example of what Robert Graves has called "true myth": it is an instance of "the reduction to narrative shorthand of ritual mime."

Exactly *why* Rip was allowed to witness this mystery is a secret which, since he was ignorant of the reason himself, he has been able to keep for many generations. So, in all likelihood, was Irving unaware of the original reason for the outsider's presence at the ceremony: even by Peter Klaus's time the myth had so badly deteriorated into folklore that only the fragments we are deciphering remained. But the secret is out by now: Rip and Peter were initiates. Rip goes right through the steps. While he sits dreamily and alone on the green knoll the period of preliminary isolation passes; then he is summoned by name. Helping to carry the heavy keg up the side of the ravine, which he may have had to volunteer to do, is a sort of test. There followed a kind of procession, and something like a vigil, and finally the experience of communication with the divinity and his disciples. Rip is even given a magic drink, which as a novice he is first required to serve, and after this he is plunged into the magic sleep. When he wakes he is in a new phase of life, and on this level the great changes he finds about him are symbols of the changes in him, and of the differences in his situation, now that he is initiate.

Rip has also been reborn in another, reinforcing way, for the imagery of his emergence into a new life inevitably and unavoidably suggests an issue "from the womb." This concept,

---

* The thunder that Thor made came ordinarily from the roar of his chariot, of course, but the method described in the myth Irving drew on is by no means unknown. Grimm reported that on hearing thunder North Germans were likely to remark, "the angels are playing at bowls"; and in our own country there is a close parallel in the mythology of the Zuni Indians of New Mexico, whose warriors when they die go off to make lightning in the sky, where rainmakers cause thunder with great "gaming stones."

which is often thrown about gratuitously, really urges itself here, for Irving's description of the entrance to the mountain, taken from "Peter Klaus," is extremely arresting—almost as pointed, say, as accounts anthropologists have given of pits dug in the ground by primitive tribesmen, and trimmed about the edges with overhanging shrubbery (which ditches the men dance about in the spring, while brandishing their spears and chanting that these are no ditches, but what they were built to represent). The imagery is the same when Rip is led eerily through the ravine till he comes to the bottom of a hollow, surrounded by perpendicular precipices, over the brinks of which hang the branches of trees.

From this setting he is delivered into his old age. Ripe for escape before, he has experienced an escape only one step short of death. Apparently well into middle age, and saddled with a wife who had completely lost her desirability, he laid down his gun and entered the mountain. Here he witnessed some symbolical activity—which, in the severely censored form of the pins and bowling balls, has overtones of human, as well as vegetable, fertility—and he saw it all as joyless and melancholy. Magically confirmed in his own feeling about the matter, he drank, slept like a baby, and was released into the world he had longed for—into an all-male society, the perpetual men's club that used to meet at the inn, which his wife can no longer violate as, unforgivably, she had done before. His gun is ruined and useless, and his wife is gone. But it makes no difference now; he has slept painlessly through his "change of life."

The trouble with this story as some kind of "male-menopause myth" is that the reading is partly based on a misinterpretation attributed, perhaps unfairly, to Rip. Lacking the information we have, he made a mistake: the men were lifeless and unhappy at their bowling because they were dead. More than that, they were still the followers of Thor, whose sign was lightning and whose emblem was a hammer. Thor was god of power, and of human as well as vegetable fertility. He was god of the vital moistures in general, an ithyphallic, not a detumescent, god. Even dead, his worshippers made a great deal of noise in his service. In short, the bowling which sends thunder across the Catskills is violently masculine symbolic activity in a very feminine mountain. And in this last vague but massive symbol is a final irony, for the mystery revealed to Rip had thus two aspects, animal or human, and vegetable—one for each of Thor's two fertility powers.

Of what pertinence were all these revelations to Rip? What does it mean to him that the strange men he saw have come down to us from the men of Thor, or that he was initiated into an ancient mystery and shown the sacred secrets of all life? No relevance at all to him and no meaning whatever. And that is the ironical point. Befuddled, unwitting, and likeable old Rip: no man in the valley, luxuriantly green already, thought less or as little about the crops, and no man he knew could have been chosen to witness the secrets of human fertility and found them more sleep-provoking.

III

What would have interested him, and what did he want? Concentrating somewhat anthropologically on the story's central scene in an attempt to get at the bottom of it, we have not got to the bottom of the character. But if for a moment we will think more as psychologists, and consider the story as a sort of dream—as a product of the unconscious, itself a kind of anthropologist—we open a whole new and remarkable area of meaning. Suddenly everything seems illusive, unreal; time goes into abeyance and the sense of history is lost; the very identity of the central figure is shaken, and reason dissolves.

The easiest entry to the dream level of "Rip Van Winkle"

passes through that inn where Rip once sat with his friends—
the inn which was "gone," and replaced by a hotel straight
out of nightmare: " a large rickety wooden building . . . with
great gaping windows . . . mended with old hats and petti-
coats"—and in front a sign with a familiar face all out of
place in its setting. Soon, however, "idle with impunity" and
"reverenced as one of the patriarchs of the village," Rip "took
his place once more on the bench at the inn door." A conflict
in Irving explains the confusion. He wanted to show the great
changes a revolution had brought, but wished more deeply to
feel, and wanted us to feel, that aside from the happy loss of
his wife nothing had really happened to Rip. Toynbee, re-
sponding fully to this ab-sense of time and change, made
what amounts to the same mistake. But it is a meaningful
slip, and on one level they are both right. For Rip, time and
history *have* ceased operation. Nothing *has* happened, and the
inn is there to signal the fact.

What, then, are we to think when we come to the start of
the very next paragraph and are told (in a kind of preliminary
postscript at the end of the tale proper) that Rip is now telling
his story "to every stranger that arrived at Mr. Doolittle's hotel"?
The inn is there, is gone and replaced, is there again, is gone
again. Reality is slithering away; and so it must eventually do,
for this is not ultimately its world. Nor is this truly the world
of fiction, unless of Kafka's. It is the world of the unconscious,
where time and history are not suspended, exactly, but do not
exist—where everything exists at once. It is the region where
people and things are always appearing in unreasonable
places, and everything is passing strange: but distorted toward
some hard-to-recognize truth. The recurring transformation
of Irving's hostelry belongs in this night world. It represents a
"willful accident," and as such makes its own kind of sense.
Irving was groping very darkly in a world of symbol, myth,
and dream for meanings beyond awareness.

In this strange new world Rip's identity is harder to establish
than the identity of that shifting meeting place. Removed as
he is from time, the confusion of generations is appalling, and
he is hard pressed to know in which of at least three generations he really "belongs." It will be next to impossible to know
for sure, for the truth is he had almost as little part in his own
generation as the one he slept through. This was entirely clear,
had we the wit to see it, when we first met him. He was not
an adult, but a child playing with children, a kid with a dog.
He lived with his wife, to be sure, but only in a manner of
speaking, for he accepted instead his "only alternative": "to
take gun in hand and stroll away into the wood." Or, more
striking, he would escape her by sitting on a wet rock with
a rod in his hand "as long and heavy as a Tartar's lance, and
fish all day . . . even though he should not be encouraged by
a single nibble." "A great favorite among all the good wives of
the village," he ran their errands and did "such little jobs as
their less obliging husbands would not do for them"—not, by
pointed implication, what their husbands would do: "As to
doing family duty . . . he found it impossible."

At the inn with the menfolk, Rip shows that he wants to be
a father. But at home he is a son, and not up to it: he is the
son who wants to be the father but his mother won't let him.
He represents, to be technical for a moment, the ego arrested
at the infantile level in an Oedipal situation; under pressure
he reverts all the way back to the sleep of the womb.

The scene in the mountain now takes on a new and different
suggestiveness. It is at once the dream of a child and an adult
dream reflecting Rip's own predicament. The great noses of
the mountain men give the next phallic clue, as they must
likewise have done in the ancient Teutonic mythology. (The
psychoanalytic and the anthropological mix well: they are
both—the first personally, the second culturally—"regres-
sive.") From this viewpoint the dwarfs are really disguised

little boys with pins and balls practicing, in highly activated silence, a forbidden rite; Rip is not invited to play, too, and they make him work, so he sneaks their drink and goes off to sleep. On the other hand the dwarfs are also so many mirrors to the "adult" Rip, held up as revelations which his consciousness is not likely to read: they are aged little men playing games, who have grown old but not up. Our protagonist, then, is both gerontion and child—or is neither, precisely. He has nor youth nor age, but as it were an after-dinner's sleep, dreaming on both.

On his return to the village, the sense of the decomposition of his "self" becomes even more awesome. His wife-mother is gone, but he is still a child as much as he is anything, and as such he must find his role in a relationship to someone else. But now it is completely bewildering. He is soon confronted with the very "ditto of himself," a negligent loafer named Rip—actually his son. Worse, he faces a woman who seems both strange and, as his poor mind struggles into recollection, hauntingly familiar. She had, she says, a father named Rip, and she carries in her arms a child of that name. Who, then, is our protagonist? His own unaccepted and "impossible" self, or the son of his wife that he used to be and emotionally remains? Or his own son, the loafer leaning there against the tree and, after the ravages of twenty years that passed as a night, looking more like the man Rip impersonated than he suddenly does himself? Or perhaps another Rip, the child of his daughter, now surrogate for his departed wife, and the sign of his true emotional state? Or even, conceivably, the husband of this replacement wife-mother, and the father of this son—or of that one, or of himself? The sense of generation is shattered; his daughter's house, in which he lives, is a whole house of mirrors, and everywhere he looks he sees a different distortion. He has one moment of panicked insight: "God knows . . . I'm not myself—I'm somebody else—that's me

yonder—no—that's somebody else got into my shoes. . . . "
Small wonder he takes his leave of all these people for the
security of the role he can play at Mr. Doolittle's.

It is clear now that Rip escaped no change of life, but his
very manhood—went from childhood to second childhood
with next to nothing in between. It is not just his wife he has
dodged, either, but all the obligations of maturity: occupation,
domestic and financial responsibility, a political position, duty
to society in a time of war. His relation to history is so ambiguous that—ridiculous suspicion—he is thought a spy.
Charming and infantile, he narcissistically prefers himself; he
will tell his tale of twenty years' sleep at Mr. Do-little's, where
Irving leaves him for the last time. It has become a symbol
for the sleep that has been his life.

Considering the universality of his fame, it is a wonder that
no European, say, has pointed gleefully to this figure as a
symbol of America, for he presents a near-perfect image of the
way a large part of the world looks at us: likeable enough,
up to a point and at times, but essentially immature, self-
centered, careless, and above all—and perhaps dangerously—
innocent. Even more pointedly, Rip is a stereotype of the
American male as seen from abroad, or in some jaundiced
quarters at home: he is perfectly the jolly overgrown child,
abysmally ignorant of his own wife and the whole world of
adult men—perpetually "one of the boys," hanging around
what they are pleased to think of as a "perpetual men's club";
a disguised Rotarian who simply will not and cannot grow up.
In moments of candor we will probably admit that a stereotype with no germ of truth in it could not exist: some such
mythic America, some such mythic American, exist both
actually and in the consciousness of the world. Rip will do
very well as their prototype.

"Rip Van Winkle" is then, and finally, a wonderfully rich
tale—the richest in our literature—and an astonishingly com-

plex experience arising from a struggle among many kinds of meaning. On the "prehistoric" level we are dimly aware of immemorial ritual significance, on the psychological of an extraordinary picture of the self arrested in a timeless infancy —rich appeals, both, to the child and primitive in everyone that never grow up and never die in anyone. These awarenesses conflict in the story, as they do in life, with the adult and rational perception that we do indeed grow old, that time and history never stop. In much the same way, our affection for Rip himself must oppose our reluctant discovery that as a man we cannot fully respect him.

But in addition to all his other sides, this remarkable Van Winkle also, of course, projects and personifies our sense of the flight—and more: the ravages—of time. And this is what wins us ultimately to his side. We know perfectly well that as an adult this darling of generations of Americans will not entirely do. But if he does seem, finally, meek, blessed, pure in heart, and if we mock him for what he has missed we do it tenderly—partly because it is something hidden in ourselves we mock. And this is not just our own hidden childishness. It is all our own lost lives and roles, the lives and roles that once seemed possible and are possible no more. In twenty years all springs are over; without mockery it might be too sad to bear. Today would grieve, and tomorrow would grieve; best cover it over lightly.

And so here is Rip at the end: Lazarus come from the dead, come back to tell us all. He will tell us all, and badgering any who will listen, he tries: Well now—have you heard what happened to *me?* But it won't do; he doesn't know. And that is a pity, truly. Here is a man in whom rest complexities and deficiencies a lifetime might contemplate, as the world has done; a man who has peered toward the dawn of civilization, witnessed ancient mysteries, and stared at his essential nature; a man who now in town is looking at the future and realizing a dream of the ages. And he cannot communicate his visions.

But supposing that he could, that he could tell us all: would it have been worthwhile? Visions, revelations like these are private. To translate what the thunder meant, to confront the meaning of life and the future of all our childish selves, we all have to go up into our own mountains.

1960